THE UNIVERSITY

READERS' GUIDES TO ESSENTIAL CRITICISM

CONSULTANT EDITOR: NICOLAS TREDELL

Published

Series Standing Order ISBN: 1403901082

Hanif Kureishi

EDITED BY SUSIE THOMAS

Consultant editor: Nicholas Tredell

First published 2005 by
PALGRAVE MACMILLAN
Houndmills, Basingstoke, Hampshire RG21 6XS and
175 Fifth Avenue, New York, N. Y. 10010
Companies and representatives throughout the world

PALGRAVE MACMILLAN is the global academic imprint of the Palgrave
Macmillan division of St. Martin's Press, LLC and of Palgrave Macmillan Ltd.
Macmillan® is a registered trademark in the United States, United Kingdom
and other countries. Palgrave is a registered trademark in the European
Union and other countries.

ISBN-13: 978– 14039–2056–0   hardback
ISBN-10: 1–4039–2056–7   hardback
ISBN-13: 978– 1–4039–2057–7   paperback
ISBN-10: 1–4039–2057–5   paperback

This book is printed on paper suitable for recycling and
made from fully managed and sustained forest sources.

A catalogue record for this book is available
from the British Library.

A catalog record for this book is available
from the Library of Congress.

10   9   8   7   6   5   4   3   2   1
14   13   12   11   10   09   08   07   06   05

Printed and bound in China

CONTENTS

Situates Kureishi's work in the context of new ways of being British; summarizes the initial critical debates about the 'politics of representation' and the more recent controversies surrounding Kureishi's treatment of heterosexual relationships in a post-feminist era.

Foreplays: *The King and Me* (1980), *Outskirts* (1981), *Borderline* (1981) and *Birds of Passage* (1983)

Explores Kureishi's original contribution to the 'Fringe' and looks at the review responses to these early works, showing how they highlighted topics that would be important in criticism of the screenplays and prose fictions.

'Class, Race, Fucking and Farce': *My Beautiful Laundrette* (1985)

Surveys the initial controversial reception with extracts from Leonard Quart's enthusiastic review; Mahmood Jamal and Perminder Dhillon-Kashyap's critique of Orientalist attitudes; Rushdie's robust defence of 'warts-and-all' representations of minority communities; Norman Stone's right-wing attack on the film as 'agit-prop', and Kureishi's reply. Includes extracts from two later assessments: Stuart Hall's seminal essay on 'New Ethnicities' and Radhika Mohanram's sophisticated discussion of 'postcolonial spaces and deterritorialized homosexuality'. Concludes with Ruvani Ranasinha and Elizabeth de Cacqueray's contrasting interpretations of the representation of women.

identity'; Maria Degabriele's lively account of the web of pop allusions; and Frederick M. Holmes's penetrating discussion of form.

Looks at Kureishi's analysis of fundamentalist Islam as an ideology constructed in relation to western capitalism and postmodernism. Follows the continuing controversy over the representation of Muslims as fanatics by Ruvani Ranasinha; and Bart Moore-Gilbert's account of the film's engagement with *Taxi Driver*.

Includes reviews from a range of newspapers and literary journals exploring the perceived change of focus from 'race' and class to personal relationships; the autobiographical controversy; the 'new restlessness' and the male testimonial in a post-feminist era.

Continues reviewers' discussion of the politics of the body and Kureishi's more compressed and spare prose style; the continued interest in identity and authenticity; and London as an increasingly 'semi-detached metropolis'.

Points to some present and future projects.

A NOTE ON REFERENCES AND QUOTATIONS

U nless stated otherwise, quotations from Hanif Kureishi's work are taken from the following editions published in London by Faber & Faber. References to these editions appear in brackets in the text with the indicated abbreviations.

The Black Album (1995)	(BA)
The Body and Seven Stories (2002)	(B)
The Buddha of Suburbia (1990)	(BS)
The Faber Book of Pop (1995)	(F)
Gabriel's Gift (2001)	(GG)
Intimacy (1998)	(I)
London Kills Me (1991)	(LKM)
Love in a Blue Time (1997)	(LBT)
Midnight All Day (1999)	(MAD)
My Beautiful Laundrette and Other Writings (1996)	(MBL)
My Son the Fanatic (1997)	(MSF)
Outskirts and Other Plays (1992)	(OOP)
'The Rainbow Sign'	(RS)
Sammy and Rosie Get Laid (1988)	(SRGL)
Sleep with Me (1999)	(SWM)
'Some time with Stephen'	(SS)

In any quotation, a row of three dots indicates an editorial ellipsis within a sentence or paragraph, and a row of six dots (that is, two ellipses) indicates an editorial omission of a paragraph break, or of one or more paragraphs. Interpolations in critical extracts by the Guide author are in square brackets and standard type, except for dates, which have been inserted in extracts where required without typographical differentiation.

ACKNOWLEDGEMENTS

The editor would like to thank Hanif Kureishi for his help during the preparation of this book.

Also, the editor and publishers wish to thank the following for use of copyright material:

Maria Degabriele for 'Prince of Darkness Meets Priestess of Porn: Sexual and Political Identities in Hanif Kureishi's *The Black Album*', in *Intersections: Gender, History and Culture in the Asian Context*, Issue 2, May 1999, online *http://wwwsshe.murdoch.edu.au/intersections/*

Sight and Sound/BFI for Philip Dodd, 'Requiem for a Rave', in *Sight and Sound*, 5:1, September 1991, pp. 9–13.

The Modern Language Association of America for Rita Felski, 'Nothing to Declare: Identity, Shame, and the Lower Middle Class', *Proceeding of the Modern Language Association* (2000): pp. 37–8.

South End Press for bell hooks, *Yearning: Race, Gender and Cultural Politics* (1991), pp. 158–9, 160–1 and 162–3.

Mahmood Jamal for his review of *My Beautiful Laundrette*, *Artrage*, 1988, pp. 21–2.

Wasafiri for Seema Jena, 'From Victims to Survivors: the Anti-Hero as a Narrative in Asian Immigrant Writing with Special Reference to the Buddha of Suburbia', *Wasafiri*, 17, Spring 1993, pp. 3–6.

University of Texas Press for Kenneth C. Kaleta, *Hanif Kureishi: Postcolonial Storyteller* (1998).

Hanif Kureishi for his Introductions to *My Beautiful Laundrette* and *Sex and Secularity*, © 2002 Hanif Kureishi. Reproduced by permission of the author c/o Rogers, Coleridge & White Ltd, 20 Powis Mews, London W11 1JN.

Greenwood Publishing Group for Gita Rajan and Radhika Mohanram, *Political Discourse and Changing Cultural Contexts: Theory and Criticism.* © 1995 by Gita Rajan and Radhika Mohanram. Reproduced with permission of Greenwood Publishing Group, Inc., Westport, CT.

Manchester University Press for Bart Moore-Gilbert, *Hanif Kureishi* (2001).

Cinéaste Magazine for Leonard Quart's review of *My Beautiful Laundrette*, *Cinéaste*, 15:1, 1986, pp. 38–9.

Ruvani Ranasinha and Northcote House Publishers for Ruvani Ranasinha, *Hanif Kureishi* (Writers and Their Works Series) (2002).

Boydell & Brewer for Sukhdev Sandhu, 'Pop Goes the Centre: Hanif Kureishi's London', in Laura Chrisman and Benita Parry, eds., *Postcolonial Theory and Criticism* (1999), pp. 140–3 and 151–2.

The London Review of Books for Sukhdev Sandhu, 'Paradise Syndrome', *London Review of Books*, 18 May 2000, pp. 33–5.

Sage Publications Ltd for Berthold Schoene, 'Herald of Hybridity: the Emancipation of Difference in Hanif Kureishi's "The Buddha of Suburbia" ', *International Journal of Cultural Studies*, 1:1, 1998. © Sage Publications Ltd (1998).

Routledge/Taylor & Francis Books, Inc. for Gayatri Spivak, 'Sammy and Rosie Get Laid', © 1993 from *Outside in the Teaching Machine* by Gayatri Spivak.

Every effort has been made to trace the copyright holders, but if any have been inadvertently overlooked the publishers will be pleased to make the necessary arrangement at the first opportunity.

Introduction

■ You would flatter yourself if you thought you could change things by a film or a play or whatever, but perhaps you can contribute to a climate of ideas ... It is important to ask questions about how we live sexually, how we live racially, what our relations are with each other emotionally. Asking these questions seems to me to be the things that artists can do rather than change society in any specific way.[1] □

Before Hanif Kureishi there was *It Ain't Half Hot Mum* (1974–79), *Mind Your Language* (1977–79) and Peter Sellers waggling his head from side to side singing 'Goodness Gracious Me'. In mainstream popular culture, 'Pakis were unknown material, off the cultural radar', as Sukhdev Sandhu says, and 'young Asians had no cultural ambassadors or role models'.[2] But the work of Kureishi (born 1954) was life-changing, and as a writer and filmmaker he has achieved iconic status. Amitava Kumar describes his first encounter with *My Beautiful Laundrette* (1985): 'Hanif Kureishi swam into my universe like a new planet. Here was an entirely other world.'[3] Sandhu reels off a list of artists Kureishi has inspired:

■ Ayub Khan Din, who in 1988 played opposite Frances Barber in *Sammy and Rosie Get Laid*, has gone on to write *East Is East*: it packed out the Royal Court Theatre in 1997 and was made into a ... film which has ... become the highest-grossing fully British-funded movie. Chart-topping Cornershop had a song called 'Hanif Kureishi Scene' on the B-side of their curry-coloured first single ... Meera Syal, one of the sour-faced lesbians in *Sammy and Rosie Get Laid*, is well-known as a writer and as one of the stars of *Goodness Gracious Me*, the all-Asian television comedy.'[4] □

As Sandhu insists, 'If there is one figure who is responsible for dragging Asians in England into the spotlight it is Hanif Kureishi ... [who] has presented their lives to mainstream audiences with unrivalled wit and candour.'[5]

Although there is a long tradition of literature by and about Asians in Britain, Kureishi's were the first works by a British-born writer of Asian descent.[6] Unlike Salman Rushdie (born 1947) or V. S. Naipaul (born 1932), he is not a displaced postcolonial writing *back* to the centre; he writes *from* the centre.[7] Moreover, the optimism with which he tackles cultural dislocation and racial issues has little in common with Naipaulian misanthropy. Rushdie was an early mentor, but magical realism had no impact on Kureishi's novels, which belong to a tradition of comic realism. Arguably, it has been Kureishi's work that has paved the way, not just for Meera Syal and Ayub Khan Din, but for writers such as Zadie Smith (born 1975), Shyama Perera, Atima Srivastava (born 1961) and Monica Ali (born 1968).[8]

Kureishi not only inspired young British Asians and altered the popular perception of Asians in mainstream culture; he has also been hugely influential in changing monocultural definitions of British national identity. This is the subject of his landmark essay, 'The Rainbow Sign' (1986), in which he describes growing up in Bromley with his English mother and Pakistani father:

■ In the mid-1960s, Pakistanis were a risible subject in England, derided on television and exploited by politicians. They had the worst jobs, they were uncomfortable in England, some of them had difficulties with the language. They were despised and out of place.

From the start I tried to deny my Pakistani self. I was ashamed. It was a curse and I wanted to be rid of it. I wanted to be like everyone else. I read with understanding a story in a newspaper about a black boy who, when he noticed that burnt skin turned white, jumped into a bath of boiling water.[9] □

The childhood experiences he describes – racial abuse on the streets, in school, and his friendship with a skinhead (known behind his back as Bog Brush) – were developed in his first film, *My Beautiful Laundrette*. The essay records, too, the racist calls by Enoch Powell (1912–98) for the repatriation of 'unassimilable' immigrants, Powell's lurid vision of rivers of blood, and Duncan Sandys's speech in 1967: 'The breeding of millions of half-caste children would merely produce a generation of misfits and create national tensions.' Like Karim in *The Buddha of Suburbia*, Kureishi describes himself 'as desperately embarrassed and afraid of being identified with these loathed aliens ... "the Pakis" ' (RS 28). But as Karim discovers, racism is not a private problem, it is society's unreason: 'I wasn't a misfit; I could join the elements of myself together. It was the others, they wanted misfits, they wanted you to embody within yourself their ambivalence' (RS 27–8).

'The Rainbow Sign' also shows how little political understanding of racism existed in England at that time. Kureishi contrasts this with the American Civil Rights Movement of the 1960s. He rejected the extremist views of Elijah Muhammad and Malcolm X : 'the separatism, the total loathing of the white man as innately corrupt, the "All whites are devils" view, was equally unacceptable. I had to live in England ... with whites. My mother was white' (RS 30). But he describes the liberating effect of reading black American writers such as Richard Wright (1908–60) and, above all, James Baldwin (1924–87): 'Baldwin, having suffered, having been there, was all anger and understanding. He was intelligence and love combined' (RS 29). Kureishi's attempt to understand, rather than demonize, racists, and his later criticism of anti-western Muslim extremists, has opened him up to the same charge of being self-hating and sycophantic towards whites that Eldridge Cleaver levelled at Baldwin (RS 31). But Kureishi has never succumbed to hate; his work is intelligence and love combined.

In the third part of 'The Rainbow Sign', Kureishi records his return to England after his first visit to Pakistan, 'the land of [his] ancestors' (RS 53),[10] and his surprise on realizing how British he feels. But reading of the fire-bombing of an Asian family in the East End in which a child was killed, he is enraged and thinks: 'who wants to be British anyway?' Meditating on the meaning of belonging and home, Kureishi rejects the patriotic faith in tolerance of George Orwell (1903–50) and calls for a 'new way of being British':

> ■ In the meantime it must be made clear that blacks don't require 'tolerance' in this particular condescending way. It isn't this particular paternal tyranny that is wanted, since it is major adjustments to British society that have to be made.
> I stress that it is the British who have to make these adjustments.
> It is the British, the white British, who have to learn that being British isn't what it was. Now it is a more complex thing, involving new elements. So there must be a fresh way of seeing Britain and the choices it faces: and a new way of being British after all this time. □   (RS 55)

As Kureishi stresses, it is not a matter of insisting 'minorities assimilate' and be exactly like the British, because even then the British will reject them. Nor is it about 'a small group of irrelevant people who can be dismissed as minorities', but about the humanity, equality and justice of British society as a whole (RS 56).

With the exception of *London Kills Me* (1991), all Kureishi's work up to *Love in a Blue Time* (1997) has engaged with issues of racism and new forms of Britishness. Given the prominence his work achieved and the paucity of opportunity for British Asian writers and filmmakers, Kureishi proved a controversial figure. The controversy arises out of what Kobena Mercer has called 'the burden of representation': the assumption that the minority artist speaks for the entire community from which they come, which Mercer argues not only limits the artist but is based on the racist assumption that 'every minority subject is, essentially, the same'.[11] The debate about the politics of representation in Kureishi's work, which forms the basis of the critical discussion in chapters one to four and six to seven of this study, has been succinctly summed up by Nahem Yousaf:

■ Kureishi has ... been judged according to a cultural studies agenda of the 1970s that expressed the need to formulate 'positive images' that would perform a public relations exercise for the community to which the artists belonged.[12] But he has simultaneously found himself judged according to the tenets of a typically 1980s political agenda that has sought to articulate raced subject positions in ways that prove them to be both heterogeneous and sophisticated. Kureishi has been caught between a rock and a hard place ... □

(Nahem Yousaf, 'Hanif Kureishi and "The Brown Man's Burden" ', 1996)[13]

In works such as *My Beautiful Laundrette, Sammy and Rosie Get Laid* and *The Buddha of Suburbia* (1990), Kureishi was attacked for failing to provide positive images of British Asians. In *The Black Album* (1995) and *My Son the Fanatic* (1997), he was accused of reinscribing stereotypes of Muslims as fanatics. But he has also been praised by notable writers and commentators, including Stuart Hall, Salman Rushdie and Gayatri Spivak, for his complex representations of minority experience and for enabling solidarities between different groups. He has been hailed as the 'herald of hybridity', celebrating the 'in-between', the commingling of cultures and peoples.

Kureishi's middle works, discussed in chapters eight and nine of this Guide, have focused less on race. This in itself has been contentious since there is still the expectation that so-called 'minority' writers should confine themselves to questions of ethnicity. Kureishi has always refused to be limited in this way: from his first published play, *The King and Me* (1980), through *London Kills Me*, to his most recent play, *Sleep with Me* (1999), set in an English country house, the white British have been his subject. But the main debate about Kureishi's middle works has centred not on representations of ethnicity but on masculinity. Here the critical divide has been between those who see Kureishi exploring new forms of masculinity in a post-feminist era, tackling the contemporary breakdown of heterosexual relationships with honesty and insight, and those who argue that these works are misogynistic. In addition, much of the critical discussion about *Intimacy* (1998) raises the issue of whether Kureishi used his private life in a way that was hurtful to others and unjustified.

This Guide devotes a generous amount of space to *The Buddha of Suburbia*, which is the subject of chapter four, because of the enormous critical interest that this novel has generated. Studied in schools and universities across the world, it is undoubtedly one of the most significant postwar British novels. This is not in any way to imply that Kureishi's other work is less important, and there are full discussions of the early plays in the first chapter of this Guide; of the groundbreaking films, *My Beautiful Laundrette* and *Sammy and Rosie Get Laid* in chapters two and three; of Kureishi's second, condition-of-England novel, *The Black Album* in chapter six; and of his haunting return to film with *My Son the Fanatic* in chapter seven. However, partly because Kureishi's work has been primarily viewed through the lens of postcolonial theory, *London Kills Me*, which is discussed in chapter five, has not attracted much critical attention. Nor have critics quite caught up with Kureishi's middle works, from the spare and melancholy tales in *Love in a Blue Time*, considered in chapter eight, through to the exploration of identity in Kureishi's most recent fable, 'The Body', which is one of the subjects of the final chapter.

The extraordinary range of Kureishi's preoccupations and diversity of genres – plays, films, novels, short stories, and his lucid essays on culture and politics – are unparalleled in Britain. Unlike Martin Amis (born 1949), Julian Barnes (born 1946) and A. S. Byatt (born 1936), who have ignored multiculturalism, or the work of writers such as Andrea Levy (born 1956) and even Sam Selvon (1923–94), which can been pigeonholed as 'ethnic' literature, Kureishi has brought the margins into the mainstream. As he himself indicates, it was a deliberate and radical project:

■ A jejune protest or parochial literature, be it black, gay or feminist, is in the long run no more politically effective than works which are merely public relations. What we need now, in this position, at this time, is imaginative writing that gives us a sense of the shifts and the difficulties within our society as a whole.

If contemporary writing which emerges from oppressed groups ignores the central concerns and major conflicts of the larger society, it will automatically designate itself as minor, as a sub-genre. And it must not allow itself to be rendered invisible and marginalised in this way.[14] □

The critical essays explored in this Guide testify to the central importance of Kureishi's imaginative writing to society as a whole.

CHAPTER ONE

Foreplays: *The King and Me (1980), Outskirts (1981), Borderline (1981) and Birds of Passage (1983)*

K ureishi launched his career in London as a playwright. Although he refers to his early plays as apprentice pieces – 'a setting-out of the themes that would absorb me for a long time, as if I were beginning to discover what my subject would be' (OOP xix) – he achieved considerable success in the theatre.[1] He won the Thames Television Playwright Award in 1980, the George Devine Award for *Outskirts* in 1981, and, in the same year, *Drama* magazine's Award for the Most Promising New Playwright. In 1982 *Borderline* was judged best play in Thames Television's Bursary Scheme. He not only discovered his subject in these plays; the theatre would itself become the subject of *The Buddha of Suburbia*.

In the introduction to *Outskirts and Other Plays*, he recounts that he first sent a play to the Royal Court Theatre when he was 18. To Kureishi, the Royal Court was 'hallowed ground, and the walls of its perfect auditorium breathed accomplishment and integrity'. Much to his amazement, the literary manager, Donald Howarth, invited Kureishi to the Court and for two years he sold programmes and read manuscripts while studying philosophy at King's College (1974–77). At the Court he met Samuel Beckett (1906–89), and other writers and directors, such as Peter Gill (born 1939), Bill Gaskell (born 1930), Max Stafford-Clark (born 1941), Caryl Churchill (born 1938) and Mustapha Matura (born 1939). Although nobody consciously taught him anything, it was 'an excellent education in the arts and in living' (OOP viii). In 1982 he was appointed Writer-in-Residence at the Royal Court.

Kureishi goes on to explain why he turned to the theatre. Although he started writing stories at the age of 14, he had begun to feel 'that this tiny skill, this intricate work, rather resembled lace-making. It was elegantly useless, the creation of a *frisson* for a literary minority' (OOP xii). Although not convinced by all the talk of the 'Death of the Novel' in the 1970s, the novel seemed 'posh, written by gentlemen like Graham

Greene (1904–91), and published by upper-crust Bloomsbury types' (OOP xiv). Film, although it reached a larger audience than the novel, was too hard to break into, while television serials at that time seemed 'shallow' and were subject to censorship. Theatre, in contrast, was radical, popular and accessible. In the following extract, Kureishi refers to the concept of 'hegemony' developed by the Italian Communist Antonio Gramsci (1891–1937): the pervasive system of beliefs and values, or ideologies, that shapes the way things look and what they mean for the majority of people within a particular culture:

■ The plays, when they were about anything, concerned left and anarchist politics, sex roles, rebellion and oppression. They flourished all over London, in basements, above pubs, in tents, in the street and even in theatres. They used nudity, insult, music, audience participation and comedy. They attacked the Labour Party from the left. This was good enough for me ...

After the age had caught up with Gramsci's Leninist analysis of hegemony, the whole cultural area was now being seen as political, as presenting values, assumptions, practices, all seemingly invisible, but which kept late capitalism intact. Part of the state's use of force was the coercive nature of implicit ideas, which were, partly, disseminated by the state's media. Naturally, as the media multiplied, its influence was grasped as being politically significant in many ways, as was, therefore, the analysis of its workings and cultural defiance of its paradigms.

The subsidized theatre was relatively free from state, economic or institutional censorship, compared to television or film; it could be an independent political forum, dealing with sexuality, the security services, Northern Ireland and the corruption of politicians and the state, without the obstruction that TV projects sometimes faced. □   (OOP xiv–xv)

As Kureishi says, part of the appeal of fringe was that it attacked the Labour Party from the left. Labour had been in government from 1964 to 1970 and 1974 to 1979, and was seen as clinging to power while unemployment soared, the economy declined and the Welfare State cracked under the strain. In *Borderline*, the Labour headquarters has not one pane of glass left, its only attempt to 'make the Party more accessible' (OOP 177). While Kureishi is perhaps best known for declaring war on Thatcher (see chapter three), he has always been a fierce critic of the failings of the Left. From David in *Birds of Passage* (1983), through Terry in *The Buddha of Suburbia*, Brownlow in *The Black Album* and on to Barrie in *Sleep with Me*, working-class socialists wait in vain for the revolution, while champagne socialists, such as Pyke in *The Buddha of Suburbia*, send their sons to private schools.

Although exposing and challenging the dominant ideology could not be further from lace-making, Kureishi soon realized that no play was going to topple the state. The main problem with fringe was that it actually only reached a tiny proportion of the population. It was not *really* popular, despite the vigorous efforts of its practitioners. Looking back, Kureishi reflected that alternative theatre could seem as complacent and exclusive as the bourgeois theatre it challenged:

■ Little was gained in numbers or poetry by trying to annex drama to the cathartic ecstasy of a pop concert. The pop audience didn't much like the theatre and if there was rock'n'roll in a play they found the acting interrupted it. And if anything, this kind of play – using agit-prop, song, caricature and, usually, clenched-fist salutes as the end, in a kind of music-hall on speed – was even more elitist and esoteric than conventional theatre. It rarely appealed to those elusive 'wider audiences', and least of all to the working class it was often about, though not addressed to. It was depressing: there was no breakthrough. Like other vestiges of the 1960s, the fringe became self-indulgent.

   ... You could sit through some terrible evening and hear the writer or director say in the pub afterwards, 'At least the point was worth making,' confirming a leftish audience in its prejudices just as much as a bourgeois audience was confirmed in its own. □   (OOP xv)

Despite the self-indulgence of fringe, Kureishi's political consciousness was formed by its radical class politics, the anti-racist, feminist, and pro-gay agenda. Moreover, even if alternative theatre turned out to be less inclusive in terms of audiences than had been intended, Kureishi acknowledges the support the new writing venues such as the Royal Court and the Riverside Studios gave him. He sees himself as having benefited from 'the liberal desire to encourage work from unmapped and emergent areas':

■ They required stories about the new British communities, by cultural translators, as it were, to interpret one side to the other. Anyone with one eye open could see that Britain had changed. It wasn't merely a matter of black workers doing the dirty jobs in the hospitals and on the buses. This was the end of something – the psychological loosening of the idea of Empire – and the start of something else, which involved violence, the contamination of racism and years of crisis. The questions that a multi-cultural society had to ask had hardly been put. □   (OOP xvi)

Kureishi was involved with drama between 1976 and 1984, an exciting period in postwar British theatre, which saw the introduction of new production techniques and new political energies. After the abolition of stage censorship in 1968, almost anything could happen on stage and frequently did. Kureishi's plays made a significant contribution to the understanding of a changing Britain. It was in the theatre that he began his investigation into the condition of England and he had important stories to tell, about immigration and racism.[2]

THE KING AND ME

The King and Me debuted on 9 January 1980 at the Soho Poly Theatre. Set in a council flat, the play introduces themes of stagnation, poverty, and the dreams of escape that have so often fuelled Kureishi's writing. The 30-year-old Marie neglects her children (who remain off-stage) and fantasizes about Elvis Presley (as Stone will also in *London Kills Me*) as a way of enlivening the dreariness around her. She pushes her overworked husband, Bill, into an Elvis lookalike competition, although her sister, Nicola, says 'he'll need plastic surgery if he's going to win' (OOP 9). Marie waits in the flat, which she never seems to leave ('It's ugly out'), while Bill sets off in his costume. Inevitably, he fails and, on his return, he attempts to change their lives by clearing out the Elvis paraphernalia: 'We can work. The King's finished.' But Marie remains with her eyes firmly shut, dreaming: 'I'm a human cinema' (OOP 27).

In the early plays, this one in particular, Bart Moore-Gilbert detects the influence of Beckett, whom Kureishi had met at the Royal Court during rehearsals of *Footfalls*.

■ At the level of theme, the evidence of Beckett is evident in a number of areas: the feelings of entrapment, whether in physical environments like the flat in *The King and Me*, imprisoning cultural/geographical locations like South London, or in relationships, which Kureishi's characters so often prove unable to escape from, however much they at times may desire to; the problems of non- or failing communication between characters; the burden on them of the unfulfilling present (and its evasion through fantasy or nostalgia); the endless waiting (or 'hanging about'); the at times almost unendurably repetitive and ritualistic nature of life. If all these are staples of both writers' work ..., so are the positive elements which prevent either writer's vision from collapsing into mere bleakness: the humour, the solidarity between characters and the stubborn will to endure. □ (Bart Moore-Gilbert, *Hanif Kureishi*, 2001)[3]

Although *The King and Me* was clearly the work of a young writer, it was well received. Irving Wardle of *The Times* declared: 'We have acquired a good new playwright.'[4] But Ruvani Ranasinha notes that Kureishi was seen as an Asian playwright and contrasted with his British contemporaries: 'Kureishi's skill in not allowing his outlook to be influenced by his "Asianness" is praised! [Wardle] notes approvingly Kureishi's "capacity to write about working class Britons [read white] without the least trace of ethnic bias." '[5]

In *The King and Me*, then, we can see Kureishi's interest in marginalized characters, in pop culture, and in the desire for change – social,
political and personal. We can also see the critical confusion that often
arises when a writer, deemed 'ethnic' by the mainstream, deals
with white characters. The expectation that Kureishi will write about
British-Asian characters persists in some quarters even today, despite
the fact that he is now more often seen as British.

OUTSKIRTS

Outskirts was first performed at The Royal Shakespeare Company's
Warehouse Theatre on 28 April 1981. It consists of 12 scenes, which
flash back and forth between 1981 and 1969. In the present, Bob, who
is unemployed, lives with his elderly mother and his wife in a council
estate in south London. Bob's childhood friend, Del, now a teacher,
comes back for a visit during which they recall their violent assault on
an Indian man 12 years before. Del is ashamed of his past actions; Bob is
proud. *Outskirts* and *The King and Me* both show characters who are
stuck in low-paid work, or unemployed, and in unhappy marriages; Bill
in *The King and Me* tried and failed to 'better himself' through education,
Del succeeds and gets out. Education and social mobility continue to be
key themes in Kureishi's work. In *Outskirts* he also begins to explore the
causes of racism.

Ranasinha praises the 'short, compressed but powerful scenes' and
the skilful building up of dramatic tension: 'The scenes alternate
between tense domestic interiors and the rubbish heap under the
motorway, where the boys used to meet and where the attack took
place: it is symbolic of urban wasteland and alienation.'[6] As Ranasinha
argues, the audience's sympathies are not 'divided diagrammatically'
between the protagonists since Del's spouting of 'multiculturalist
rhetoric comes across as hollow' (OOP 63) when we realize that it was
Del who had to be 'pulled … off the little Indian' by Bob (OOP 74). She
continues:

■ In his introduction, Kureishi locates Bob's fascism 'in the context of
unemployment and nationalism of the late 1970s, and the despair they
caused' (OOP, p. xx). Bob insists 'This country, if anything, that's the ill
one; not me' (OOP 63). To an extent, the link between unemployment
and fascism is maintained: the bleakness and stagnation of Bob's present life is powerfully conveyed and suggests why his viciousness became
strengthened where Del's has dissipated: Del's teaching career has initi-
ated his social mobility. He has moved beyond the 'outskirts'. However,
what emerges from the play is that the brutal assault itself cannot be

rationalized. The gratuitous violence of the act is clear. Del suggests that they attacked the Indian man because they were bored and 'wanted sensation' (OOP 65). Bob's mother wistfully observes that in contrast to Bob, Del had 'brains and background' and 'attention' from his dad (OOP 59). While this may have facilitated Del's move to the middle classes, it did not prevent him taking the initiative in the offence. □

(Ruvani Ranasinha, *Hanif Kureishi*, 2002)[7]

Moore-Gilbert's reading of the play emphasizes Kureishi's 'nuanced approach' to the issue of racism. While conceding that 'Bob is himself largely responsible for his parlous situation', Moore-Gilbert contends that 'set against Bob's political brutishness ... is the enormous tenderness which he shows towards his ailing mother and, despite the obvious strains in their relationship, his love for Maureen'. He goes on:

■ Perhaps most indicative of Kureishi's nuanced approach to the issue of racism is the fact that Bob's political views are shown to be intimately bound up with the sense of frustration he feels as a member of a white 'under-class' which was emerging in the wake of the recessions of the 1970s (as well as being unemployed himself, Bob's mother has been laid off and his sister has been forced to emigrate). Bob explains the make-up of his neo-Nazi group in the following terms: 'Men worn down by waiting. Abused men, men with no work. Our parents made redundant. Now us. No joke. Wandering round the place, like people stranded on holiday' (OOP 64). To this extent, Bob is depicted as the victim of enormously powerful currents of social and historical change. His attachment to the far Right, with its attempt to make immigrants into scapegoats for developments of which they are the symptom and not the cause, is testimony to the disruptions generated by the long-term decline of a working-class sense of security, identity and community. It is for this reason that Bob's claim to have the support of ordinary (white) people in the area has credibility and why he – and the class fraction that he represents – are depicted with some sympathy. As Del comments to his friend's exasperated wife: 'There's a whole machinery down on him, Mo. You've got to see that' (OOP 82). □   (Bart Moore-Gilbert, *Hanif Kureishi*, 2001)[8]

According to Ranasinha, it is precisely this sympathetic portrayal of the white attackers that caused the favourable reception of *Outskirts* in the white-dominated press:

■ *The Times* review of *Outskirts* suggests that as 'a British-born Pakistani who writes with some sympathy about the white urban working class, Hanif Kureishi is an inexpressibly welcome figure on the racial scene'. However, the reviewer [Wardle] goes on to discuss Bob's portrayal in a manner that verges on a rationalization of his racist behaviour

that is not present in Kureishi's text. He refers to Bob's 'courageous independence ... he knows who he is. In a sense he rejected the system before the system threw him on the scrap heap.'[9] This suggests the way texts can be made to take on meanings by dominant critical views. □
(Ruvani Ranasinha, *Hanif Kureishi*, 2002)[10]

Ranasinha's point here is an important one: to try to understand (the motives of neo-Nazis) is not to condone. How characters are read by audiences becomes a major preoccupation in Kureishi's later work, while the sympathetic portrayal of white working-class fascists, found in *Outskirts*, also causes controversy in *My Beautiful Laundrette*.

The characters in *Outskirts* are all white – 'the little Indian' never appears. In his next play, Kureishi switches attention from the causes of racism to explore the resistance to racism, with a larger cast of characters, most of whom are Asian.

BORDERLINE

In this play, first performed at the Royal Court on 2 November 1981, after a short tour, Kureishi was engaged in a different kind of writing process. He was asked by Max Stafford-Clark, artistic director of the Court, to write a play with Joint Stock, the ensemble founded by David Hare (born 1947) and William Gaskill, among others. Kureishi describes the company's 'unique way of making plays':

■ After casting, the actors, writer and director would spend six months researching the idea, improvising around characters met and gathering information about the subject ... [in this case] the lives of immigrants and their children in Southall, a predominantly Sikh area of West London. After this period of collective effort, the writer would spend ten weeks writing the script, using the gathered material. Eventually the play would be rehearsed in the normal way, though over a longer period than is usual in the British theatre, allowing more valuable time for rewriting. □
(OOP xviii)

The idea behind this experiment was to 'produce well-informed drama about contemporary events, a mixture of information about the state of things, polemical journalism and theatre' (OOP xviii). Research would make the drama 'relevant' and this bottom-up, collaborative method would ensure that 'the democratic will of the company was sovereign, rather than that of the individual writer's imagination' (OOP xix).

The main focus, then, was not on the artist's unique voice but on exploring the 'new British communities'. As Ranasinha points out, the general context for *Borderline* was 'a series of black uprisings' in Toxteth, Southall and Brixton, which forced 'the British establishment to confront the extent of white racism and the degree to which black people were alienated and marginalized'.[11] She goes on to describe the play:

■ *Borderline* explores the different ways in which an immigrant family (Amjad, Banoo and their daughter Amina) has adapted to life in Britain. The play charts Amina's political radicalization, as she becomes increasingly involved in the Asian Youth Front led by Anwar and Yasmin. The youth movement's mobilization in response to racism, and their combative assertion that Britain is home and they are 'here to stay', are defined against their parents' reactions. The play closes with Yasmin reminding Amina 'We can't go home like your mother' and instructing her to keep the lights on in the Asian Youth Front Office so 'people know we are here' (OOP 168). However, not all the young Asians agree on this approach: Amina adopts an activism that her clandestine boyfriend Haroon rejects. Meanwhile, Anwar and Yasmin are initially hostile to a white journalist, Susan, who wants to join their fight against racist oppression. □ (Ruvani Ranasinha, *Hanif Kureishi*, 2002)[12]

In choosing to set his play amongst a group of activists, Kureishi challenges the media stereotype of Asians as passive and depoliticized; a stereotype of the victim often constructed in contrast to a supposedly more militant African-Caribbean youth. In addition, Moore-Gilbert contends that 'Kureishi's representation of increasingly self-assertive and politically engaged young British-Asian women like Amina and Yasmin challenges the common perception in mainstream society that such women passively accept their apparent status as the most oppressed members of an oppressed constituency.'[13] Ranasinha points out that Kureishi disrupts notions of a 'monolithic Asian community' by depicting competing class, generational and gendered differences. As an example of class conflict, she cites Haroon's father exploiting illegal immigrants in his restaurant as cheap labour, and then turns to issues of gender and generational tensions:

■ *Borderline* deftly points to the various, complex factors that impinge upon immigrant experiences and the diverse responses to immigration. It presents a poignant portrait of first-generation immigrants rationalizing their decision to emigrate, weighing up the gains with the costs. The husband Amjad stresses the economic benefits that he as the male 'provider' has worked hard to secure for his family in Britain. He tells his wife Banoo that he does not want to return to Pakistan to 'be loved by your relatives' (OOP 106) ... Banoo acknowledges their material gains but ruefully observes 'they haven't made us happy' (OOP 127). She misses her family, her village and feels estranged from her daughter Amina who has become too 'English ... grown so far from us ... ' and 'understands life here more than us' (OOP 126–7). Banoo sees Amina's education in terms of a class mobility that exacerbates the distance between them: 'We are poor people. Where we come from, education is for the rich. But it has changed her and we can't understand' (OOP 125).

The play highlights the gendered nature of some intergenerational conflicts. At first Amina finds ways to secretly elude the constraints her parents impose on her freedom, but by the end of the play she rejects the marriage arranged for her and symbolically cuts her long hair: a marker of 'traditional' South Asian femininity. Amina's internalization of these conflicts, manifested as a sense of guilt, is effectively delineated. Kureishi emphasizes the gap between parental expectation and reality by juxtaposing Amjad's attempts to police and obstruct Amina's sexuality and insistence that she is his 'baby girl', with scenes indicating her active sex life with her boyfriend Haroon. Her friend Jasmin prefigures the outspoken feminist anti-racist Jamila of *The Buddha of Suburbia*: 'for women like us, too much is dictated by other people. By our parents. And tonight by white racists' (OOP 167). We learn that Yasmin's father began to starve himself to death when she refused to accept an arranged marriage (OOP 116). This is developed more fully as a subplot in *The Buddha of Suburbia*. Amina and Yasmin are the first in a series of Kureishi's British Asian female protagonists who find they cannot explore intellectual and sexual independence while remaining within the family. At the same time, Susan tells Amjad that her parents 'do mind' about her career as a journalist and that they 'think it's time [she] married an architect and had kids' (OOP 127). This points to the gender constraints and patriarchal expectations in white British culture and prevents a simplistic contrast between a progressive white Britain and its 'backward' minorities.

Amina's family diverges in its response to their neighbours' racist attack on Amjad. Despite having suffered the racial assault, Amjad insists that a 'few' English racists should not force them to leave. He takes a court case against his aggressors, maintaining his belief in British democracy and the British legal system. In contrast, Banoo speaks of the failure of the police to uphold the law and protect them: 'the law wasn't there when the neighbour knocked you down ... the police ... said: go to hospital in a rickshaw' (OOP 107). Kureishi's irony repeatedly foregrounds the discrepancy between vicious racial attacks and Britain's vaunted reputation as a liberal, tolerant society. For Banoo, living in fear of further racial hostility is unbearable: she wants to return to Pakistan, and does so after Amjad's death. For her daughter, this is not an option: Amina says 'I belong here. There's work to be done. To make England habitable' (OOP 158). □
(Ruvani Ranasinha, *Hanif Kureishi*, 2002)[14]

Moore-Gilbert's reading of the generational differences in *Borderline* emphasizes the older generation's faith in economic emancipation and their desire to assimilate to the norms of British society, at least outside the home:

■ Such characters ... tend to see the economic sphere as the key both to integration and empowerment in contemporary British society. Haroon explains his father's attitude as follows: 'He says "What I want to see in England is a day when you won't find a single Pakistani on the shop-floor. You never see Jews in overalls. We've got to develop our businesses, our power" ' (OOP 138).

However, *Borderline* suggests a number of problems with the strategy of the older generation. Their belief that assimilation in the 'public sphere' can be squared with the continuing sway of custom and tradition in the domestic domain is predicated on the belief that the two spaces can be kept entirely separate. Thus, Amjad can claim: 'Our Amina was born here, as you know. But she's Pakistani through and through' (OOP 153). As his daughter's experience suggests, however, this division of roles and spheres is hard to sustain ... Moreover, the older generation's misplaced faith in the institutions of the 'public sphere' to deliver social justice is highlighted in a number of ways. As Yasmin points out, material prosperity provides no safeguards against racism – as is made evident by the terrifying experience of Haroon's parents during the Southall riots and, as Amjad's ordeal at the police station when he complains about racial harassment also makes clear, the forces of law and order can be as much part of the problem of racism as its solution. □   (Bart Moore-Gilbert, *Hanif Kureishi*, 2001)[15]

For these reasons, Moore-Gilbert sees the play as an endorsement of the younger characters' activism.

Ranasinha emphasizes that the play does not uphold a clear-cut generational divide and cites Banoo's spirited response to her attackers: 'but I am not afraid. They do their things to us, but I will fight them' (OOP 126). She also refers to Avtar Brah's influential study, *Cartographies of Diaspora* (1996), which affirms the importance of not erasing the parents' struggle against racism. She goes on to relate this to the portrayal of the older generation in *Borderline*:

■ Kureishi locates the Asian Youth Front's adoption of an alternative politics (to that of their parents) in terms of the militant protests against the escalating right-wing activities of the late 1970s. Avtar Brah observes that in the late 1970s, the media portrayed the Asian youth militancy as a new phenomenon and defined it in contrast to the political behaviour of their more 'docile' parents: this erased the history of the first generation's militant struggles in the 1950s, 1960s and early 1970s. □
(Ruvani Ranasinha, *Hanif Kureishi*, 2002)[16]

Although Ranasinha concedes that Kureishi is in danger of reinforcing this 'discursive erasure', she finds that while he 'explores *inter*generational disagreements, he does not homogenize the divisions within each generation'.[17] The youth struggle against racism may take a more visible form than the parents' strategy but the older Asian characters in *Borderline* are never simply passive. Moreover, within each generation, there is considerable diversity and debate about the best means to 'make England habitable'.

Ranasinha discusses this younger generation in terms of the arguments for and against separatism and political activism: 'the ambivalence and implications of solidarity to an "ethnic" community and the competing demands of self and group':

■ Haroon explains why he chooses to pursue education rather than the separatist activism of the Asian Youth Front: 'We've got to engage in the political process. Not just put out fires when they start them. Yasmin and Anwar – they're brave. But they're separatist. I say we've got to get educated ... And get inside things. The worm in the body ... ' (OOP 118). Haroon articulates the argument that separatism reinforces boundaries between groups, and minorities remain at the socio-cultural margins of the body politic, while power remains at the homogeneous centre. Haroon desires instead to 'get inside things' and subvert them from within. Yasmin refutes Haroon's exhortation to abandon 'pointless' demonstrations and instead 'join parties, sit on committees' on the grounds of the inadequacy of and 'slow progress' of 'existing machinery' while 'people are being burnt to death' (OOP 150). Yasmin counters Haroon's arguments, but in a manner characteristic of Kureishi, Haroon's points are not completely dismissed or negated. So while Yasmin feels it is 'crucial we defend ourselves', she contests those who 'imagine that all our work can be done with broken bottles and knives' (OOP 164) ... On the evening of the demonstration, she agrees with Anwar that 'Tonight [protest is] the only possible response', but insists that she is 'already thinking about tomorrow' (OOP 164). Yasmin's counter-argument asserts the importance of balancing confrontational activism (which involves both self-defence and retaliation) with a more proactive approach that will strengthen the community's status in the long term. In this way her stance is not so far removed from Haroon's. In this instance, Kureishi moves beyond a separatist/anti-separatist dichotomy in showing the relationship between the two positions as overlapping and complex. □ (Ruvani Ranasinha, *Hanif Kureishi*, 2002)[18]

For Moore-Gilbert, too, '*Borderline* can be interpreted as an early exploration of the possibilities of a "third way" of responding to the worsening racial situation.' But where Ranasinha locates this in Yasmin's direct activism coupled with forward planning, Moore-Gilbert finds it embodied in Haroon's 'long march through the institutions. The black mole under the lawns and asphalt of England' (OOP 159), which

Moore-Gilbert sees as a means of avoiding both the parents' 'quietism' and the danger of 'ghettoisation' inherent in Yasmin's position.[19] But this privileging of Haroon's politics in *Borderline* is not entirely convincing, not least because Haroon's motives are portrayed, in part, as self-centred. Ranasinha sees Haroon as the embodiment of Kureishi's own individualism and ambivalence about community: 'Haroon feels "cramped" and "stifled" by the community', 'Shut in for safety' (OOP 117), and wants to get out of this 'place and the past' (OOP 100). For Ranasinha, Haroon's dilemma is presented sympathetically in the play but he is certainly no herald of the 'third way':

■ First, solidarity is presented as difficult: it demands a self-sacrifice that Haroon resists. In contrast to the commitment of the militants, Haroon's refusal to engage with the activism of the Asian Youth Movement appears to be a rationalization of his personal ambitions to become a lawyer. Amina and the others perceive his individualism as a disloyal self-interest that prevails over his obligations to the community. At the same time, the suggestion that solidarity can be painful is treated sympathetically. Haroon demurs, partly because he does not wish to confront and adopt an embattled existence. For Amina (and the others) political engagement gives her a sense of belonging ('we were a community') and direction, Haroon plaintively observes, in contrast, 'I want to live a normal life ... I suppose' (OOP 149). For Haroon, distancing himself represents independence and freedom. Yasmin tells Haroon that his independence is far from liberating because it stems from an internalization of 'race and contempt' as if 'it was some kind of personal problem you can work through on your own' which is ultimately self-destructive. She compares this to externalizing conflicts in the collective struggle against white racism, insisting: 'you can't live like that ... It'll tear you apart in the end. No, we've got to organise and retaliate' (OOP 149). Her description of Haroon echoes Kureishi's accounts of his childhood as marked by a sense that racism was a private problem. □

(Ruvani Ranasinha, *Hanif Kureishi*, 2002)[20]

One could also see Haroon as an early version of Karim in *The Buddha of Suburbia*, looking for fulfilment through personal success rather than political engagement. Haroon may represent some of Kureishi's own dilemmas but, in Ranasinha's reading, he does not represent any answers.

Interestingly, Moore-Gilbert also makes autobiographical parallels but in a very different way. He sees Haroon's plan to change the nature of the dominant order from within as similar to Kureishi's own politically subversive theatre practice. In this model, 'fringe' is a third space, between mainstream and minoritarian theatre (such as Temba and the Black Theatre Cooperative), enabling Kureishi to address the majority ethnicity without excluding a minority audience. By choosing to work in fringe theatres, Kureishi was endorsing the 'cultural politics of the "in-between" position', planting the 'ethnic worm' in the body of 'white' theatre.[21]

But the role of the 'in-between' is a tricky one: the community being represented may feel misrepresented by the appointed cultural translator; or the audience may misinterpret in the light of their own preconceptions and prejudices. Moore-Gilbert asserts that 'what is distinctive about Kureishi's drama ... is its attempt to address the predicament of Asian Britain from the inside'.[22] Kureishi himself, however, explicitly disavows any such insider knowledge:

■ Unfortunately, the idea behind *Borderline* was impossible. It was using a method, journalism, as the tool for a different form, art or theatre. The result could only be external, sketchy, an impression. We knew the subject was there but we couldn't get at it, not from this far outside – it was too big, too vague – and not from the inside either: we didn't know enough. A play is not an article in a newspaper. What did we think we could bring back, apart from the acceptance of our ignorance, and the knowledge that the British Empire had released forces that would transform much? □ (OOP xix)

Not everyone would accept such a clear-cut division between art and journalism (which have often informed each other), but Kureishi's belief that this method had failed led him to autobiography: 'I knew I had to find a way of knitting ideas to specific characters, events and emotions, based on my own experience' (OOP xix). Writing *Borderline* was a pivotal moment, then, confirming that political theory and documentary observation are not enough without intimate understanding.

Moore-Gilbert gives a very perceptive account of the play's debate about liberal interventions on behalf of oppressed groups, and he goes on to apply the issues raised in the play to an exploration of the method used to create the play in the first place. He begins his discussion by looking at the role of Susan, the liberal journalist who is conducting research into ethnic minorities for a documentary. Despite her genuine sympathy, Moore-Gilbert suggests that she could be seen as a contemporary version of the 'benevolent missionary' who believed she was 'raising up' the colonized:

■ Anwar ... questions whether Susan's programme is not an appropriation of the voice of his community, a danger to which he suggests that interventions 'from outside', however benevolently motivated, are perhaps inevitably liable: 'I've said you take our voice. Use our voice. Annexe our cause. Because you like a good cause don't you, a good solid cause to tie yourself behind ... Now for a few days you've borrowed our little worry' (OOP 132). Kureishi's criticism of Susan metacritically [in other words, a criticism *of* the play *in* the play] and self-referentially questions the ethics underpinning the interest of radical theatre groups like Joint Stock (which commissioned *Borderline*) in the politics of race, which might be deemed to run the same kind of risks as Susan's investigative project. □ (Bart Moore-Gilbert, *Hanif Kureishi*, 2001)[23]

Here Moore-Gilbert refers to Joint Stock as outsiders, who like Susan, run the risk of patronising Southall's Asian community and appropriating their stories. But as Kureishi was Joint Stock's writer, this seems to contradict Moore-Gilbert's earlier view of Kureishi as an insider. In any case, it is not clear whether *Borderline* suggests that outsiders should not get involved. As Susan says, it is not necessary to have personal experience of a particular oppression to want to oppose it.

Moore-Gilbert goes on to compare Haroon's role in the play with Kureishi's in writing it:

■ The issue is further complicated by the ambiguous implications of Haroon's desire to write about Asian Britain, which inevitable invites reflection on Kureishi's own role as a writer about 'his' community. Yasmin suggests that Haroon's proposed vocation is in some sense parasitic on the very people from whom he affects to want to distance himself. She caricatures his novel as follows: 'It's full of feeling, I've heard. It's subtle with suffering. Whose suffering, Haroon?' (OOP 148). One inference to be drawn from this debate is that a shared ethnicity or roots in a particular marginalised community grants no *a priori* privileges to the intellectual or artist in the context of the question of the right to represent that community's oppressions. □
(Bart Moore-Gilbert, *Hanif Kureishi*, 2001)[24]

But there is a contradiction here: is Haroon to be interpreted as a 'parasite' or as 'an embodiment of the third way'? Is it possible for him to be both? The issue of who can speak for whom is a controversial one and the politics of representation is a major issue in discussions of Kureishi's work – both in the reception of *My Beautiful Laundrette* and as a preoccupation in *The Buddha*. Here it could be argued that although *Borderline* interrogates the motives for, and efficacy of, both Susan's and Haroon's interventions, it also raises the more general question of whether *anybody* is entitled to represent a minority community. If all attempts to speak on behalf of others are necessarily biased and incomplete, does that mean the alternative is silence?

Kureishi is not necessarily offering a 'message': *Borderline* is best read as an investigation of questions rather than a source of definitive answers. The play succeeds in including a number of different, sometimes clashing perspectives and voices, and the reader or audience is encouraged to examine their own moral and political assumptions. As in Brecht's *Mother Courage* (1939), which Kureishi adapted (1984), the aim is to start debate. The Brechtian aesthetic, of provoking audiences into questioning their preconceptions, is one that informs all Kureishi's work up to and including *My Son the Fanatic*.

Having considered the role of the writer, we now come to the other side of the curtain and the question of how audiences actually responded and how critics have interpreted this response. Kenneth Kaleta (who does not discuss the play itself), provides an account of the reviews in the mainstream press:

■ [T]he play provided Kureishi with his first major popular success. '*Borderline*, a study of the Asian community in Britain, is the best thing by Kureishi that I have seen,' wrote the *Sunday Times* reviewer [James Fenton], who went on to describe it as having 'some accurate charcterization, funny dialogue and supple political analysis' ... ... Reviews ... recognized that he had defined an area of interest. '*Border-line* is a portrait of a community under threat. Running through it is the fear of violence and intolerance that will compress all its subtle distinctions into one stark antithesis,' wrote the *Times Literary Supplement* reviewer. 'Kureishi describes himself as a beige liberal. His picture of the diverse and contradictory values of the immigrant community is a fine example of the possibilities of investigative theatre.' ... ... Another critic [Irving Wardle] agreed that 'where [*Borderline*] comes marvellously to life is in its treatment of the individual characters irrespective of any issue they represent.' But again, this otherwise positive review opened by chastising Kureishi for lacking authorial objectivity because this spokesperson for liberal causes had 'his heart definitely in the right place to please white liberals.' □

(Kenneth Kaleta, *Hanif Kureishi*, 1998)[25]

As Kaleta notes, reviewers interpreted *Borderline* in terms of Kureshi's 'racial' background: either 'categorizing [him] as the Asian voice crying out in white London or as the speaker for white sensibilities in a dusky body'.[26] It could be argued that the very fact that Kureishi was seen in the white press as both the 'voice of the ghetto' and, at the same time, a 'coconut', suggests he was neither. Ranasinha also explores the contradictions that result when reviewers pigeonhole Kureishi as an ethnic writer. She notes that it is Kureishi's use of farcical characters and situations that appeals to white reviewers:

■ Kureishi sometimes resorts to generating humour by invoking facile stereotypes. Ravi [an illegal immigrant befriended by Susan] is a clichéd figure of a sex-starved, randy Asian who arrives from India, imagining Britain as a sexual haven peopled with sexually available white

women: 'You are English, please – undress' … (OOP 121) … . It is significant that *The Times* review singles out this hackneyed Asian character
for praise and describes the scenes with the 'accident-prone Ravi' as
'simply the work of a fine dramatist with no axe to grind'. □
(Ruvani Ranasinha, *Hanif Kureishi*, 2002)[27]

The use of farce, as a way of disarming audiences and readers, is a characteristic of much of Kureishi's work and Ravi could be seen as an early
version of Changez in *The Buddha of Suburbia*. Ranasinha also considers
that *Borderline* is an easy play for white liberals to find sympathetic
because it does not show Asian youth in Britain as utterly alienated.
Even Yasmin, the most radical character in the play, is a responsible
rebel who insists that she is not 'against things here. I want them to
be improved' (OOP 167). Ranasinha goes on to contrast this with more
confrontational works, such as Ceddo's *The People's Account*, which
Channel 4 refused to transmit.[28]

But what was the response of the British-Asian audiences on whose
behalf the play was developed? This is much more difficult to discover.
According to Ranasinha, *Borderline* was never staged in Southall as
originally intended because of objections by local British Asians. In a
footnote, she speculates about possible reasons: 'These may have origi-
nated from a perception that the play was oriented towards a white
audience.'[29] In other words, the play was not radical enough for
Southall. Moore-Gilbert, in contrast, favours Kureishi's own view that
local activists were outraged by the play's 'boldness' in putting sexually
explicit language into the mouths of British-Asian women.[30] The problem, in this view, is the sexual conservatism of British-Asian audiences.
In a footnote, Moore-Gilbert also refers to the recollection of one of the
original cast members, Vincent Ebrahim, that the main objection in
Southall was to the fact that white actors played some British-Asian
characters.[31] It may be that this was intended as an example of
Brechtian 'defamiliarization' – a challenge to audience preconceptions
about ethnic difference – but was interpreted by British Asians as insen-
sitivity, or a sign that their story was being appropriated by outsiders.

The major irony here is not only that the attempt to provide a
platform for the views of a minority community was rejected by that
community, but also that there is little knowledge as to precisely why; an
irony compounded by the fact that both Ranasinha and Moore-Gilbert
relegate their speculations on the British-Asian response to the footnotes,
while Kaleta does not discuss it at all. This might confirm the suspicion,
first articulated by Gayatri Spivak in her work on the 'subaltern', that
attempts by western radicals to represent the views of the marginalized
paradoxically only perpetuate their subordination.[32] None of the
available discussions of *Borderline* includes any voices from Southall.

Nonetheless, *Borderline* successfully explores racism, resistance, the politics of representation, generational and gender differences within the British-Asian community, and the tensions of group solidarity and individualism. Its critical reception also raises questions about ethnic minority and mainstream audiences, which will surface again, most notably in *The Buddha of Suburbia*, where Pyke's radical improvisation bears marked similarities to the working methods of Joint Stock.

BIRDS OF PASSAGE

Kureishi did not repeat this experimental method of writing plays in his next work, *Birds of Passage*, which is more traditional in approach and structure. First performed at Hampstead Theatre on 15 September 1983, it centres on Asif, a wealthy Pakistani student who buys the house of his unemployed landlord, David, and his wife Audrey. He has a brief affair with Audrey's sister Eva, who is unhappily married to Ted. Audrey and David's daughter, Stella, has got out of south London; their son, Paul, is joining the fight against racism.

As Ranasinha notes, the play bristles with various forms of racist and class tensions:

■ In *Birds of Passage*, Kureishi explores the intersection of race and class: the way race relations are inflected by class politics. Kureishi employs a strategy of anti-racist discourse, inversion to reverse the Manichean aesthetic of colonial discourse. Asif's remarks are rather self-consciously emblematic of the transposition of hierarchies: 'I'm going to be an expansionist ... this house is the beginning of my empire' (OOP 215). In contrast to Asif's entrepreneurial spirit, the landlord's children Paul and Stella are rootless and derailed. Stella becomes an upmarket sex-worker. This contrast between Asian immigrant success and the white working-class failure resurfaces in *My Beautiful Laundrette*.

Not that class privilege always protects one from racism, as evidenced in the account of the reception of Asif's father ('a high up' in Pakistan where 'no one can touch him') experienced in Britain: 'The last time he came here someone spat on him' (OOP 185). A recurrent feature of Kureishi's characterizations of wealthy Asians is, as Gayatri Spivak describes, the migrant élite's 'comic yet ugly self-separation from the less advantaged from the former colony'.[33] Spivak is referring to Rafi in *Sammy and Rosie Get Laid*, but Changez in *The Buddha of Suburbia* makes similar snobbish observations on immigrants in Britain. Kureishi first articulates this tendency through Asif, who comments: 'Most English don't realize that the immigrants who come here are the scum of Pakistan: the sweepers, the peasants, the drivers ... They've given us all a bad reputation here because they don't know how to behave' (OOP 200). □   (Ruvani Ranasinha, *Hanif Kureishi*, 2002)[34]

As in *Borderline*, there is also a debate about the best way to deal with racism (and who can be involved), but with an increased emphasis on class differences:

■ Asif and Paul debate whether vigilante activism or material empower-ment is the most suitable weapon for combating racism. Here Paul takes on the activist role, joining Asian vigilante groups against the 'lumpen racists' (OOP 215). He says: 'It's good to see them organizing and resist-ing' (OOP 200). Asif mocks such militancy, insisting that 'There are other ways of achieving social peace. I've got some ideas. Prosperity is a great quietener, you know' (OOP 200). Asif abandons his education, and decides to create a capitalist enterprise supported by his father's money. Asif dismisses Paul's involvement in the anti-racist movement: 'We don't need your help. We'll protect ourselves against boots with our brains. We won't be on the streets because we'll be in cars. We won't be throwing bricks because we'll be building houses with them. They won't abuse us in factories because we will own the factories and we'll sack people' (OOP 215). That Asif's capitalist dream is available for only the privileged few is underlined in Paul's retort: 'Will everyone own factories or only those of you with wealthy fathers in Western-supported Fascist countries?' (OOP 215). In *My Beautiful Laundrette*, the protagonist Omar rejects education (the path to empowerment outlined in *Borderline* by Haroon) in favour of Asif's capitalist ethic. □

(Ruvani Ranasinha, *Hanif Kureishi*, 2002)[35]

In addition to the connections between *Birds of Passage* and the later works that Ranasinha mentions here, it is also clear that, from the beginning, Kureishi refused to counteract racist stereotypes by producing positive images of British Asians. His decision not to produce 'cheering fictions' will be explored more fully in the next chapter.

Moore-Gilbert discusses the influence of Joe Orton (1933–67), Ibsen (1828–1906) and Chekhov (1860–1904) – very different playwrights who, nonetheless, have all had an abiding effect on Kureishi's work. Although Moore-Gilbert does not cite a specific Ibsen play as a source, he argues that Kureishi admired Ibsen's naturalism and concern with social and moral issues. In the following extract, Moore-Gilbert explores *Borderline* in relation to Orton and Chekhov, two unlikely bedfellows, whose later coupling in *Sleep with Me* is discussed in chapter eight.

■ *Birds of Passage*, ... like [Orton's] *Entertaining Mr Sloane* (1964), revolves around a lodger who progressively usurps the 'host' family.[36] Just as Kath welcomes Sloane as a replacement for the son she has lost, so Audrey greets Asif as a 'new son'. Just as Kath and Sloane become lovers, so do Asif and Audrey's sister Eva in Kureishi's play. Kemp expresses similar kinds of racist sentiment to Eva's husband Ted. Sloane's relations with Ed are at first conflictual, with each struggling for ascendancy, before the relationship settles into a co-operative one of mutual benefit, a pattern largely followed in Asif and Ted's relationship. Like Sloane, Asif is without apparent shame or guilt for the way he behaves in his private life. Stylistically, the debt is most evident in Kureishi's dramatic language, which in many of his plays echoes Orton's somewhat mannered and aphoristic phrasing as well as his colloquial register.

... The naturalistic conception of character, stage time and structural development in *Birds of Passage*, and its interest in moral as much as social issues, especially the conflict, repression, hypocrisy and secrets characteristic of family life, all suggest Ibsen's influence. An even more important source for *Birds of Passage* is Chekhov. The link is signposted by Asif, who asks Stella what she thinks of the Russian dramatist (OOP 216). *The Cherry Orchard* (1904) is the key intertext here in terms of character, action and theme. Thus, Paul's conviction that 'Sydenham's a leaving place' (OOP 173) echoes Yasha's desire to quit the backwoods for the metropolis. Just as David and Audrey long for a life of contemplation in Wales, Varia yearns to improve herself in 'holy places'. Gayev has the same kind of 'progressive' attitudes as David, and their politics, about which each likes to hold forth at length, are represented as equally out of date. Kureishi combines the roles of the student Trofimov and the businessman Lopakhin in Asif. Audrey greets Asif as her new son, just as Liuba sees Trofimov as a surrogate for Grisha. Both Asif and Lopakhin are represented ambiguously, insofar as their energy and ambition is admired while their disdain for traditional moral values is decried. Like Asif, Trofimov is a restless 'bird of passage'. Like Liuba, Stella returns home after a period away, with a dark secret which is uncovered in the play. As with Liuba and Gayev, her parents are afflicted by feelings of failure and the sense that their best days are behind them. This grounds the main social issue of both plays, the exploration of the decline of the class which these respective pairs of parents represent. Just as Lopakhin, whose parents were family serfs, takes over Liuba's house, so Asif, whose parents were colonised subjects, takes over David's.

... While the earthiness of Kureishi's humour and the characteristic coarseness of his principal protagonist prevent his play from attaining the refined poignancy and bitter-sweet timbre of Chekhov's, there are undoubted hints of an attempt to produce a similar sense of the pathos (and dignity) of human life and relations within the quite different social contexts of late twentieth-century, multi-racial, Britain. □

(Bart Moore-Gilbert, *Hanif Kureishi*, 2001)[37]

Perhaps more than any specific debt to a particular play or playwright, Moore-Gilbert's discussion highlights the way a writer's style and preoccupations are shaped as much by other texts as personal experience. It is possible to see in this early work the two sides of Kureishi's aesthetic: the Chekhovian interest in subtle analysis of character on the one hand; and on the other, the concern with social justice found, in different forms, in Ibsen, Brecht and Orton. Moreover, the ten years Kureishi spent in the theatre, in particular the Royal Court and the Riverside Studios, surrounded by people engaged in intense, engaged and radical artistic endeavours – people for whom culture really mattered – seem to have been profoundly influential.

These early plays, then, provide insights into Kureishi's later work. As he says in the introduction to *Outskirts and Other Plays*: 'A character from *The King and Me* ... turned up in *London Kills Me*. The lives of the suburban couple ... from *Birds of Passage* were extended in *The Buddha of Suburbia*, and the boys from *Outskirts* were the genesis of the boys in *My Beautiful Laundrette*' (OOP xx). But these foreplays are not just an indication of later developments; they constitute an important contribution in their own right to Kureishi's long-standing commitment to telling stories about a changing Britain, a contribution which in turn changed the way the British have seen themselves. In *My Beautiful Laundrette*, Kureishi revisits the zoo of South London as skinheads and anti-racists, British Asian entrepreneurs and intellectuals, parents and children, conflict and collide – and critics engage in even fiercer battles over representations.

CHAPTER TWO

'Class, Race, Fucking and Farce':
My Beautiful Laundrette (1985)

After the reception of his first plays Kureishi anticipated that *My Beautiful Laundrette* would create a furore: '[the Asian community] think that I'm perpetually throwing shit at them anyway. They'll think that this is the last straw: now he's showing us as drug dealers, sodomites and mad landlords'.[1] Kureishi was attacked by some members of his family and criticized by many in the Asian community for giving ammunition to racists. But he vigorously defended his refusal to provide 'useful lies and cheering fictions', to play the role of 'the writer as public relations officer, as hired liar'.[2] Instead of 'positive images' he aimed to make 'the characters rounded and human'. At the same time, Kureishi was aware of the political implications of his representations of minorities: as he said, 'you'll notice that none of my Asian characters are victims'.[3] Most significantly, Omar, the protagonist, is a 'wog' to the white fascists and an 'in-between' to his Pakistani relatives; but far from feeling himself a misfit, he is confident that he can make it in Britain.

From a contrasting quarter, right-wing English critics attacked the film for failing to produce PR for Britain: why show a semi-derelict London, riddled with unemployment, poverty and racist violence? Although the film hardly warmed the hearts of Thatcherites, it was a runaway success at the Edinburgh Film Festival and went on to become one of Britain's most commercially and critically successful films of 1986. It launched Daniel Day-Lewis's career, established Stephen Frears as a major filmmaker and earned Kureishi an Oscar nomination for best screenplay of 1985.[4]

Kureishi explained that he turned from theatre to TV and film because by the 1980s the energy and experimentalism of fringe had got lost. He blamed the 'catatonic' state of new British drama on the lack of imagination of theatre managers and on reactionary, bourgeois critics, unsympathetic to progressive work. Dramatists such as David Hare (born 1947), Trevor Griffiths (born 1935), David Edgar (born 1948) and Kureishi decamped to Channel 4 and other independent film companies in order to 'make large statements about the state of England' and to reach wider audiences.[5] In his introduction to *My Beautiful Laundrette*, he recounts that he was working on the script for the film at the same time as his adaptation of Brecht's *Mother Courage*; and Brecht's strategy of presenting conflicting perspectives to provoke audiences into questioning assumptions can be seen as an important influence. Kureishi explains his initial aspirations:

■ The film started off as an epic. It was to be like *The Godfather*, opening in the past with the arrival of an immigrant family in England and showing their progress to the present. There were to be many scenes set in the 1950s; people would eat bread and dripping and get off boats a lot; there would be scenes of Johnny [played by Daniel Day-Lewis] and Omar [played by Gordon Warnecke] as children and large-scale set pieces of racist marches with scenes of mass violence.

We soon decided it was impossible to make a film of such scale. That film is still to be made. Instead I set the film in the present, though references to the past remain.

It was shot in six weeks in February and March 1985 on a low budget and 16mm film. For this I was glad. There were no commercial pressures on us, no one had a lot of money invested in the film who would tell us what to do. And I was tired of seeing lavish films set in exotic locations; it seemed to me that anyone could make such films, providing they had an old book, a hot country, new technology and were capable of aiming the camera at an attractive landscape in the hot country in front of which stood a star in a perfectly clean costume delivering lines from the old book.

We decided the film was to have gangster and thriller elements, since the gangster film is the form that corresponds most closely to the city, with its gangs and violence. And the film was to be an amusement, despite its references to racism, unemployment and Thatcherism. Irony is the modern mode, a way of commenting on bleakness and cruelty without falling into dourness and didacticism. And ever since the first time I heard people in a theatre laugh during a play of mine, I've wanted it to happen again and again.

We found actors – Saeed Jaffrey [who played Omar's uncle, Nasser], for whom I'd written the part; and Roshan Seth [who played Papa] I'd seen in David Hare's play *Map of the World* (1983), commanding that huge stage at the National with complete authority. I skidded through the snow to see Shirley Ann Field [Rachel, Nasser's mistress] and on arriving at her flat was so delighted by her charm and enthusiasm, and so ashamed of the smallness of her part, that there and then I added the material about the magic potions, the moving furniture and the walking trousers. It must have seemed that the rest of the film was quite peripheral and she would be playing the lead in a kind of 'Exorcist' movie with a gay Pakistani, a drug-dealer and a fluff-drying spin-drier in the background.

Soon we stood under railway bridges in Vauxhall at two in the morning in March; we knocked the back wall out of someone's flat and erected a platform outside to serve as the balcony of Papa's flat, which had so many railway lines dipping and crisscrossing beside and above it that inside it you shook like peas in maracas; in an old shop we built a laundrette of such authenticity that people came in off the street with their washing; and I stood on the set making up dialogue before the actors did it themselves, and added one or two new scenes. □

(Hanif Kureishi, Introduction to *My Beautiful Laundrette*, 1986)[6]

Several aspects of this introduction are worth stressing: the ambition of the original conception (even though this had to be scaled down); the collaborative nature of the project (reminiscent of Kureishi's work with Stafford-Clark and Out of Joint); the use of irony as a means of avoiding dourness and didacticism; and the way the realism of the run-down locations was offset by the surrealistic elements in the plot. Indeed, one of the charms of the film is this blend of gritty documentary realism, wit, and flamboyant fantasy. All of these are strikingly evident in the transformation of the decayed laundrette, Churchill's (ironically invoking the Battle of Britain and past imperial splendour), into the palace of spin-driers, Powders (ironically named after Omo, the powder that washes whiter, and alluding to the drugs that financed the laundrette).

We can begin by considering some of the first reviews – both appreciative and hostile – and then go on to look at how these arguments are developed in later, more sustained, theoretical analyses. Many of the initial responses sound surprised that grim social issues could be made into an entertaining and moving film. David Robinson enthused:

■ The marvel of the film is that it deals with such tough issues – class, race, sex, corruption, ignorance, prejudice, Britain here and now – yet remains not only watchable but very comic; that it never compromises, yet proposes no ready-made villains or victims, unless (fulfilling both functions) it is the hopeless little knot of National Front punks who hang around dismally waiting for something or someone to smash. □

(David Robinson, 'Only Sentiment', 1985–86)[7]

Robinson gives much of the credit to Stephen Frears for making a film look this good for £600,000 and concludes by praising the film's ending: 'The boys still have each other. Kureishi and Frears, without self-consciousness or shame, leave us with one of the most delicate and touching love scenes in contemporary cinema.' Harlan Kennedy, too, was impressed by the fact that a film funded by TV manages to cover so much: 'it's a British movie about modern British life that has a color, craziness, and wit worthy of the big screen'.[8]

Several reviewers praised Kureishi for his sympathetic but complex portrait of immigrant life. Leonard Quart, for example, notes that *Laundrette* acknowledges that immigrants adjust in a variety of ways:

■ *My Beautiful Laundrette* provides an ironic, comic portrait of upper middle class Pakistanis on the make in an England where young, native Cockneys have only the dole and street violence to console them. The Pakistanis are ambivalent about Thatcher's England, but are not put off by its racism, knowing that 'there is money in muck.' They feel contempt for the English who lack the energy and drive to 'squeeze the tits of the system.' Still, they sometimes become nostalgic about their past privileged life in Karachi: and Nasser continues to run his home in the traditional style, with an illiterate wife who conjures up potions, and daughters who obediently cut his toe-nails and soothe his brow while he lies in bed and holds court like a rajah.

It's England, however, with all its dangers and opportunities, not Pakistan 'sodomized by religion' or the Pakistani, which claims their ultimate loyalty. As Nasser states, 'We're professional businessmen not professional Pakistani,' and what comes first is making money, not ethnic loyalty. Nevertheless, despite their corruption – and in the case of the fashionable, reptilian Salim, their vicious sadism – this inside view of Pakistani immigrant culture is not an unsympathetic one.

Nasser may be an exploiter and domestic autocrat – he is absolutely insensitive to his sharp, liberated daughter Tania's desire for sexual and intellectual independence – but he is a warm, generous, life-loving man. He genuinely loves Omar, his brother (Omar's father), and his sensual, knowing English mistress Rachel ... In the context of the film, his crude materialism and hedonism turn out to be more attractive than the impotent, self-pitying idealism of Omar's eloquent father, whose socialist teachings never make any headway with the working-class young – 'the working class,' he says, 'has been a great disappointment to me.' In fact, it's the racism of the National Front rather than dreams of class struggle whose call they hear and march to.

My Beautiful Laundrette almost always succeeds in subverting the predictable. The once colonial Pakistani are now the wielders of economic power in this slice of London, while the native English punks and skinheads can only froth and indulge in menacing behaviour. While the film's central relationship – between pleasant, adaptable, handsome Omar and silver streak haired, decent Johnny – is spontaneous, natural and even tender at times, there are suggestions of something darker lying underneath. What's fresh in this film is that the insidious elements are not sexual in nature. In fact, there isn't a hint of self-consciousness or intimation of anything psychologically problematic about their sexuality. It's the need for power and status that are the potential destructive forces here. For Omar, having had a taste of English racism, takes keen pleasure in his role as employer, asserting his power over Johnny and ordering him about. Omar is also a man without a defined identity or set of moral values, who has begun to fantasize and plan about making big money. He's a Salim in the making, and he will probably betray or sacrifice Johnny when it's in his interest to do so. □   (Leonard Quart, 1986)[9]

Pam Cook, too, emphasizes that the relationship between Johnny and Omar is not depicted as 'psychologically problematic' but as determined by colonialist politics and history: 'Moments of tenderness, warmth and humour are set against those in which power relationships deriving from deep-seated colonialist attitudes are shown to be all-pervasive.'[10]

My Beautiful Laundrette, then, was not seen as a film about being gay. Kureishi himself confirms that he did not set out to explore issues around gayness:

■ The two boys are really the two sides of me: a Pakistani boy and an English boy, because I'm half Pakistani and half English. I got the two parts of myself together ... kissing ... It seemed perfectly natural, not strange or even particularly interesting. I hadn't set out to explore issues around gayness: writing about the effect of a gay relationship on a Pakistani family or Johnny's friends would have made it into a different kind of film. I preferred just to take it for granted, the way we live our lives now. □   (Jane Root, 'Scenes from a Marriage', 1985)[11]

Indeed, appearing during the homosexual panic engendered by the AIDS crisis, the fact that the boys' love affair was not a problem was radical in itself. The film was hailed as 'an early and definitive example of New Queer Cinema; for the two gay characters' gayness is open and matter-of-fact, loving and sexual and, most importantly, not troubling to themselves'.

But while the reviewers quoted so far praised the complex and unsentimental depiction of Asian immigrants and the refreshing treatment of the central gay relationship, some Asian critics were more sceptical about both. The poet and filmmaker Mahmood Jamal, who produced *Majdhar* (1984) and *Hotel London* (1987), wrote a polemic entitled 'Dirty Linen' in which he accused Kureishi of peddling cheap stereotypes and selling out to an English audience:

■ In this respect, *My Beautiful Laundrette* is an honest film reflecting the author's thinking. It is a state of mind that I can only describe as neo-orientalist. Edward Said in his book, *Orientalism* (1978), described orientalism as a set of attitudes and assumptions through which the Orient was incorporated in western thought by European scholars. Neo-orientalism best describes the way the Asian community is incorporated within contemporary culture by Asian intellectuals who have been laundered by the British university system.

The main Asian characters in the film are a young man (gay), his uncle (an adulterer and money-crazed businessman who keeps throwing out poor tenants from his houses), his father (a bedridden alcoholic), his cousin (a dope dealer), his uncle's frustrated daughter, and his superstitious wife who makes magic potions. As if all this were not enough, the saving grace of the film comes in the form of an ex-fascist who happens to fall in love with this white-washed Asian boy, a supposed example of what assimilated Pakis should be like viz; as much like their white counterparts as possible. The story is about how this young man drifts through life aided by his white lover whilst constantly being harrassed [sic] by his pig of an uncle and embarrassed by his own kind. The only person who makes a moral choice of any serious kind in the film is his gay lover, a white knight in shining armour ... What is surprising about the film is that it expresses all the prejudices that this society has felt about Asians and Jews – that they are money grabbing, scheming, sex-crazed people. It's not surprising therefore, that it was popular with European audiences. It says everything they thought about us but were afraid to say.

... It is not as some critics have described it, a view of Thatcher's Britain. To me it is a view of Britain as it has always been, seen through the rose tinted spectacles of a liberal offering love between two individuals as a solution to historically based social contradictions, a solution which does not take us into account. Apart from all the other issues, this, to me, is the film's greatest weakness. The soggy liberalism that seems to hang out of the door of the washing machine, the underclothing left by someone too timid to arouse attention to himself by daring to move it and sling it in the dryer of harsh reality ... ... □

(Mahmood Jamal, 'Dirty Linen', 1987)[12]

While Jamal recognizes that 'being misrepresented in the media can make one unbearably sensitive to issues of stereotyping', he insists that his objections to *My Beautiful Laundrette* do not result from over-sensitivity. The crux of his argument is the controversial use of humour, which he sees, not as Kureishi intended – as a way of avoiding dourness and didacticism – but as offering cheap laughs for a white audience. However, it could certainly be argued that all the characters are treated with mockery: the white working-class fascists as much as anyone. Jamal's polemic is perhaps best seen in the context of the 1980s, when there were few opportunities for black and Asian filmmakers to tell their own stories and when there was considerable urgency in the project of counteracting negative stereotypes. Although Jamal acknowledges that the attempt to counteract misrepresentation in the media can lead Asian artists 'to indulge in rhetoric and one-dimensionality', it may have seemed, at the time of the film's release, that Kureishi had squandered a rare chance to show Asian characters in a more dignified way. Implicit in Jamal's criticism is the demand that the minority artist should be didactic and provide 'cheering fictions': a role that Kureishi has refused. Moreover, it is not at all clear, despite Jamal's assertion, that the film suggests that 'assimilation' is the answer. Nor is it the case that all Asians in the film are money-grubbing: Omar's socialist father sees education and not money as the solution to combating racism and class inequality. As he says to Johnny: '[Omar] must have knowledge. We all must, now. In order to see clearly what's being done and to whom in this country. Right?'[13] Papa may have been 'done in' by this country but Kureishi here employs a classic device to avoid obvious didacticism: giving the strongest argument to the weakest character. Pickled in vodka and occasionally self-pitying, Papa is nonetheless 'right'.

Perminder Dhillon-Kashyap, like Jamal, accused Kureishi of serving up 'ever more sophisticated stereotypes' for a white audience. He not only explores what he considers to be negative stereotyping in *My Beautiful Laundrette*, but is also concerned that protest from the Asian community is invariably disregarded as uninformed and 'reactionary'. But according to Dhillon-Kashyap, the stereotypes of the corrupt Asian businessman and the oppressed Asian woman are so obsessively repeated in the British media that any reworking is indefensible. His critique focuses on the central gay relationship, which had been praised by white critics, but which he sees as creating a new victim, the 'white fascist':

■ The problem with *My Beautiful Laundrette* is not that it depicts an Asian gay male or that it has trivialised racism by fusing love between a racist white male and an Asian gay, but that it has subtly reworked the stereotypes thereby adding an 'authenticity' to them. By fusing racism and sexuality, the film has created a new victim, the white fascist – a victim of economic circumstances who is being exploited by petty bourgeois Asian businessmen. Consider the opening scene of the film – two white fascists have been thrown out by black heavies on the orders of Salim (Derrick Branche). Instantly, the film attempts to engage the spectator's sympathy towards these fascists ... ...

Laundrette seems to be less interested in exploring issues of class, corruption or sexuality and more in sensationalising them in order to win a white audience ... Making Tania (Rita Wolf) bare her breasts does not, *pace* Hanif Kureishi, give 'Rita a chance to be liberated for a few moments'.[14] Because *My Beautiful Laundrette* seems to operate predominantly as a white male fantasy, Tania must bare her breasts to the audience's voyeuristic gaze.[15] □

(Perminder Dhillon-Kashyap, 'Locating the Asian Experience', 1988)[16]

The difficulty here is that Dhillon-Kashyap suggests that the sympathetic treatment of white fascists is being used to justify racism, whereas what the film is exposing is the ruthlessness of Thatcher's enterprise culture, which thrust many, white and black, on to the scrap heap. The exclusive focus on race can obscure the importance of class, but the film demonstrates their interconnection. Salim's money, for example, cannot protect him from 'Paki-bashers', but Omar's educated father and wealthy relatives provide him with more of a future than the white-working class on the streets of south London. As we will see, critics will return to the issue (raised by Jamal) of whether offering love between two individuals as a solution to social contradictions is a liberal cop-out, and to the controversy surrounding Tania bearing her breasts. But first we can consider Salman Rushdie's talk on 'Minority Literatures in a Multi-Cultural Society' (1986), which very clearly sets out the pressures exerted on the minority writer and provides a robust defence of Kureishi's *My Beautiful Laundrette*.

Rushdie begins by exploring the multiculturalism of Shakespeare (1564–1616) and James Joyce (1882–1941) in order to emphasize the extent to which great writing has always been hybrid rather than parochial, and discusses the new literatures that have emerged from the old empire before considering the role of the minority writer in a multiracial society. One aspect of this 'giving voice' Rushdie calls 'anthemic' (the singing of anthems or hymns of praise): 'which is telling one's own people in songs or stories what they find pleasing or beautiful, what they know to be true'. The other kind of 'giving voice' is 'an exercise in shouting across ... "a gulf in reality", the chasm which exists between white and black perceptions of the world'. This retelling of stories creates a literature of the highest importance and value.[17]

Having set out the two main roles of the minority writer in a multiracial society, Rushdie goes on to explore the problems of marginalization. The established literary world will try to place this writing on 'the periphery' and maintain its own centrality. There is also the danger of 'marginalization from within': the construction of defensive walls around a culture: 'In any group that sees itself – with good reason – as being on the defensive there is a risk that new orthodoxies will be erected ... works which do not speak to us only, to the inside, become suspect; that is to say, parochialism instead of being considered a weakness becomes a virtue.'[18] The criticism that *Laundrette* was setting out to please a white audience could be seen as the expression of defensive orthodoxies.

Rushdie continues 'that if you know a community by virtue of being a member of it then you know it, warts and all' but to show this honestly 'lays you open to the serious charge of lending ammunition to your enemies'. Despite this danger, Rushdie insists that the writer should not avoid 'all mention of warts'. He goes on to describe *Laundrette* as a sharply written satire of Thatcherism and Asian fat cats and praises the film because the satire, however uncomfortable for the Asian community, rings true:

■ *My Beautiful Laundrette* is very far from being some kind of nihilistic sneer, it is funny, touching, passionate, to my mind one of the finest works of art to emerge from the new generation of black British writers, and I think that a substantial part of its quality has to do with the writer's courage, his decision simply to say what he sees and stand by it. The film's central relationship is between Omar and a white ex-school friend, called Johnny, who has flirted with fascism, but who actually loves Omar. The love of these two is presented very explicitly and is both extremely sensual and very moving. It is not often that a film love affair looks like an adult relationship, but this one manages to do just that, and it is also of course a metaphor of hope. The relationship is subject to colossal stresses, both from the Asian and the white side. Johnny's former fascist friends smash up the laundrette and beat him up, but the film ends with the love surviving, literally bloodied, but surviving. There is a kind of heroism, but it is not the kind of heroism which will satisfy people who want positive images of blacks. I doubt that a community as sexually silent and conservative as the Asians would take kindly to a gay hero who makes love to a former National Front member. I would defend *My Beautiful Laundrette* against all colours, even though it will upset some Asians. In fact there are some fat cat Asian businessmen that I would not mind upsetting. Even though, more seriously, some white viewers will find in it material which will satisfy their wish to dislike Asians ... The reason for my defence is that there is nothing in it that is imaginatively false, and because it seems to me that the real gift which we can offer our communities is not the creation of a set of stereotyped positive images to counteract the stereotyped negative ones, but simply the gift of treating black and Asian characters in a way that white writers seem very rarely able to do, that is to say as fully realized human beings, as complex creatures, good, bad, bad, good. To do anything less is to be kept captive by the racist prejudices of the majority, and that complexity is what Kureishi's script strives for. □

(Salman Rushdie, 'Minority Literatures in a Multi-cultural Society', 1987)[19]

Rushdie's defence is all the more convincing because he takes seriously the political consequences of such warts-and-all representations (which would have dire repercussions for him and for the Asian community after the publication of *The Satanic Verses* in 1988).

If the film outraged some in the Asian community, it had an equally negative response in the right-wing English press. Both camps argued that there were subjects that should not be discussed. Norman Stone of

Worcester College, Oxford University, contrasted a golden age of well-made British films (each with a beginning, middle and an end) with a crop of 'worthless and insulting' 1980s films, 'which might have come straight from the agitprop department of the late GLC' (the Greater London Council, abolished by Thatcher in 1986, at the height of Ken Livingstone's left-wing leadership). Two of Stone's targets are *My Beautiful Laundrette* and *Sammy and Rosie get Laid*:

■ Each of them has been stamped with approval, and sometimes more than that. ... They are all very depressing, and are no doubt meant to be. The rain pours down; skinheads beat people up; there are race riots; there are drug fixes in squalid corners; there is much explicit sex, a surprising amount of it homosexual and sadistic; greed and violence abound; there is grim concrete and much footage of 'urban decay'; on and off there are voice-overs by Mrs Thatcher, Hitler, etc.

Plots are desultory, messy, and in one case non-existent. Endings are melodramas of the corpses-on-the-stage type, revealing that the makers have either run out of money or, more likely, of ideas. A few of the actors make a decent show of keeping these confections together, but wood and ham are otherwise much in evidence.

Somehow, their visual world has been dominated by a left-wing orthodoxy: the done thing is to run down Mrs Thatcher, to assume that capitalism is parasitism, that the established order in this country is imperialist, racist, profiteering, oppressive to women and other minorities ... ...

Theirs is a flat, two-dimensional ideology. Yes, there are nasty patches in modern Britain, and parts of our great cities are a disgrace. And yes, it is right for film makers to be concerned with these bad patches if they can be converted into meaningful film in the long and worthy tradition of social-realist films. But the vision of England they provide has nothing to offer an overwhelming majority of the potential audience. They represent at best a tiny part of modern England, and, more likely, a nasty part of their producers' brains. □　　　　(Norman Stone, 'Through a lens darkly', 1988)[20]

Stone's attack is both political and aesthetic. Any criticism of the status quo is written off as 'agitprop'; a sleight-of-hand that attempts to maintain that the kind of films of which he approves are without ideology, rather than admitting that they subscribe to a different, conservative, one. The aesthetic is also conservative, with the use of collage or non-naturalistic strategies wilfully misunderstood as plotless and messy. But as Sukhdev Sandhu has argued: 'Collage is a democratic art ... [which] creates a new imaginative space where no individual can insist on preserving a privileged zone or an unpolluted sphere from which members of other races or classes are barred.'[21] It was, perhaps, not the 'mess' but the 'democracy' to which Stone took exception.

According to Stone, the 'shift to the left' by intellectuals began in the 1930s with W. H. Auden and the Left Book Club, then spread from the written word to theatres such as the Royal Court (where Kureishi started), and from there infiltrated film. Stone sees a glimmer of hope in the fact that a few good films 'of a traditional kind' are still being made, notably *A Passage to India* (1984) and *A Room With A View* (1986). Despite Stone's assertions, this battle for representations is clearly ideological. David Lean's *A Passage to India* was one of several films described by Rushdie as 'Raj Revival': a genre which aimed to glamorize Britain's imperial past and ignore the contemporary consequences. James Ivory's *A Room with a View* belongs to the genre of nostalgic and self-congratulatory 'Heritage' cinema, which presents an ethnically homogeneous and monocultural vision of England. Both Raj Revival and Heritage cinema were engaged in constructing a very narrow definition of national identity, precisely the view of Britain and its Empire that Kureishi was setting out to challenge.[22]

Kureishi replied to Stone's criticism with relish:

■ He ... calls our films 'worthless and insulting' and adds: 'The vision of England they provide had nothing to offer an overwhelming majority of the potential audience.' This is certainly not true of *My Beautiful Laundrette*, which has been seen all over the world, both on TV and in the cinema, and in Thatcherite terms was an overwhelming business success.

Stone accuses us of dwelling on depressing aspects of British life like 'homosexuals,' 'grim concrete' and 'race riots.' He says: 'The done thing is to run down Mrs Thatcher.'

... ... Similarly, last September *The Sunday Times* wrote a leader in which they complained of Britain's intelligentsia always 'sniping from the sidelines.' I think this is [a] euphemism for being critical. God forbid that any artist should mention unemployment, or racism, or poverty. Like Norman Stone and *The Sunday Times* and Mrs Thatcher, like the obnoxious and arrogant English cricket team, we should all be batting for Britain too. Everyone should bat for Britain or shut up and not say that Britain is a depressing place for millions of people, or that black people don't fight back against the violence, prejudice and discrimination that cold-hearted and wretched British whites inflict on them every day.

... *Passage To India* and *Room With A View* [of which Stone approves] are stories of the over-dressed British abroad, set against ravishing landscapes. They are romanticised escapism, glamorised travesties of novels by the great E. M. Forster, the sort of meaningless soft-core saccharine confection that Tory ladies and gentlemen think is Art.

It is easy to forget that Forster himself is a formidable part of a tradition of dissent – didn't the old scoundrel love his homosexual friends more than England? – a tradition that includes Dickens, Wilde, Lawrence

and Edward Bond, writers – however different to each other – who recognised it as part of their job to say what is not normally said; to show what
is forbidden; to reflect seriously on our actual lives, both private and public; and to show us how we live. □

(Hanif Kureishi, 'England, bloody England', 1988)[23]

Stone presents himself as attempting to preserve a great tradition;
Kureishi invokes a different but equally great tradition, of dissent
(Dickens, Wilde, and so on) and adroitly outflanks Stone by exposing
the way E. M. Forster – a gay anti-imperialist who could only raise two
cheers for democracy – has been misrepresented and appropriated by
little Englanders.

Laundrette's initial, contradictory, reception – disliked by some in the
Asian community for warts-and-all depictions of Asian characters and
by the right-wing English for failing to show a picture-postcard view of
England – highlights how very differently work will be interpreted,
depending on the location of the viewer. These early reviews not only
suggest that this difference is likely to be pronounced in an ethnically
diverse society, but, as Kobena Mercer has argued, they also show the
extent to which 'image-making has become an important arena of
cultural contestation'.[24]

Later on, the film was interpreted differently. Two critics in particular, Stuart Hall and Radhika Mohanram, have explored it in terms of
new ways of thinking about being British. For Hall, Kureishi's work is
viewed as enabling solidarities between different ethnic minorities
and between differently disadvantaged groups, while Mohanram
focuses on the links between colonization, sexuality and nationalism in
multicultural England.

Drawing on the work of George Mosse,[25] Mohanram explores the
relation 'between forms of sexuality and the formation of the national
subject'.[26] She uses the example of German nationalism: heterosexuality represented a strong nation, homosexuality was categorized as
abnormal and disrespectable. She continues: 'In sum, the effete
homosexual body, like the racialized body, signifies a threat to the myth
of ontological purity of the nation.'[27] Mohanram's argument focuses on
the overlapping concerns of sexuality and race:

■ I want to begin my discussion of *My Beautiful Laundrette* by focusing
on a very dramatic scene. The scene which depicts the opening of the
laundrette, contains a homosexual couple (Johnny and Omar) in a room
with a one-way mirror, sexually imitating the courtship of the heterosexual pair (Omar's uncle Nasser and his mistress). I would like to pick up on
two things in this scene. The trajectory of the camera's gaze reveals its
position behind the homosexual couple who are themselves behind a

one-way mirror, and the heterosexual couple are then aligned with the homosexual couple. In effect, the one-way mirror might reflect Nasser and his mistress, but the audience knows that behind the mirror, miming the two, are Johnny and Omar. Heterosex mimes homosex and vice versa and becomes interchangeable. The discourse of illicit desire (homosexuality) can only be slid secretly behind the discourse of permitted desire (heterosexuality). However, in this instance, even the heterosexual desire expressed is itself illicit in that Nasser is having an affair with this Englishwoman. What is revealed is a hierarchy of desires in the text. Nationally approved legitimate heterosexual desire is predicated on illicit heterosexuality. But heterosexuality itself is dependent on its opposite homosexuality for its inscription and elaboration.

If a national identity is in fact implicated in a heterosexual identity to the extent that both are mutually interchangeable, *My Beautiful Laundrette* brings up the question of the part played by interracial homosexuality within such an economy. The braided tropes of sexuality and the economy appear to form a rigid nationalistic backdrop which forecloses any attempt at the creation and location of a homosexual discourse within the confines of that text. In at least three separate instances the film maintains silence on this subject. One incident occurs when Salim, a slimy cousin of Omar's, witnesses an intimate moment between Omar and Johnny in the side mirror of his car. This arouses Salim's suspicions sufficiently for him to spill the beans to Nasser, the financial patriarch of the family. Yet Salim cannot articulate his horror of homosexuality. Instead, he voices his suspicion of Johnny and states the fact that he cannot be trusted with the family money. He ends with an ambiguous, 'There's some things between them I am looking into.' Obviously, one cannot discern if his dislike of Johnny is because he is untrustworthy, or because he is seducing Omar, or because he is white.

The text records another moment of ambiguity when Johnny and Omar, walking in an alley, kiss for the first time. The societal disapproval of their unnationalistic sexual desire is recorded when they are interrupted by loud noises caused by Johnny's skinhead buddies. In this exchange, one of them states, 'I don't like to see one of our bloods grovelling to Pakis. They came over to work for us. That's why we brought them over ... Don't cut yourself off from your own people. They don't want you.' This instance is only one of several. Every time homosexuality rears its subversive head, the text veers into a discussion of race. In yet another instance, Omar gives Johnny a ride home in his car. After they kiss each other goodnight, Johnny states that he wishes he could ask him in but knows that Omar has to go home and take care of his ailing father. Omar's response again registers a shift from sexual desire to race. He bitterly points out how Johnny had behaved like a fascist, demonstrating against Asians in Britain.

At this juncture, I want to point out that the foreclosure of homosexuality in these scenes causes it to function as nationalism's Other, thereby providing the nation with its identity through opposition. Thus homosexuality has to be situated outside representation: it is an absence, a negativity. It has to be repressed for the nation to consolidate its unitary identity and gather coherence. This repression is because nationalism's close relationship with the notion of respectability necessitates the repression of this subject. Thus, in these two instances, race becomes the expression for the unnatural and unnationalistic sexuality present in the text.

However, the conflation of race with homosexuality is problematic in itself in that unitary nationalistic identity is based upon the premise of one race for all the nation's people. Therefore, the notion of different races, like homosexuality, is also tainted with the same brush of degeneration and immorality and a general absence of self-discipline. And, in fact, the nationalistic text seems to discern the degeneration that has infiltrated John Bull [*OED:* a personification of England or the typical Englishman, represented as a stout red-faced farmer in a top hat and high boots. It was originally the name of a character representing the English nation in John Arbuthnot's satire *History of John Bull* (1712)] and denies it nationalistic sentiments which are more polyphonic or less rigid. Nasser, the family patriarch, who among his many enterprises is a slum landlord as well, hires Johnny to help him get rid of an unwanted, black, Rastafarian tenant. As the two of them throw the tenant's belongings out of the window, Johnny comments that it 'doesn't look too good. Pakis doing this sort of thing' to other minorities. Nasser retorts, 'I am a professional businessman, not a professional Pakistani. And there's no question of race in the new enterprise culture.' In this way Nasser and the text create identity by class within diasporic space [in postcolonial theory 'diaspora' is sometimes used interchangeably with 'migration' and is generally, as here, invoked as a means of interrogating ethnic identity and cultural nationalism] and not by any originary, natural essence. Like homosexuals, the racial other threatens the integrity of the society and by his or her very existence confirms its standards of behavior; moreover, the racial Other, like the homosexual, is a site from which distinctions between the normal and the abnormal can be drawn.

Notice the progression of meaning in these scenes. In the first two scenes, race has to be inscribed centrally with the marginalization of illicit sexuality. Eventually there is a foreclosure of any discourse on sexuality because race has to be privileged. In the last scene discussed, Nasser insists there is no question of racial difference in the new enterprise culture. In this way, the text averts focus away from race as well as sexuality. England functions as one. In this instance, inappropriate racial mixes as well as illicit sexuality function as protective dyads [twofold protection] or discursive shifters [grammatical elements which have no precise meaning but which acquire meaning from the context in which they occur] which eventually manage to prevent any substantive discussion of either. Through this double act of containment of the Other, homosexual as well as racial panic is avoided within the text of national-ism. The Kureishi/Frears team concentrate on and unravel the mecha-nisms through which England attains proper subjectivity and coherence. The condition upon which the English national subject gains coherency is through the expulsion of the impure and the disorderly. However, what Kureishi and Frears uncover is that the homosexual and the black are the underside of a stable subjective identity, the abyss at the borders of the subject's existence. Being neither subject nor object, they are, in fact, the recognition of the impossible, untenable identity the subject projects onto and derives from the other. The superimposition of Johnny and Omar's images at the inauguration scene of the laundrette referred to earlier points out that the identity of Johnny, the fascist who wants Pakis to go home, is always teetering on the brink of a yawning hole which contains the figure of Omar. Omar is always a reminder of Johnny and John Bull's fading unstable identity. In the same way, in this film homo-sexuality functions to remind us that heterosexuality, the scaffolding on which nationalism rests, is an unstable identity. □

(Radhika Mohanram, 'Postcolonial Spaces and Deterritorialized (Homo)Sexuality', 1995)[28]

We can contrast this penetrating and subtle analysis of the film's treat-ment of homosexuality, race and nationality with earlier reviews which dismissed the odd couple's affair as a soggy liberal evasion of complex social and historical conditions. Instead, Mohanram argues that Kureishi and Frears show how 'the threat of difference is no more outside the boundary but instead questions the dictum of the nation modelled on its people as one'.[29]

Stuart Hall used *Laundrette* as a culmination and illustration of his argument about 'Old and New Identities, Old and New Ethnicities'. He begins by discussing the ways in which old ideas of a fixed and stable identity have been 'de-centred': after Marx had positioned the individual in history and Freud had shown how little we know about ourselves, the self began to seem 'a pretty fragile thing': not autonomous, but deter-mined by history and by the unconscious. The logic of identity was fur-ther undermined by developments in linguistics, in particular the thesis of Ferdinand de Saussure (1857–1913) that language exists prior to us so that: 'philosophically, one comes to the end of any kind of notion of a perfect transparent continuity between our language and something out there which can be called the real, or the truth, without any quotation marks'.[30] Given all this, it becomes almost impossible to say anything about individual identity at all. Hall goes on to show the ways in which social and collective identity have also become more complex and frag-mented, partly because we no longer believe in totalizing accounts or 'master concepts' such as class, and partly because of increasing social diversity and plurality. But, Hall argues, these theoretical decentrings are politically problematic because we still need to be able to think about identity, both individual and social. 'The old discourse of the subject was abolished' but, through psychoanalysis and feminism, we have begun to think about other ways of conceiving identity. We have become 'aware that identities are never completed, never finished; that they are always as subjectivity itself is, in process'.[31] This new way of thinking rejects the notion that 'identity has to do with people who look the same, feel the same, call themselves the same' and recognizes that 'identity is always in part a narrative, always in part a kind of representation'.[32]

Hall then turns to changes in the politics of social identity. He refers to 'Identity Politics One', which he argues 'had to do with the constitution of some defensive collective identity against the practices of a racist society'. With this act of mobilization 'the margins begin to contest, the locals begin to come to representation. The identity which that whole, enormous polit-ical space produced in Britain ... was the category Black.' As Hall goes on to explain: 'Black is not a question of pigmentation ... [It] is a historical category, a political category, a cultural category.'[33] The positive use of the term 'Black' by people from diverse cultures and societies – from the Caribbean, East Africa, the Asian subcontinent – was an important moment in the anti-racist struggle because it allowed for solidarity: 'there is more that unites us than what divides us'. Hall argues that during the 1970s, the enemy was 'multiculturalism', which Hall identifies as another version of the 'exotic': 'we would all come and cook our native dishes and sing our native songs and appear in our native costume'.[34]

Although Hall suggests that the policy of multiculturalism was tanta-mount to divide and rule, he also argues that that the collective Black identity, so essential in resisting racism, has its own problems. It silenced the specific experiences of Asian people, not all Black people identified with it, Black women were silenced, and it did not allow for solidarity with the white working class, who suffered deprivation as well. Hall goes on to ask:

■ What then does one do with the powerful mobilizing identity of the Black experience and of the Black community? Blackness as a political identity in the light of the understanding of any identity is always com-plexly composed, always historically constructed. It is never in the same place but always positional ...

That is the politics of living identity through difference. It is the poli-tics of recognizing that all of us are composed of multiple social identi-ties, not of one. That we are all complexly constructed through different categories, of different antagonisms, and these may have the effect of locating us socially in multiple positions of marginality and subordina-tion, but which do not yet operate on us in exactly the same way. □

(Stuart Hall, 'Old and New Identities, Old and New Ethnicities, 1991)[35]

Out of this much more complex view of individual and collective identities, Hall argues, has come some of the 'most exciting cultural work now being done in England' and he hails *Laundrette* as 'one of the most riveting and important films produced by a black writer in recent years':

> ■ If you have seen *My Beautiful Laundrette* you will know that it is the most transgressive text there is. Anybody who is Black, who tries to identify with it, runs across the fact that the central characters of this narrative are two gay men. What is more, anyone who wants to separate the identities into their two clearly separate points will discover that one of these Black gay men is white and one of these Black gay men is brown. Both of them are struggling in Thatcher's Britain. One of them has an uncle who is a Pakistani landlord who is throwing Black people out of the window.
>
> This is a text that nobody likes. Everybody hates it. You go to it looking for what are called 'positive images' and there are none. There aren't any positive images like that with whom one can, in a simple way, identify. Because as well as the politics – and there is certainly a politics in that and in Kureishi's other film [*Sammy and Rosie Get Laid*] but it is not a politics which invites easy identification – it has a politics which is grounded on the complexity of identifications which are at work. □
>
> (Stuart Hall, 'Old and New Identities, Old and New Ethnicities, 1991)[36]

And if we are surprised to read Hall's description of Johnny as a 'Black gay man', that is because we invariably do think of 'Black' in terms of skin pigmentation rather than as a political category.

But although Kureishi has been seen as opening up a more creative space for the representation of new forms of identity and ethnicity, and praised for refusing to engage in simplistic protest or in PR, there are those who criticized the film from a feminist perspective. Ranasinha discusses the arguments that have been made about the film's treatment of gender:

> ■ Tania provides a critique of her father's business ethic, but she is structurally marginalized in this narrative of the two male buddies. Inderpal Grewal argues that in *Laundrette* Kureishi 'does not do too well with feminist issues. The hero's cousin, a young girl who rejects the accepted role of women in both the English and Pakistani cultures, ulti-mately cannot be accommodated in the film. She disappears at a railway station, and this disappearance seems to be the only *solution* for a femi-nist Asian woman'.[37] Grewal's response points to the expectations of critics who seek overt political solutions especially perhaps in a text authored by a minority artist. Perhaps Kureishi suggests leaving home may be the 'solution', which underlines the way he gives you politics but not in a way you might want or expect. At one level, Tania's running away

follows a clichéd trajectory, although it can be argued that here Kureishi depicts the way some British Asian women are faced with such stark choices. At the same time, responses such as Grewal's register an implicit disappointment that Kureishi fails to promote change or present alternative possibilities for circumventing cultural and sexual positioning.[38] What Tania's disappearance makes clear is the way the film (and this is true of Kureishi's work in general) is not centrally interested in the women characters or what happens to them. While Kureishi skilfully delineates complex, realistic Asian and western female protagonists and takes pains to empower them, often giving them the sharpest lines, they function primarily as foils to the men. □

(Ruvani Ranasinha, Hanif Kureishi, 2002)[39]

Ranasinha goes on to suggest that Kureishi's characterization of Tania as 'fearless, outspoken and sexually free ... contests the trope of the submissive Asian daughter and undermines stereotypes of Asian women as passive and desexualized'. However, she agrees with Dhillon-Kashyap's view that when Tania bares her breasts this 'positions her literally in the "voyeuristic gaze" of white male fantasies of the sexually exotic other' and she concludes that Kureishi's portrayal of Tania is 'marked by patriarchal flaws'.[40]

In contrast, Elizabeth de Cacqueray argues that the 'configuration of space within the screen plays an important role in determining attitudes towards gender'. Noting first the separate space allotted to men and women in Nasser's household, she follows the camera angles to show how Tania 'has to find her place in society':

■ Bilquis, Nasser's wife, is often shown hovering on a threshold looking into a space occupied by others which she herself cannot enter or share: either watching Tania and Omar in the game room or looking outside her house towards the street. Again the filmmaker has chosen the point of view with care: Bilquis is looking toward the camera placed outside the house, the spectator is not symbolically sharing the character's space, she alone is trapped inside. Tania is also shown looking into the defended male space, when she looks in on her father's guests. It is also a space shared by the male characters and by the spectator from which she is excluded, but she is already, at this early stage of the film, differentiated from her mother as she manages, from her theoretically 'excluded' position, to taunt the men, revealing her breasts to a drunken Pakistani who thinks his vision is due to excess of alcohol. She will eventually free herself from parental oppression and set out on her own journey of initiation. □   (Elizabeth de Cacqueray, 'Space for Dreams', 1997)[41]

In this reading, Tania's gesture is a challenge to the male gaze, with the magical realist ending showing her escape from the confined space her mother occupies (an escape that also contrasts with Papa's miserable little room).

While it is true that Kureishi is more interested in the boys (later, Kureishi attributed *Laundrette*'s success in America to the fact that it was about 'outcast boys'[42]), the female characters are portrayed with considerable sympathy. We understand Bilquis's anger and enjoy her revenge, but we are not encouraged to condemn the mistress. Although Tania taunts Rachel that for a woman to live off men is 'a pretty disgusting parasitical thing', Rachel replies, '[Y]ou must understand, we are of different generations, and different classes. Everything is waiting for you. The only thing that has ever waited for me is your father'.[43] The scene is comic (as Omar, totally disconcerted, invites Tania 'to come and look at the spin-driers'), and politically complex (as class, gender and generation all come into play), but even as it mocks the characters' mixed motives, it gives them depth and dignity. Indeed, these qualities, of political complexity, humour and humanity, are evident throughout the film – they are why *Laundrette* can be considered a contemporary classic.

Omar and Johnny's attempt to sustain a relationship despite the boundaries fixed by their 'own people' is in part heroic but also marred, first by Johnny's defection to the neo-fascists and then by Omar's bitterness: 'When we were at school, you and your lot kicked me all round the place. And what are you doing now? Washing my floor.'[44] As Omar bathes his lover at the close of the film it feels like an affirmation but, at the same time, the viewer imagines that the next day he might order Johnny to get the mop out. Kureishi has said: 'If a black and white couple are screwing, it involves colour, class, and relations between the sexes. Human relations are meeting points for a whole complex of social arrangements, and that's why I like to write about them.'[45] With this in mind we can go on to Kureishi's second film, originally entitled 'The Fuck', with some idea of the social arrangements to be explored. In addition, *Sammy and Rosie* shows a greater range of human relations than *Laundrette*, offers a more trenchant critique of Thatcherism, and takes a new direction: not towards a broader definition of Britishness but towards a view of London as the 'semi-detached metropolis'.[46]

CHAPTER THREE

World City: *Sammy and Rosie Get Laid* (1988)

Like *My Beautiful Laundrette, Sammy and Rosie Get Laid* provides a 'mixture of realism and surrealism, seriousness and comedy, art and gratuitous sex'.[1] The eponymous odd couple here are a radical social worker and a British Asian accountant. This film, too, was made outside the mainstream (for Channel 4), which meant that Stephen Frears and Kureishi could maintain control. As in earlier work, Kureishi drew on his own experience for *Sammy and Rosie*, describing it in his published diary of the making of the film, 'Some time with Stephen', as 'quite a personal story ... not in facts, but emotionally' (SS 132). The character of Rosie was based on a former lover and Kureishi admits that this opens him up to the charge of exploiting others: 'Sarah started to call the film: "Hanif gets Paid, Sarah gets Exploited" ' (SS 135).

Although *Sammy and Rosie* shares similarities with *My Beautiful Laundrette*, Gayatri Spivak argues that the second film is a much 'more collective representation' of a social text than *My Beautiful Laundrette*.[2] It cuts between whites and Asians, British African-Caribbeans, trendy liberals and the dispossessed. With the character of Rafi (Sammy's father), fleeing from the consequences of having tortured political prisoners in an unnamed country (presumably Pakistan), the film also deals 'with the effects of colonial history and the regimes that were established by national liberation struggles'.[3] During the making of the film, Thatcher was elected for a third term: homophobia, homelessness, ruthless enterprise capitalism and racist police brutality turn London into a 1980s version of 'The Waste Land' by T. S. Eliot (1888–1965).[4] But the film also explores what John Clement Ball has called 'incompatible visions of London' as Sammy's idyllic description of weekend walks, browsing bookshops and lectures at the ICA are juxtaposed with scenes of street violence and police in riot gear.[5] Perhaps most significantly, *Sammy and Rosie*'s much broader scope meant that Kureishi was writing about characters and settings with which he was not familiar. Where the film was least autobiographical, Kureishi had least confidence. The 'waste ground' scenes, for example, in which a group of squatters resist the property developers, was an integral part of the film's political purpose in showing how 'illiberal and heartless this country had become' but not something of which he had personally had experience: 'the problem was whether this material would be convincing' (SS 137).

Kureishi's film diary also pays tribute to Frears for his optimism and energy throughout the filming and, ultimately, for giving it 'a clarity and definition I couldn't find for it in the script' (SS 197). As Graham Broadstreet in an article in *Screen International* explains, the making of the film was fully collaborative: 'all members of the crew were offered profit participation points. Each, without exception, accepted. *Sammy and Rosie* was now genuinely a product of all those involved, with everyone participating in its potential success.'[6] The film was 'collective' in its mode of representation and in its production. At times, Kureishi records his surprise and pleasure at the participation, for example, the distinctive quality that Oliver Stapleton imparted to the lighting: 'He has given the film a European quality, sensuous and warm. I haven't seen a film like it made in Britain' (SS 166). Kureishi also seems to have relied on Roland Gift to bring 'much of himself' to the part of Danny; a part which Kureishi worried was 'underwritten' (SS 157, 8). As we will see, Danny's role provoked considerable controversy. At other times, it sounds as if Kureishi was dismayed or unconvinced by the particular slant a scene was given or how a character was played. There are fears that Ayub Khan Din was too nice to play Sammy and that Frances Barber's costumes were too fanciful for the part of a social worker (SS 168, 173).

It is also striking how much the screenplay changed: there were several rewrites and, during the editing, scenes were taken out and put back in, so that the process of filming was like 'a structured improvisation' (SS 191). Kureishi had considerable difficulty in deciding what to do with his characters after the 'fuck' scene and how to end the film, until he decided that Rafi should hang himself:

■ [Frears and I] talk until one-thirty about this end and worry whether it's too brutal both on the audience and as an act of aggression by Rafi against the group of characters he's been involved with. We talk about the possibility of Rafi dying of a heart attack! But this is too contingent. It's the power of the deliberate act that we like.

We discuss Chekhov's *Seagull*. I say Rafi's suicide could be like Trepliov's at the end of that play: understated, with the action off-stage, one person discovering it and then returning to the room to tell everyone else. □

(SS 143)

Later, in discussions with the cast, the suicide was seen as inconsistent with Rafi's belief in political expediency, but Kureishi emphasizes that the motive is not guilt: 'It's that he's come to the end. No one wants him. There's nowhere for him to go, neither at home nor in Britain' (SS 145). Rafi's hanging should be 'a just thing, chosen, dignified, something of a Roman act' (SS 155).

There are also several discussions in Kureishi's diary as to what should happen to Sammy and Rosie and whether there should be 'some image of reconciliation'. There were plans to shoot another scene for the very end of the film with Sammy and Rosie by the river at Hammersmith, which Kureishi was not happy about because of the danger of sentimentalizing. Such an ending would suggest that:

> ■ despite everything – the shooting, the revolts, the politics of Rafi – this odd couple end up being happy together, the implication being that this is all that matters. This is, of course, the pattern of classical narration: an original set-up is disrupted but is restored at the end. Thus the audience doesn't leave the cinema thinking that life is completely hopeless. □
>
> (SS 191)

Nor, with this kind of narration, does the audience leave with the conviction that society needs changing.

Another source of concern in the film diary was the political significance of showing black people rioting:

> ■ Frears talks about the problems of shooting the riots, especially after a friend said: Oh no, not a lot of black people rioting. So we talk about avoiding the TV news-footage approach: screaming mobs, bleeding policemen. What you don't get in news footage is detail ...
>
> In *Sammy and Rosie* you do see the circumstances from which the riot comes – the shooting of a black woman by the police. And we see, in the circumstances, how justifiable the riot is. The difficulty arises from the fact that black people are so rarely represented on TV; if when they are shown, they're only throwing rocks at the police, you're in danger of reinforcing considerable prejudice. I suppose this depends partly on how you see the riot, or revolt. □   (SS 146)

During the making of the film, Kureishi was following the Blakelock case in the newspapers. A man was sentenced to life imprisonment for the killing of a policeman during an uprising on the Broadwater Farm Estate in north London. As Kureishi explains: 'The uprising followed the death of a much respected middle-aged black woman, Cynthia Jarrett, who died of a heart attack during a police raid on her home on the estate.' Reading these accounts makes Kureishi question again the ethics and likely consequences of the riot scene in the film:

> ■ It's all depressing, as was the incident around which I based the opening of the film: the shooting of a black woman, Cherry Groce, who was

permanently paralysed after being shot during a police raid in which her son was being sought ... ...

I can't work out today if the question about the relation between the real people, the real events, and the portrayal is an aesthetic or moral one. In other words, if the acting is good, if the film is well made, if it seems authentic, does that make it all right, is the stealing justified? Will the issue be settled if experience is successfully distilled into art?

Or is the quality of the work irrelevant to the social issue, which is that of middle-class people (albeit dissenting middle-class people) who own and control and have access to the media and to money, using minority and working-class material to entertain other middle-class people? Frequently during the making of the film I feel that this is the case, that what we're doing is a kind of social voyeurism.

At the same time I can justify our work by saying it is the duty of contemporary films to show contemporary life. This portrayal of our world as it is is valuable in itself, and part of the climate of opposition and dissent. ☐   (SS 171–2)

At various points in the editing process, the scene in which a black woman is shot is taken out and finally put back (SS 196). The way this shooting was filmed forms part of bell hooks's critique of the film.

Kureishi and Frears's open approach allowed the film to respond to and be influenced by contemporary events. As the diary notes: 'the structure is secure enough now for anything odd or interesting that happens to have a place. All the bits and pieces will just have to get along with each other, like people at a party' (SS 147). Although pleased to be able to catch this contemporaneity, Kureishi was concerned that the film may be 'too diffuse ... [that it] lacks narrative force and focus' (SS 179).

Having looked at Frears and Kureishi's anxieties and aspirations, we can now look at how the film was viewed and the possible gap between intention and effect. The use of juxtaposition was the subject of early reviews. Kaleta gives a sample of the varying responses to the fragmented and episodic mode of presentation, beginning here with Leonard Quart:

■ It's [Kureishi's] belief in a life of spontaneity – free of guilt and crass self-interest which the film sets in opposition to all that is respectable, repressive and calculating in society. Frears's directorial style reinforces this vision by making use of split screen, rapid, rhythmic cross cutting, shock cuts (e.g., cutting from the police killing a middle-aged black woman to the bare, tattooed behind of a nubile woman photographer), swish pans, tracking with a hand-held camera, overlapping dialogue, vivid color (a use of bright light and red filters) – a barrage of visual and aural fireworks to help disrupt our sense of order and affirm a life lived without conventional constraints. (Leonard Quart, 'The Politics of Irony', 1994)[7] [Kaleta continues] Rafi succinctly transfers the film's surreal juxtaposition of visual and political messages into literal message when he puts the urban riots into words, on a postcard he sends back to Pakistan: 'Streets on fire – wish you were here.' ... ...

Many critics have complained that Kureishi's lack of identification with any of the large cast of characters leaves both his story unresolved and the audience uninvolved. 'The film is constantly cross-cutting between characters, events, and scene-setting images. As each character is overwhelmed to a greater or lesser degree by contradictory impulses, so is the film',[8] wrote one critic. However, other critics have praised the effect of Kureishi's distance from and lack of sympathy for his many characters. Political despot Rafi, for example, is characterized by Richard Corliss as having 'no more or less sympathy than any other character in this exuberant egalitarian stew of a movie'.[9] □

(Kenneth Kaleta, *Hanif Kureishi*, 1998)[10]

Kaleta goes on to point out that the reviews of *Sammy and Rosie* were far more mixed than those of *My Beautiful Laundrette*. He notes that 'most of the negative criticism centred on [Kureishi's] artificial language' and he quotes from Leonard Quart's ambivalent review: 'The talk is usually literate and witty (a rarity in most contemporary films) and ranges from Sammy's homage to London, to Rosie's lesson with concomitant demonstration of the different types of kissing. At times, however, Kureishi becomes too enamoured with his own eloquence and wit, and the characters just take off on interminable soliloquies'.[11] Kureishi himself expresses similar reservations in the film diary: 'I cringe throughout at the ridiculousness of the dialogue, which seems nothing like the way people actually talk. A lot of this will go, I expect ... though I am attached to some of the ideas in the more strident speeches' (SS 188). Evident here is the tension between getting across a political message, while avoiding the one-dimensionality of characters as mere mouthpieces. Some reviewers complained that the film's political content was too blatant; others that the political message was contradictory and unclear. Norman Stone's right-wing polemic against Kureishi, quoted in the previous chapter, savaged *Sammy and Rosie* as an example of 'general disgustingness' and agitprop. Perhaps ironically, Sandeep Naidoo, from a contrasting minoritarian perspective, came to a similar conclusion: 'There was no dramatic focus, too much was thrown in and one couldn't get the feeling that these were believable characters.'[12] As none of the early reviews get much further than asserting one view or the other, we will look at the more considered political analyses of later critical responses.

Probably because the use of montage, juxtaposition, irony and multiple characters means that *Sammy and Rosie* requires more than one viewing to absorb, the most interesting criticism emerged some time later. For bell hooks, the film was an example of 'stylish nihilism', which despite its good intentions, turned the representation of oppression into 'high spectacle, the alternative playground'. The difficulty for hooks is that Kureishi's use of irony needs an audience that is politically conscious enough to interpret it: the reliance on ambiguity and contradiction mean that the film's power to subvert and liberate is undermined. She begins by praising Kureishi's refreshing refusal to censor aspects of the postcolonial experience, before arguing that he 'appropriates' the pain of the oppressed. We can join her argument as she discusses the implications of the shooting of a black woman in the opening scenes and the political ambiguity of the ironic mode:

■ In *Sammy and Rosie*, Kureishi based the first scene on an actual incident in which Cherry Groce, a black woman, was paralyzed when accidentally shot during a police raid. While his intent may have been to expose viewers to the cruelty and indifference of white police as they raid this building where mostly black people live, the scene is shot in such a way that it undermines this concern. In the opening scene, a black woman is shown slinging the hot oil in which she is cooking french fries at the white police. This undercuts the idea that she is being shot accidentally, suggesting instead that, however violent the police may be, they are responding to a perceived threat. This is a very subtle filmic moment, one that happens so quickly it is easy to miss, shot as though the filmmaker could not simply depict white police shooting the woman at her stove without provocation. We watch this very violent death of a black woman, which sets off racial rioting – all of which becomes backdrop for the drama of Sammy and Rosie. If there was any intent to depict the pain of oppression and systematic violence in the lives of Britain's black underclass, it is undercut not only by the 'spectacular,' thrilling, fast paced movement of the scenes, but also by the way they are portrayed as mere farce. The realism embedded in such imagining is lost, and what lingers is solely the quality of entertaining, violent spectacle.

... This is the deep satirical message of the film, when it comes across as satire, its social critique – for it says that the cool white people, and even perhaps the cool non-whites, who supposedly 'understand' what is happening with the oppressed, really don't care in a way that counts, especially when counting means surrendering center stage, or privilege. This is best highlighted in two marvelous scenes, one where Sammy wanks off, eats his cheeseburger, listens to music, and does a little coke, while the riot goes on, and the scene where Rosie strolls right through the violent action, pausing for a moment of picture taking. Rather than these 'cool' white people appropriating the labor of black servants to build empires, they appropriate the pain and passion of the oppressed to build images of themselves as politically correct, as different from oppressive white people who do not lead a more diverse, colorful, intense life, who do not 'get down.' While audiences laughed at these contradictions, it was obvious from the comments white students from Yale were making during these scenes that they laughed heartily because they identified with Sammy's indifference, his narcissism, yet not in a critical or subversive way ... ...

[Even more than *My Beautiful Laundrette, Sammy and Rosie Get Laid*] 'amuses' as it juxtaposes the lives of those on the periphery who are against domination with those who do not know where they stand. Kureishi's irony is not always conveyed. At times he seems to be suggesting in the film that resistance to racism, sexism, and other forms of domination assumes the quality of spectacle and farce because the forces to be overcome are all-powerful, a rather despairing take. It is not surprising that some audiences miss the irony and think that the message is that one should focus on personal pleasure to have any satisfaction in life, since the oppression does not end. □

(bell hooks, 'Stylish Nihilism', 1991)[13]

The gap between intention and effect is clear here. While Frears and Kureishi wanted to celebrate rebelliousness but also to show its ironies and ambiguities, hooks seems to want a more straightforward resistance narrative, which demonstrates the effectiveness of political action.

Hooks goes on to argue that the 'black and brown women' in the film are portrayed in negative and stereotypical terms:

■ the South Asian woman character who has radical political beliefs is portrayed as 'hysterical,' one might even say as monstrous. She and her black woman lover are 'into' confrontation; they want to hold Rafi responsible for his actions. They are portrayed as uptight and uncool, as in that scene where Sammy tells her that she is a prick. Not only is there never even the slightest hint of bonding between Sammy, Vinia, and Rani, black women continually appear on the screen and are disposed of, like props taken away as soon as they have fulfilled their function ... □

(bell hooks, 'Stylish Nihilism', 1991)[14]

Hooks then turns her attention to the characterization of Danny and the other 'non-white males', which she also sees as contributing to the film's message of powerlessness against oppression, and from there she goes on to discuss the film's treatment of sexuality:

■ Danny, also known as Victoria – a name which suggests that he can be both male and female, masculine and feminine – tells Rosie that the murdered black woman cared for him as a child, yet he does not know how to respond to her death. He does not participate in the rioting, but neither does he grieve. Instead he seems to be totally distracted by his sexual desire for Rosie. Danny comes on the scene as magnificent outsider, the rebel who observes and processes before he acts. Yet he continually fails to respond to political situations, finding solace in the realm of desire. Danny's desire for Rosie blocks him from engaging in effective political response ... Throughout the film, non-white men are portrayed as lusting after white women. Alice, Rafi's lover, tells him, 'The penis has been your life-line,' critiquing both his sexism and the way it shapes and informs his sexual desire. Still, she does not refuse him. Like Sammy, Rafi and Danny use sexuality as a way to escape their inability to respond politically. It is as though the impotence these Third World men feel, their powerlessness to stop domination, to be anything but colla-borators and perpetrators through either passivity or direct action, renders them incapable of facing reality ... White women appear in this film as the consolation prize nonwhite men receive as reward for their betrayal ...

... Sammy's mother is an absent non-white female presence who was disposed of by Rafi because he considered her 'ugly.' Danny's mother is absent. The black male child he often carries has no visible black mother, and he seems to be the primary nurturer. After Rosie has sex with him, she is portrayed stroking the black child as though she has now become the symbol of nurturance and motherhood. Well, none of this should have been surprising; let's face it, the black woman as mother was wiped off the planet in the very first scene. If black women constitute the garbage to be disposed of, and black and brown men have no meaningful response to this aggression and violation ..., then the genocide is complete; culture and people are effectively 'appropriated,' destroyed, 'wiped out.'

At one point in the film Danny and Rosie fuck, Sammy and Annie fuck, Rafi and Alice fuck, to the beat of black male Rastas singing 'My Girl.' This was farce and spectacle at its best, highlighted by the fact that the dudes could sing. As a black female watching this scene, I was struck by this use of a song which emerged from segregated African-American culture as an expression of possessive love between black female and black male, evoked here to celebrate this inter-racial spectacle of non-white men with white women. I found this scene very amusing. It graphi-cally exposed contradictions. However, when I stopped laughing I found its message to be potentially frightening and even threatening, because it did not overtly promote critical reflection about the absence of black women, and could easily be seen as making light of the disposing of women of color, of sexual and racial violation of women of color by white women and men (Rosie is visibly sexually turned on when Danny shares with her that the murdered black woman nursed him as a child) ... Talking with many white viewers, I was not shocked to hear that the irony never registers, that they saw these scenes as a celebration of sex and desire, as a meeting place across race and ethnicity. (bell hooks, 'Stylish Nihilism', 1991)[15] □

Judging from the discussions of this scene in the film diary, it was intended as a rejection of Thatcher's call to return to Victorian family values (' the mean monogamous spirit of our age' (SS 188)), and, indeed, to show what hooks says white viewers saw: 'a meeting place across race and ethnicity'. Kureishi and Frears do not seem to have registered the absence of women of colour, nor its implications.

Hooks then considers the film's ending:

■ Our attention leaves Rafi and is focused again on Sammy and Rosie, who we see in the final scene reunited on the floor in their heterosexual unity, rocking back and forth crying and kissing one another, as though once again desire mediates the pain of grief and tragedy. Sammy, as Third World infant, turns for comfort to Mother Rosie, who considers abdicating her maternal role for a brief moment, but then is once again drawn back into the familial fold. This ending suggests that the cool, politically correct, (dare I say it?) 'feminist' white woman, who identifies with blacks and lesbians alike, wants to have a relationship with the Third World in which she dominates as nurturing mother, duplicating in a slightly inverted form the white male, imperialist, paternal position. At first the film seemed to subtly critique Rosie, exposing her appropriation of the pain of Third World people, our issues, and our sexuality, but the traditionally romantic ending affirms her ... ...

Rosie is a symbol of failed modern radicalism. She does not stand alone. She embodies the helplessness, the powerlessness, that overwhelms many politically aware, cool people. She is stylishly nihilistic! □
(bell hooks, 'Stylish Nihilism', 1991)[16]

Part of hooks's difficulty with the film is Kureishi's juxtaposition of the violent and the comic, intended as a way of avoiding 'dourness and didacticism', but seen by hooks as trivializing the oppression the film sought to expose. But her most powerful punches are aimed at the treatment of race and gender: the absence of the black mother and the privileging of the white feminist; the white woman as prize for self-hating non-white males; sexual pleasure not as liberating in itself, but as defeatist – an escape from harsher political realities.

Hooks looks at the film from the perspective of a black woman and is attentive to the differences between how she, and her black male friend (whose dismay at the character of Danny she describes), view particular scenes in contrast to the reactions of her mainly white students. Gayatri Chakravorty Spivak, who was born and educated in India and has taught in the United States for 38 years, is equally alert to the ways in which the location of the viewer shapes interpretations, but her reading is very different. Although Spivak concurs with hooks 'that making the police shoot the black woman in self-defense puts the film's race-perspective in some doubt', that would seem to be the only point of agreement.[17] Where hooks complains of the prominence given to Rosie, Spivak relishes Rosie's role; hooks is critical of the representation of the lesbians, Spivak is admiring; hooks sees the ending as an affirmation of 'heterosexual unity', Spivak sees nothing enduring in the reconciliation; hooks objects to 'dark-skinned blacks', Danny in particular, being relegated to the role of backdrop, Spivak sees in Danny a 'reference point for radical innocence'. Although Spivak's essay was not written in reply to hooks, we can fruitfully contrast the two readings.

Spivak is a literary philosophical critic, whose pioneering introduction to and translation of Derrida's *Of Grammatology* appeared in 1976. She brings a variety of theoretical perspectives to bear, focusing on the contradictions, gaps and ambiguities in the film. Spivak assumes 'the death of the author', that the writer has no authority over how readers interpret a text, and so is more interested in her own interpretation than in second-guessing Kureishi's intentions. She begins her essay 'In praise of *Sammy and Rosie Get Laid*' by explaining her focus; that she is looking at the film as a 'didactic' piece and that she is interested in the 'relationship between aesthetics and politics'.[18] With this in mind we can consider her reading of the 'incredible role' of Rosie:

■ It seemed to me ... that the old British ideological subject of radicalism has become very indeterminate and that Rosie was that subject in the film. She was white, deliberately downwardly class-mobile, a social worker, heterosexual ... ...

Given our general unpreparedness for knowing what is and is not radical, that beleaguered position is seen today as the white ideological subject-position of reactive welfare-state radicalism. You cannot really be against Rosie, but there is no final determination. She loves all the right people. She's a white heterosexual woman who loves lesbians, loves blacks, is in an interracial marriage, etc., etc. ... ...

... One of the most important moments in the film is when Rafi and Rosie are having their row in the restaurant. Rafi's line is that she doesn't know what it is like in decolonised space and she's giving the line about there being no excuses for torture. They're screaming at each other and everybody in the restaurant forms a sort of audience so that it becomes a public performance. At a certain moment the camera holds on a close-up of Rosie so that it almost looks like a still. Rosie has very sharp weapon-like earrings, and the profile is frozen in such a way that it looks as though a sort of caged beast has been cornered: the beleaguered position of the civilised conscience for whom torture is bad under any circumstances. In *Analysing Marx* (1984) Richard Miller takes up the question of why Marx repudiates the merely moral position.[19] It might be interesting to compare the two positions.

The elusiveness of Rosie's presentation, her aporetic quality [in the critical terminology of deconstruction, aporia is used in the sense of a final impasse: a point at which the text's self-contradictory meanings can no longer be resolved] – we can neither agree nor disagree with her and are uneasy in every way – is the predicament of a dharmic elusiveness in a rational analytic world that understands morality in systems [Spivak uses 'dharma' here in the sense of ideology]. Rosie the character *is* not this, but Rosie the bit of filmic text shows this up. Paradoxically, the same aporetic character pervades the decolonized justification of torture as the system that cures the inconvenience of mere moral systems. We cannot just dismiss Rafi without dismissing what produces him. The world of the London Asian is hung between the two. □

(Gayatri Spivak, '*Sammy and Rosie Get Laid*', 1993)[20]

This is similar to hooks's description of Rosie as a 'symbol of failed modern radicalism', but while hooks is exasperated by Rosie's 'stylish nihilism', her failure to take a stand, Spivak is less interested in what Rosie '*is*' than in the fact that she 'dramatizes this confrontation between radicalism and old-fashioned simple Enlightenment morality'. To Spivak, Rosie does not embody hooks's 'helplessness of the cool', she is the means by which the film provokes the viewer into an awareness of complexity: 'we can neither agree nor disagree with her and are uneasy in every way'; we cannot assent to torture but we have to see it as part of 'the heritage of imperialism'. The kind of radicalism that Rosie represents has failed to take responsibility for postcolonial violence.

Spivak then moves from Rosie's 'unreadability' to discuss gender and the portrayal of lesbians in the film, arguing that the black lesbians have a more complex function than the gay couple in *My Beautiful Laundrette*, 'where interraciality was presented in a lyrical way ... with all the erotic furniture of romantic heterosexuality ... [or] the erotic permissiveness of classical Greece'[21]:

■ But in [*Sammy and Rosie Get Laid*] what I like is that the interraciality embraces varieties of blackness, and I like that a lot. But in addition the lesbians go from one end of the spectrum of language use to the other. They move from an expository fact-finding use of English, in the scene in the office where the woman who speaks with a fairly heavy accent is Chinese-British, to hurling abuse in Urdu. It seems to me that this is rather bold. It's not simply that their comments about heterosexuality are always funny. It's more importantly that they are never confined to one place. Whereas in the earlier film the two boys had been kept in one place: the development of the solution to interracial problems. Although lyrical it was much more overtly didactic. So the protagonist says he doesn't want to fight and gets beaten up. And then at the end you have all the splashing-water ablution with the music welling up as the dirt is erased, so they are cleansed. The lesbians have a role that you cannot specify as a model in the same way because the didactic focus is blurred. From one perspective the central issue is Rafi and his son Sammy. On the other hand these people are not a sub-plot, their function is crucial to the film. It's because of their fact-finding that the film can utilise somewhat old-fashioned non-realistic techniques, montage, the ghost figure, etc. The film justifies its move away from realism, its stylistic transformation in terms of these two lesbians which I find quite interesting. Lesbians play a role which is much more than the gay couple. □

(Gayatri Spivak, 'In Praise of *Sammy and Rosie Get Laid*', 1989)[22]

In this reading the black women are neither 'monsters' nor 'props' (as hooks argues). According to Spivak, the lesbians are not only funny and convincing; they are 'crucial' to the film. Radhika Mohanram (whose discussion of 'deterritorialized (homo)sexuality' in *My Beautiful Laundrette* we looked at in the previous chapter) picks up Spivak's point about the 'traveling' lesbians in *Sammy and Rosie* to argue that the unconfined interracial lesbianism, the visible interracial heterosexuality and the parading of extra-marital affairs takes the critique of narrow definitions of national identity one stage further: 'If the stability of a nation can be maintained only through manliness, respectability, and heterosexuality, this film attempts to destabilise all three to critique culturally received notions of the identity of its citizens.'[23]

Although Spivak argues that the lesbian couple are not a model for heterosexuality, she does not see the film's ending as an affirmation of the values of the heterosexual couple. She speculates that this may have been Kureishi's intention (although we can see from the film diary that it was not), but this does not interest her: 'For me the important issue is that I can quite happily read the end not as a declaration for the act of heterosexual love but rather as a premonition that the idea of such a courtship is defunct':

■ I read the end ... in terms of the debate on the relationship between crisis and the everyday. We've seen enough of whatever is called the everyday in Sammy and Rosie's life to doubt the solidarity that only a moment of crisis can bring. One can think of it in terms of the relation between revolution and post-revolution, the strongest statement of this from feminists in Algeria. They became comrades during the revolution. Once the dust had settled and the transitionality of the crisis is over, they had to go back to the old sexist ways of coping with the everyday. ... ...

The final scene shows us Sammy and Rosie simply weeping in response to a crisis, as the group at the table depart ... This is how solidarities are fabricated, manufactured directly in response to crisis and such alliances are very fragile. The rest of the film has prepared us to see this fragility and we should pay attention to the rest of the film. □

(Gayatri Spivak, '*Sammy and Rosie Get Laid*', 1993)[24]

In Spivak's first version of the essay she is unequivocal in her praise of the characterization of Danny and the way the film traces 'the different position of blacks and Asians in Britain'.[25] She rejects the call for positive images of blacks (which she regards as deeply insulting) and opposes the view that the film is racist because it shows Danny as 'stupid', arguing that he is a reference point for 'radical innocence'. In the second essay, she takes into account outbreaks of 'hostility between inner-city Blacks of Afro-Caribbean, African, and Asian origin', which make her more hesitant about Danny's role as 'referent':

■ I am not sure if Kureishi ... has been able to pull it off by constructing a figure who is totally outside of crisis but reaching out, a figure of radical innocence, a cross-dressing would-be androgyne, a sweet fake drag queen, the other side of the savvy lesbians, the nicest all-round hybrid you could wish for: Danny-Victoria. But it must be admitted that he tries. A measure of his attempt is marked by Danny-Victoria's misreading of India. Danny-Victoria says to Rafi (and in the process he confuses India with Pakistan): 'after all your way is just to sit down and be non-violent and that's what we ought to learn.' And, of course, Rafi rises to the bait and is benevolent about Gandhi, a typical example of a postcolonial indigenous elite falling into a Ministry of Culture patter. But we know his standard defence of torture. And indeed Kureishi, a London Asian of Pakistani origin, is explicitly critical of the postcolonial Pakistani here, an attitude rather different from the usual ethnic-partisan root-searching. We might also remember that, although the moment is comic, it is this sort of misreading that produces great mobilizing signifiers of political action. □

(Gayatri Spivak, 'Sammy and Rosie Get Laid', 1993)[26]

In the first essay, Spivak comments that 'Martin Luther King misread Gandhi in that way too'.[27] So Spivak finds in Sammy and Rosie: 'radical innocence, not stupidity; interracial solidarity in crisis, not romantic love'.[28]

Spivak also notes that many people objected to the fact that after the black woman is killed, the film cuts to a shot of the American woman's backside with the two Ws in a way they consider racist. But Spivak would rather read this as a 'bitter comment on the roving American journalist ... than Asian anti-Africanism yet once again'.[29] Moreover, she extends her defence of humour and juxtaposition here to the overall use of montage in the film:

■ It is in keeping with the film's juxtaposition of a whole range of fact-finding, social engineering activities. The film gives us a spectrum of the social text. There is Rosie the social worker and the American woman doing her photographs and articles and there are the two lesbian women finding out facts. A whole chain of displacements in terms of which you

are shown how a quick fix or a quick judgment or a quick read is produc-
tively resisted by the film ... In the article wrongly titled in English as
'Commitment' Adorno says of Brecht that his use of montage in *The
Resistible Rise of Arturo Ui* simply turns a political problem into a joke.[30]
One hopes that Kureishi's montage technique would have satisfied
Adorno. It is much more concerned with negotiating a certain kind of
unease, a laughter tinged with unease and bafflement. □

(Gayatri Spivak, '*Sammy and Rosie get Laid*', 1993)[31]

In Spivak's reading, then, laughter is complex and provocative, not the
reduction of oppression to spectacle or stylish nihilism, although it
could still be argued (as hooks does) that it takes a politically conscious
viewer to interpret this.

Curiously, although Spivak is uninterested in the author's aims, and
therefore does not refer to the film diary (unlike hooks who does), her
reading chimes with Kureishi's intentions. More importantly, I have put
these two essays together because they are both impressively argued,
thought-provoking and acutely aware of the politics of representation,
and both come to almost completely different conclusions. It may be
that as an Indian citizen Spivak is more sympathetic to the film than the
African-American hooks. By including a broader range of characters
than *My Beautiful Laundrette*, Kureishi opened himself up to the charge
of appropriation and misrepresentation of the black characters but as
Spivak warns: 'to construct an ever-narrowing circle of politically
acceptable texts spells danger, makes us forget our common enemy'.[32]

Spivak argues that the movement from *My Beautiful Laundrette* to
Sammy and Rosie changes the focus from 'race' to 'postcoloniality' as the
latter traces the Oedipal struggle between 'the migrant son in
Thatcherite Britain and the postcolonial father from Bhutto's
Pakistan'.[33] Mohanram argues that what happens in *Sammy and Rosie* is
'that notwithstanding Margaret Thatcher, the identity of a nationalistic
England is unravelled'. However, neither critic pays much attention to
the critique of Thatcherism in the film. This is the focus of Susan Torrey
Barber's discussion of *Sammy and Rosie*. Where *My Beautiful Laundrette*
was an 'ironic salutation to the entrepreneurial spirit in the eighties that
Margaret Thatcher championed', Barber sees *Sammy and Rosie* as a much
more 'acrimonious critique'.[34] Her main interest is in the 'waste ground'
scenes, the last refuge of those made unemployed and homeless by
Thatcher's divisive social policies. She cites the fact that in Brixton in
1981 unemployment ran close to 70 percent and she sees in Danny 'the
disenfranchisement and alienation of blacks'.[35] Barber's analysis of the
first film emphasized the difficulties but also the optimism of relationships that 'cross class/ethnic/sexual boundaries'.[36] Her focus in the second
film is not on Sammy and Rosie but on Rosie and Danny's potential 'for

a mutually beneficial and fulfilling relationship'. But in this film the odd couple are pulled apart. Barber notes the irony of Thatcher's valorization of the nuclear family and the way the film suggests 'the absolute break-down of this unit under economic pressures'.[37] As all the relationships disintegrate – Danny and Rosie, Rosie and Sammy, Sammy and Anna, Alice and Rafi – Barber concludes:

> ■ As *Sammy and Rosie* shows, the crushing pressures of Britain's economic and social upheaval render impossible heterosexual relationships that cross ethnic and class boundaries, those that have the potential to create harmony and order. Yet the film applauds a few tattered survivors: a strong group of heterosexual and lesbian females who bond together, as Rosie, Vivia, Rani, and their friends do in one of the film's final scenes. These self-appointed guardians take care of England's increasing numbers of underprivileged, while also looking out for political terrorists such as Rafi. While *My Beautiful Laundrette* demonstrated how Omar and Johnny assumed a leadership role as entrepreneurs, bringing two diverse communities together and creating a new hybrid community made stronger by the benefits of their enterprise, in *Sammy and Rosie* leaders like Rosie, Rani, and Vivia defiantly remain at odds with the businessmen who tragically destroy their communities. This pitched battle is played out when the landowners/developers, under the auspices of the government, raze the waste ground, thus destroying the fragile settlement and creating another group of homeless and alienated people. Though *Laundrette* and *Sammy and Rosie* both link sexual diversity to the preservation of communities, *Laundrette*'s optimism that enterprise can build a stronger society shifts to a bleaker message in *Sammy and Rosie*: that enterprise is obsessively self-serving. □
>
> (Susan Torrey Barber, 'Insurmountable Difficulties and Moments of Ecstasy', 1993)[38]

Although the film certainly was, as Frears said, 'screaming at Margaret Thatcher', it was also a celebration of London. The capital city represents the quintessence of Englishness, but in *Sammy and Rosie*, London is detached from the rest of England: a world city that both Sammy and Rosie are proud to identify as theirs. This representation of London is arguably the film's most radical project, its finest achievement, and so we will conclude with extracts from Sukhdev Sandhu's brilliant and wide-ranging essay on Hanif Kureishi's London.

Sandhu emphasises that Kureishi's metropolis is not a place of alienation but of possibility. At the heart of the following extract is Sammy and Rosie's love for their city:

> ■ Kureishi's archetypal London landscape consists of young people abandoning their rooms and cruising through the streets of the capital,

passing by myriads of multi-ethnic shops, restaurants and people; they'll smile, laugh, and imbibe both high and low culture. All of this will take place to the accompaniment of loud, pounding beats which capture young London's density, its ricocheting medley ... And it's with this aspect alone of London society – deregulated, energized, pop – that Kureishi's characters identify. They relate to the city not in terms of particular places – Selvon's Bayswater Road or Kwesi Johnson's Brixton street corners[39] – but as a mood, an attitude of openness and brio. More than just a space, London represents an ideal – that of possibility, change, the transformation of both self and society. This ideal may be naive, absurdly utopian perhaps, but it's all the more 'pop' because of that. Sammy enthuses to his baffled father about the joys of kissing and arguing on Hammersmith towpath, strolling through Hyde Park, watching alternative comedians in Earl's Court abuse the Government and attending semiotic seminars at the ICA where Colin MacCabe discusses 'The relation between a bag of crisps and the self-enclosed unity of the linguistic sign', before concluding 'We love our city and we belong to it. Neither of us are English, we're Londoners you see' (SRGL 33).

It's an interesting remark and one which flies in the face of the doomy portraits of immigrant life in the metropolis normally painted by literary scholars and race relations experts. Though Kureishi's declaration of metrophilia is unusually explicit,[40] it joins a tradition of positivity about London which ranges from Sancho's invocation of 'our grand metropolis' right through to Lamming's affectionate accounts of cosmopolitan Hampstead,[41] Rushdie's *The Satanic Verses* (1988) and *Junglist* (1995) by Two Fingers and James T. Kirk. These writers don't deny that life in the city can be jarring and turmoily, but they also feel that its diversity, ebullience and phatness [sociability] more than compensate. Kureishi agrees; and although there's plenty of racial violence ..., his work contains far more interracial mingling, fraternizing and couplings than that of previous writers. This is largely because Kureishi focuses on second generation Asians who are fascinated by and embroiled in pop culture, that realm at the 'fringes of the respectable world [where there is] marijuana, generational conflict, clubs, parties, and a certain kind of guiltless, casual sex' (F xix). English pop, unlike the American variety, has never been racially segregated or monochromatic. In fact, it's one of the few areas where class, race and background become subordinated to the eternal 'now' that is at the heart of pop music and where, as Rakim rapped, 'It ain't where you're from – it's where you're at'.[42] This dictum appeals to Kureishi's chief protagonists who ... don't always want to be defined by the values and beliefs of their parents.

Sammy's statement is also didactic and provocative rather than merely descriptive. It implicitly rejects the first-generation Asian view that migration and geography make no difference, and that children should cleave to their parents. Nor does it simply endorse assimilationism, a line of thought which rarely acknowledges that the host society is itself composed of a welter of classes, regions and biographies. There's no simple, uniform Englishness with which anyone, let alone an immigrant, could hope to assimilate. Sammy himself does not equate being a Londoner with being English. □

(Sukhdev Sandhu, 'Pop Goes the Centre', 1999)[43]

For Sandhu it is Kureishi's 'toleration of – and even revelling in – the more fractured, fallen aspects of London life that distinguishes him from other Asian and Caribbean writers. His characters harry, lope and arterialize their ways through the capital with queer abandon'.[44] Unlike V. S. Naipaul, they are not interested in 'finding the centre'. 'Such a notion was more poignant for pre-Independence writers who'd grown up believing – and being taught – that they were on the outskirts, the margins of English culture.' But Kureishi, second generation, born in Bromley, does not suffer from 'cultural cringe', and his relaxed attitude to the possibilities of change and his celebration of the '(pop) cultural capital' lead Sandhu to hail him as 'perhaps the first – and certainly the best and most important – Asian chronicler of London'.[45]

The money earned from *My Beautiful Laundrette* and *Sammy and Rosie* earned Kureishi a two-year period to work on his finest London chronicle, *The Buddha of Suburbia*, in which the protagonist explores the 'limitless palette of intellectual, social and sexual combinations'[46] available in the city, neither cleaving to his parents nor attempting to assimilate. But first he has to get out of the suburbs.

CHAPTER FOUR

Modern Everyman: *The Buddha of Suburbia* (1990)

'Fuck you, Charles Dickens, nothing's changed.' (BS 63)

*T*he *Buddha of Suburbia* is the most significant contemporary example of the English picaresque since *Great Expectations* (1860–61) by Charles Dickens (1812–70). As 'fuck-yous' go this seems to be an affectionate one, which recognizes Karim as Pip's descendant: both are restless, dissatisfied with their drab lives, yearning for more, but both novels achieve their deepest poignancies from the protagonists' ultimately serious and saddened awareness of loss. Indeed, with its young man on the move and on the make, naive but opportunistic, engaged in comic and often humiliating amorous adventures, *The Buddha* extends a tradition that stretches back through the 1950s novels of social mobility by John Braine (1922–86), Kingsley Amis (1922–95) and Alan Sillitoe (born 1928), through Dickens, to the eighteenth-century picaresque. Published in 1990 but set during the 1970s, it begins with the fag-end of hippiedom, through punk rock to Thatcher, and anticipates Cool Britannia. The sexual confusion and experimentation, the break-up of the traditional family; the movement from India to England, from the suburbs to the city, and from London to New York, capture the contemporary sense of displacement and surging aspiration. Shadwell, the (otherwise moronic) theatre director in *The Buddha*, is right: 'the immigrant is the Everyman of the twentieth century' (BS 141).

Most strikingly, this English picaresque is about the immigrant and minority experience. Haroon, from Bombay, boasts that 'They are looking forward to me all over Orpington' (BS 21) while Karim, born in Bromley, confides that he 'really wanted to be the first Indian centre-forward to play for England' (BS 43). But *The Buddha* is not in any sense an ethnic novel, written for or about a particular minority. Rather, as A. Robert Lee states: 'it proceed[s] from, and inscribe[s] a quite ineradicable and historic multicultural Englishness or Britishness ... [I]t 'speaks out of, and to, the absolute centre of "England," ' changing the 'script' of what it means to be English.[1]

It is an extraordinarily rich and multi-layered novel which ranges across class, race, left-wing politics, gender, sexuality, pop culture, literature and the theatre; all of which are explored in the following extracts. In addition, there are discussions of *The Buddha* in terms of genre: the picaresque, the *Bildungsroman*, the 'Condition of England' novel. It is also a pleasure to introduce significant critical writing from France on the novel's treatment of sexuality. While much of the critical debate has focused on hybridity and the politics of representation, I have included criticism that pays attention to the comic and literary qualities of *The Buddha*. One reason why it won the Whitbread Award for Best First Novel in 1990, and has sold over half a million copies and been translated into more than twenty languages, is not only because of its importance as a cultural document, but also because of its writerly vitality.

Several critics draw on the concept of cultural hybridity, the mixing of cultures celebrated by Salman Rushdie in *Imaginary Homelands* (1991), and theorized in the writing of Homi Bhabha, its most influential proponent. While Rushdie sees hybridity as a combination of cultures, ideas and identities, which allows new cultural forms to come into existence, Bhabha argues that any identity is always already hybrid and, moreover, that cultural differences are not synthesized into a new 'third term' but continue to exist in a hybrid 'Third Space'. This place of hybridity or in-betweenness is a way of conceptualizing cultural differences between formerly colonized cultures and First World cultures sharing the same metropolitan space.[2] Although cultural hybridity is a highly contested term in postcolonial theory, it is politically useful as a means of resisting cultural nationalism within the 'host' society, which sees merging as undesirable; as a way of countering assimiliationism, which requires minorities to give up their culture of origin; and, in contrast, as a corrective to multiculturalism which insists that mingling is a loss of authenticity.[3] As we will see, many critics have fruitfully explored Kureishi's novel as an embodiment and complication of Bhabha and Rushdie's celebration of cultural hybridity. Indeed, the *Buddha* draws on and deepens many of the concerns in Kureishi's earlier works, all of which, to a greater or lesser extent, deal with what the theatre director, Pyke in *The Buddha*, refers to as 'class, race, fucking and farce', and which I used as the heading for the chapter on *My Beautiful Laundrette* (with which it shares many similarities). I have begun with 'race' since Kureishi's exploration of new ways of being British is a central concern.

With the novel's opening sentence, the much-quoted 'My name is Karim Amir, and I am an Englishman born and bred, almost', Kureishi signals his intention to explore post-imperial Englishness. As we saw in the Introduction, Kureishi makes it plain that if a multiethnic society is to work, it is 'the white British who have to learn that being British isn't what it was. Now it is a more complex thing, involving new elements'; the demand that minorities simply assimilate into British society is untenable. It is not just the myth of tolerant England that is blown apart in the novel but the myth of a homogeneous Englishness. Instead, the novel shows Englishness as changing and unstable, varying according to class and gender as well as over time. National identities in *The Buddha* are invariably presented as a matter of cultural performances, rather than essential or inherited characteristics. This is important, because if 'English' is not itself a coherent category, what exactly are immigrants being asked to assimilate into? In general, critics have not paid much attention to the Anglo-English characters in the novel but Berthold Schoene kicks off his discussion of Karim as 'the herald of hybridity'[4] by arguing that the 'ethno-English' are just another minority who, like all minorities, are in the process of assimilating to and remoulding the notion of Britishness:

■ Kureishi investigates what has become of the English colonizers, not all of whom have found it feasible to sustain a nostalgic self-image anchored in memories of their erstwhile imperial superiority. The English middle classes, who find themselves demoted from the cultural centrality of colonial civil stations to the politically inconsequential realm of post-imperial suburbia, are presented as especially suffering from severe cultural dislocation. Their dislocation is exacerbated by the fact that they now see their socio-economic status, cultural prestige and national identity challenged by immigrant populations from the British ex-colonies, who gradually ascend the social ladder to further equality and sameness. As Kureishi demonstrates, this is the moment when racism as an irrational, if perfectly functional gesture of fading power – as the last desperate resort of the culturally beleaguered to ascertain their difference and phantasmic superiority – takes purchase. 'We don't want you blackies coming to the house', precariously asserts Hairy Back, the ogre of white middle-class suburbia, in Kureishi's first novel (BS 40) [Hairy Back might more accurately be described as petit-bourgeois or lower-middle-class]. It is also the moment at which the post-imperial Greater English identity reveals its spurious, essentially fictitious nature ... ...

One possible strategy, the assimilation of alterity [difference] to overcome one's own cultural emaciation, features prominently in *The Buddha of Suburbia*. Kureishi's suburbanites seem desperate for the exotic, which has become a highly marketable commodity. As Karim reports, Eva (his father's new English lover) regards him as a desirable fashion accessory :'Then, holding me at arm's length as if I were a coat she was about to try on, she looked me all over and said, "Karim Amir, you are so exotic, so original! It's such a contribution! It's so you!" ' (BS 9). The exoticism of Indianness exudes a panacean [from panacea, a universal remedy] irresistibility believed to be able to fill the gaping void at the disheartened core of middle-class suburban Englishness, 'this great hole in your way of life' (BS 264), as Haroon describes it later in the novel. In this atmosphere Haroon quickly becomes a saviour figure eagerly worshipped amongst the fetishized paraphernalia of a formerly alien, now alternative culture, 'the sandalwood Buddhas, brass ashtrays and striped plaster elephants which decorated every available space' (BS 30). The centre is about to assert its power again, this time not by aggressive, missionary dissemination but by the centripetal forces of an overwhelming need for cultural substantiation. After the disappearance of a central authority endowing their lives with a strong, legitimate identity, Kureishi's English characters – most notably Eva and her son Charlie – find themselves in a limbo marked by acute disorientation. Pertinently, Mr Kay, the husband and father, is absent, recovering from a nervous breakdown in a nearby therapy centre. The traditional hierarchy grounded in a patriarchal imperialism has broken down, releasing formerly subordinate identities into a world in urgent need of meaningful re-assemblage ... ...

... Charlie, decentred by post-imperial circumstance, just like his mother who is desperate 'to scour that suburban stigma right off her body' (BS 134), eschews a confrontation with the hollow core of Englishness by masquerading as a punk hero. Mistaking fashion-imposed acts of borrowing a succession of alternative personae for his own consistent personal development, Charlie turns into a pop commodity, 'selling Englishness' (BS 247). Only Karim sees through the artificiality of Charlie Hero, who appropriates working-class youth culture as his mother appropriates Indianness, and for the same reason, which is to become culturally visible at any cost ... □

(Berthold Schoene, 'Herald of Hybridity', 1998)[5]

Although Schoene does not mention her, the character who epitomizes an utterly defeated sense of suburban Englishness is Margaret. In a passage both comic and pathetic, Karim evokes his mother's shattered confidence: 'At supper we sat eating our curled-up beefburgers, chips and fish fingers in silence. Once Mum burst into tears and banged the table with the flat of her hand. "My life is terrible, terrible!" she cried. "Doesn't anyone understand?" We looked at her in surprise for a moment, before carrying on with our food' (BS 19). As she says self-pityingly: ' "I'm only English" ' (BS 5).

Schoene's discussion of the 'ethno-English' characters is part of his larger argument about hybridity. According to Schoene, Kureishi is setting out to redeem the previously decried process of 'societal homogenization', which does not necessarily mean 'anglicization', but rather a genuine polyculturalism (a term used by Homi Bhabha to reflect the difference between cultural diversity and cultural difference).[6] But Moore-Gilbert warns that there is a form of colonialism that operates within Britain, which attempts to leaven the 'dull Saxonism of English culture' with metropolitan minorities whilst still maintaining control. Moore-Gilbert argues: 'Thus, in contrast to Schoene's reading of Kureishi, which stresses how the author reveals "the gaping void at the disheartened core of middle-class suburban Englishness", one might see the "centre's" selective appropriation of "alien" cultures ... not as a symptom of "lack", but of a confidently enduring neo-colonial mentality.'[7]

Even with this caveat, Schoene's emphasis on Englishness as a cultural performance is a useful one, particularly as it detaches notions of national identity from ethnic origin. The creation of compliant mimic Englishmen in the Empire was a strategy that was repeated when the immigrant was expected to assimilate (although he would never be accepted as a 'real' Englishman). One of the most important features of Kureishi's handling of race is his undermining of the notion that mimicry is an exclusively postcolonial problem. It is particularly ironic that the golden boy of Beckenham should busk it as a Cockney.

Despite the fact that there is no coherent English identity to assimilate into, *The Buddha* shows that immigrants are still not accepted. With their love of England and desire to be a part of it, Haroon and Changez epitomize not a failure to assimilate, but England's failure to change its very narrow definitions of national identity. In the end, Haroon, who arrived from Bombay after the war eager to discuss Byron's poetry in the pub with the locals, declares: ' "I have lived in the West for most of my life, and I will die here, yet I remain to all intents and purposes an Indian man. I will never be anything but an Indian" ' (BS 263). Haroon's assertion that he is an 'Indian man' might suggest that Kureishi has succumbed to what Paul Gilroy has called 'the lure of ethnic absolutisms'.[8] However, Schoene argues that Haroon's Indianness is as inauthentic as Charlie's working-class stereotype. Haroon starts off as the mimic Englishman and, when this fails, he becomes a mimic Indian. John Clement Ball also sees Haroon's 'embrace' of ethnicity as taking place at 'the level not of identity but of artifice and image'. Like Karim, 'father and son both become faux-Indians, successfully marketing back to the English warmed-over versions of their own popular appropriations of Indian culture'.[9] Ranasinha argues that Haroon substitutes his initial attempt at assimilation for an assertion of cultural difference: 'Yet, in responding to the vogue for the spiritual sustenance of the exotic east, this "abrogation" or assertion of difference is dictated to according to the norms of the host society and remains a form of assimilation.'[10] But what each of these interpretations omits is the degree to which Haroon's masquerade corresponds to a genuine internal need: 'Beneath all the Chinese bluster was Dad's loneliness and desire for internal advancement' (BS 28). Kureishi suggests that posing can be a rehearsal for the real thing; just as children learn by imitation, so adults can change and develop through acting a role. Karim suspects Daddio is a 'charlatan' (BS 22), Jamila is convinced he is a 'complete phoney' (BS 72), but Haroon's career as a wise man gains credibility when his brother-in-law turns to him for help. Even Karim is impressed: 'Ted was Dad's triumph; he really was someone Dad had freed' (BS 101). By the end of the novel Haroon is not merely masquerading as a Buddhist: he leaves his dreary job in order to meditate and teach; he has found a 'meaning' (BS 266) in his life and has something to offer others. Despite its emphasis on transformation and multiple identities, the novel does not entirely dispense with the notion of an 'authentic self' (BS 219), however imaginary or indefinable: there has to be a connection between the inner self and its public performance; without this 'you are as obvious as a Catholic naked in a mosque' (BS 219). A clear distinction is made between masks that are merely opportunistic, such as Charlie's, and those that serve as a means of self-development, as in Haroon's impersonation of a Buddha.

Moreover, as national identity is a largely a matter of performance, characters can attempt to disguise their origins. When Karim goes to Millwall football ground he forces Changez 'to wear a bobble-hat over his face in case the lads saw he was a Paki and imagined I was one too' (BS 98). But the novel also shows how it is not always possible to escape the way that others see you; this emerges most clearly in Karim's theatrical performances.

As we saw in earlier chapters, the reception of Kureishi's work has often been at the centre of controversies about the politics of representation: this becomes a major preoccupation within *The Buddha*. There are three performances which stage the debate: first, Karim's role as Mowgli in Shadwell's production of *The Jungle Book* (1894) by Rudyard Kipling (1865–1936); second, the controversy in the novel over Karim's decision to base his character in Pyke's political improvisation on Anwar; and third, after this decision is rejected, his portrayal of Changez as Tariq. Through Karim's job as an actor, Kureishi can look at the politics of representation and explore the construction of identity through performance, both of which overlap in the following discussions. There have been several, widely diverging, responses to the novel's treatment of these issues. Seema Jeena uses the Mowgli and 'me-as-Anwar' scenes in order to illuminate Kureishi's use of the anti-hero as a narrative strategy: Karim's role in the novel parallels the dilemmas facing the 'second-generation immigrant' writer in relation to both the 'white gaze' and the minority community. We can join her discussion at the point where she explores the difficulties of addressing two cultures:

■ This tension is seen in the novel when Karim is asked to play the role of a Mowgli in *The Jungle Book*; he quickly overcomes his initial revulsion when he realizes that he is going to be the 'pivot of the production': 'One strong feeling dominated me: ambition' (BS 155) ...

Earlier I had mentioned the immigrant writer constantly under the scrutiny of the 'white gaze', and the traumatic situation the writer has to face writing in a predominant white society where he can be accused of misrepresenting his community by failing to portray positive images of it, whilst at the same time [having] to be aware of how little choice he has operating in a society that will always want him to write about specific subjects. This dilemma is seen in the novel when Karim joins the theatre company of Matthew Pyke, an alternative theatre director ... Urged by Pyke to 'concentrate on the way your position in society has been fixed' (BS 169), Karim decides to build his character on his uncle Anwar ... Contrary to the congratulatory reception he expected, he is faced with the consternation of the other 'minority' member of the cast, the black actress Tracey: [Jeena quotes Tracey's objections (BS 180)]

This highlights my earlier assumption that an immigrant writer's representation of the community *will* be seen as representative. Though Karim might intend his portrayal of Anwar's hunger strike to force his daughter into an arranged marriage as the psychological portrait of 'one old Indian man', it will be received by the predominantly white audience as representation of fanatical black people ...

We find a different Karim from the one who was introduced to us in the beginning of the book, when he decides to research on Changez, when for the first time in his life he was aware of 'having a moral dilemma': 'If I defied Changez, if I started work on a character based on him, if I used the bastard, it meant that I was untrustworthy, a liar. But if I didn't use him it meant I had fuck-all to take to the group after the "me-as-Anwar" fiasco' (BS 186). In spite of this pang of responsibility Karim goes on to portray Changez, in a 'spirit of bloody-minded defiance'. To his surprise Pyke announces that the Tariq (Changez) character will be a part of the play, not only locking Karim into a ridiculous stereotype but at the same time presenting almost allegorically the authority of the white judge/director in choosing the way in which an Asian character will be represented, regardless of the moral dilemmas and conflicts of Tracey or Karim. □

(Seema Jena, 'From Victims to Survivors', 1993)[11]

Seema Jena argues that Karim's performances show the danger of 'selling out'. Jena states that at the end of the novel, when Karim feels 'happy and miserable at the same time', 'he is "miserable" because ... he realizes he has become a non-person, a coward who couldn't face the hard facts of life'.[12] Following the logic of Jena's reading, the status of Karim's future performances in a soap opera would be ambiguous. Would playing 'the rebellious student son of an Indian shopkeeper' mean that he was continuing to 'sell out' by performing ethnicity? He refers to it as 'shoddy' work done by 'trashy jumped-up people' and seems most excited by the prospect of money and fame ('I'd be recognised all over the country' BS 259). Or would it mean that he was at last facing 'hard facts'? The soap opera 'would tangle with the latest contemporary issues: they meant abortions and racist attacks, the stuff that people lived through but that never got on TV' (BS 259).[13] Typically of the novel, one could interpret it either way; it is both selling out and 'changing the script of what it means to be English'.

Moreover, is Tariq, as Jena claims, necessarily a 'ridiculous stereotype'? After all, to prepare for the role, Karim says, he walked 'round the flat as Changez, not caricaturing him but getting behind his peculiar eyeballs' (BS 225). Sangeeta Ray does not think so. And Ray has a slightly different reading of the Mowgli performance, too, emphasizing the varied responses to it within the novel. He points out that a 'simple, mechanistic correspondence between an Indian and the Mowgli represented on stage is completely undermined by Changez's (the latest Indian immigrant to enter England) unequivocal enjoyment of the play as sheer entertainment'. According to Ray, the novel does not allow any single interpretation to be privileged: 'No one position is favoured, and yet the various voices arguing and interfering with each other do question both the structures of the nation state and the constraints of ethnicity and national particularity.'[14] We can now follow Ray's slightly different view of cultural performance as he discusses Karim's role as Tariq:

■ in the second play directed by an avant-garde playwright, who couches a similar desire to deny cognitive capacity to an ethnic minority by using left-wing, jargon loaded clichés, we see Karim actively trying to resist the clutches of a paternalistic and tyrannical racist discourse. The intervening time has changed Karim. Jamila's father makes him realize that these 'strange creatures [...] the Indians [...] in some way [...] were my people, and that I'd spent my life denying or avoiding that fact. I felt ashamed and incomplete at the same time, as if half of me were missing, and as if I'd been colluding with my enemies, *those whites who wanted Indians to be like them*' (BS 212, emphasis mine). This awareness does not cause him instantly to rush off and attack Pyke, the director, for his inimical ethnocentrism. He continues to play the role of an Indian immigrant, but this time, he

uncovered notions, connections, initiatives, I didn't even know were present in my mind [...] I saw that creation [of an identity] was an accretive process which couldn't be hurried, and which involved patience and, primarily, love. I felt more solid myself, and not as if my mind were just a kind of cinema for myriad impressions and emotions to flicker through. □

(BS 217) (Sangeeta Ray, 'The Nation in Performance', 1998)[15]

Ray adds that when Changez says to Karim, ' "I am glad in your part you kept it fundamentally autobiographical and didn't try the leap of invention into my character" ' (BS 231), we should not read 'this enlightening passage as an instance of Changez's wilful blindness'.[16] Changez's failure to recognize himself in Tariq points to the way that Karim has discovered something about himself in the process of impersonating another. Spivak makes a similar point when she says: 'We are not surprised that Karim is represented as creatively happy when he puts together his stage Indian. The intimate enemy, a violation that enables.'[17] In contrast, Ranasinha argues: 'but while Karim feels the invention "added up the elements of my life" (BS 217), Kureishi implies when the performance (theatrical or otherwise) ends the question of subjectivity remains uncertain'. She sees the novel concluding with Karim as 'confused as ever over his cultural dilemma (BS 284)'[18] – a reading which is diametrically opposed to Schoene's account of Karim as the only character not engaged in a scramble after identity.[19]

While most critics see the Mowgli performance as making an unambiguous point about caricature, they note that Karim is not merely a victim but subverts the stereotype by switching between a Peter Sellers Indian accent and deliberately 'relapsing into Cockney' (BS 158).[20] Schoene goes one stage further: he argues that Karim's 'farcical ethnic drag act' is a way of challenging a 'binarist discourse' of black vs. white:

■ Shadwell's prescription of these measures [the brown make-up and the accent], reluctantly implemented by Karim in order not to jeopardize his budding career as an actor, illustrates how the latter's difference is not at all as unmistakably obvious to the public gaze as Shadwell claims: ' "Everyone looks at you, I'm sure, and thinks: an Indian boy, how exotic, how interesting, what stories of aunties and elephants we'll hear now from him" ' (BS 141). What Kureishi exposes here is the contrived nature of concepts of ethnicity which accentuate difference while eradicating all traces of potential sameness. The postcolonial dilemma of dislocation, of 'belonging nowhere, wanted nowhere' (BS 141), is a result of deliberate acts of Orientalist alienation, imposed upon the 'other' at the moment of his most challenging emancipation. Emerging from *in between* the imperialist black vs. white rhetoric of racial segregation, the unprecedented ambiguity of Karim's difference threatens to permeate the rigid structures of psychic and ideological Anglo-British territorialism. Not only has Karim become unidentifiable within the framework of binarist discourse, his indeterminacy questions the conceptual accuracy and purpose of all epistemological attempts at ethnic identification. It is symptomatic of the panic of the erstwhile hegemonic English self that Shadwell should try to remould Karim's cultural unintelligibility into something more clearly recognizable, using ample lashings of 'the brown muck' (BS 146) of Orientalist differentiation. However, Shadwell's strategy backfires.

Rather than further clarifying what is already commonsensically obvious to him, his (re)production becomes a parody and Karim's central perform-ance some kind of farcical ethnic drag act. The credibility of the stereo-type collapses due to Shadwell's overemphasis on accuracy, and with it evaporates the very idea of originary ethnic authenticity.

... Ultimately, Karim's ethnic drag act opens up the possibility of imag-ining the proliferation of individual identities beyond the bounds of racial originality or ethnic authenticity, that is, the gradual coming-into-being of black Englishmen or white Indians. □

(Berthold Schoene, 'Herald of Hybridity', 1998)[21]

If Shadwell is clearly satirized for spouting a multiculturalist rhetoric which insists on difference and a spurious authenticity, it is far less clear whether it is Tracey or Karim who is being mocked in the 'me-as-Anwar fiasco'. Moore-Gilbert makes the point that 'what Karim objects to in Tracey's "Black" politics is its tendency to assume that all minority groups are oppressed equally in the same way'.[22] Schoene, too, argues that Pyke's theatre group fails 'to register Karim's actual multitude of intrinsic differences', and that Tracey has internalized multiculturalist discourse. He continues that for Tracey:

■ Blackness is simply defined as non-whiteness. Such a categorical collocation of all non-white ethnicities allows for no individual departures from the norm, using skin colour to minoritize individuals of non-European extraction, while failing to imagine the possibility of cultural black/white hybridity or the emancipation of individual identity from perceptions of allegedly innate ethnic propensities and characteristics. Kureishi's stance on the matter is unequivocal. Everybody is entitled to their own singular cultural ethnicity. □

(Berthold Schoene, 'Herald of Hybridity', 1998)[23]

Spivak offers a wholly opposite reading: she sees the scene demonstrat-ing Tracey's political maturity as opposed to Karim's political naiveté.[24] The difference between these views rests on the distinction between, on the one hand, the usefulness of maintaining a 'Black' politics as a way of combating racism and maintaining solidarity between marginalized groups and, on the other hand, the importance of what Schoene, quot-ing Eagleton, refers to as 'the emancipation of difference' (see Hall's discussion of this in Chapter 3). It is not coincidental that Schoene focuses almost exclusively on Karim and largely ignores the dilemmas of characters such as Jamila and Anwar. While it is certainly true that 'Kureishi rejects communal difference as an individual's destiny',[25] it is not at all clear, as Schoene claims, that Karim cheerfully inhabits an 'ethnicity-free no-man's-land'.[26] He may wish to, but he still has to contend with how others see him. Moreover, while communal difference may not mean destiny, it can be a valuable resource. Jamila, for example, although not in any way a separatist, does not want to ditch her ethnic identity altogether and is described admiringly as 'an Indian woman' living 'a useful life in white England' (BS 216).

Much of the critical writing devoted to *The Buddha* can give the impression that cultural hybridity is the only game in town and that battles over representations are more important than the 'reality'. But Jamila scoffs at Karim's performances and accuses him of ignoring the real world, 'the shit people have to deal with' (BS 195). Proponents of cultural hybridity seem pretty keen to ignore this too. Not all the characters in *The Buddha* discover their identity through performance: some are stuck or get lost in translation, such as Anwar; and there is also the contrasting position of Jamila, who advocates anti-racist action. She is clearly an important character and the novel's treatment of ethnicity and racism is skewed if the perspective she provides is ignored.

If we turn from critics who are inspired by Bhabha's theories of hybridity and the third space, to what might be termed materialist and sociological critics, a very different novel emerges. Elaine Dubourdieu's discussion of *The Buddha* concentrates on context, on events and issues of the 1970s referred to in the novel: the rise of the National Front, Britain's racist immigration policy and statistics on racial harassment during the period.[27] Cynthia Carey follows the strand of violence that runs through the novel, much of it racially motivated, which leads to Karim's 'seemingly hopeless despair' (BS 249):

■ [T]he text of *The Buddha of Suburbia* is constructed round an interlinking, multi-level network of violence such as racist violence, police violence, vandalism, hooliganism and punk violence all reflecting 1970s England. In the words of Charlie, 'it's a fucking swamp of prejudice, class confusion, the whole thing. Nothing works over there. And no one works' (BS 256). The narrator accurately describes Callaghan's old Labour Britain ('but the bitter fractured country was in turmoil: there were strikes, marches, wage-claims' [BS 259]) and the social ills … Violence, then, was a necessary and integral element of Karim's internal and external landscapes. Punks, swastikas, shit and burning rags shoved through Asians' letter boxes, piss-heads, bums, derelicts and dealers, rockers, skins and leather chains, racist graffiti and pigs' heads thrown through Muslim shop windows are woven into the fabric of the text in a nightmarish, fetish-like fashion. Anarchy and revolution loom threateningly. □

(Cynthia Carey, '*The Buddha of Suburbia* as a Post-Colonial Novel', 1997)[28]

While it might seem that Carey slightly exaggerates the violence, or ignores the humorous tone which is often used to describe it, she is surely right to point out the more disturbing undercurrents in the novel.

Nahem Yousaf refers to critics' lack of engagement with Anwar and Jeeta, which he attributes to white reviewers' fear that Kureishi's representations of the Asian family conform to the stereotype of the authoritarian patriarch, the unhappy arranged marriage and the submissive woman:

■ Kureishi presents the Anwar family as a foil for the Amirs and in so doing he also shows that not all families are the same. However, to dismiss the Anwars as nothing more than facile caricatures would be to miss the point. In Jamila and her mother we have two very strong women who are conscious of the roles assigned to them within a traditional working-class family unit, be the family black or white. I would argue that they choose to uphold a patriarchal structure that they know to be crumbling. Furthermore, it would be grossly inaccurate to see Jamila as an uncomplicated victim of her parents, when she is, in fact, given a great deal of freedom to pursue her own interests, in contrast to the stereotypical image that would have her at the parents' beck and call, dressed in salwar kameez, head bowed and acquiescent. ... To delimit a reading of *Buddha*'s Asian women characters is to perpetuate and maintain a stereotypical hierarchy that Kureishi goes some way towards demolishing.

...... In Anwar, Kureishi demonstrates that the 'old ways' first generation immigrants are prone to cling to outside their country of birth are outmoded and redundant. Indeed, when seeking the 'buddha's' advice on the potential arranged marriage Haroon sagely responds ' "We old Indians come to like this England less and less and we return to an imagined India" ' (BS 74); it is this India of the imagination that drives Anwar, in belligerent patriarchy, into commencing his hunger strike. Anwar overlooks his own English 'freedom' which includes 'the prostitutes who hung around Hyde Park' whom 'he loved' (BS 25). Instead, by evoking Islam he represents himself as having a 'fixed identity' that originates in his 'motherland' and it is this that Kureishi deplores and satirizes. □
(Nahem Yousaf, 'Hanif Kureishi's *The Buddha of Suburbia*', 2002)[29]

As Ranasinha says, 'Anwar's metamorphosis is presented as a performance: Anwar suddenly starts "behaving like a Muslim" ' (BS 64).[30] Moreover, Anwar's return to an imagined India is a means of 'resisting the English' (BS 64) and his way of dealing with 'cultural dislocation' can be contrasted with Haroon's. The retreat into ethnic enclaves, as a survivalist tactic when under threat, is as likely a response to the experience of migration as a playful picking and mixing of cultures.

In a similar way, Ranasinha draws on the work of Paul Gilroy in order to show the potential dangers in the counter-arguments to racial essentialism:

■ While Karim perceives the Indian aspect of his identity as an 'additional personality bonus' he can create or augment at will, Kureishi shows it cannot be as easily dismissed (BS 213). Neither Haroon nor Karim can escape being perceived as black. Kureishi shows how their identities are defined by colour, a privileged visible signifier of difference. So Haroon tries to avoid getting 'stones and ice-pops full of piss lobbed at him by schoolboys' and Karim suffered racial bullying at school and is labelled as 'a little coon', one of the 'niggers' and 'blackies'. Helen's father tells him she doesn't go out with 'wogs' (BS 28, 40).[31] *Buddha's* most urgent passages draw attention to 'racialised forms of power and subordination'.[32] In the compelling delineation of the growth of the National Front and 'Pakibashing', the novel depicts the oppression of racial hatred and its impact on Jamila's family: [Ranasinha quotes the passage describing the racist attacks (BS 56).] □

(Ruvani Ranasinha, *Hanif Kureishi*, 2002)[33]

This critical attention to the ways the novel deals with 'racialised forms of power and subordination' provides an important perspective, which does not necessarily contradict Schoene and Ray's emphasis on hybridity, but certainly augments it. None of the characters lives in an ethnicity-free no-man's-land.

Perhaps the tendency to ignore the grimmer aspects of racism apparent in many responses to *The Buddha* is not just attributable to current trends in postcolonial theory but to the novel itself: narrated by a 'shaker and trembler' (BS 53) who reacts to racial harassment personally rather than politically, Karim tends to skip over racist events as being shameful or tries to shrug them off as comical. But if Jamila reminds the reader of the shit people have to deal with, Allie (Karim's younger brother) exposes the danger of rubbing the reader's nose in it. As he says: ' "I hate people who go on all the time about being black, and how persecuted they were at school" ' (BS 267). By narrating events from Karim's alternately shamed and sardonic perspective, but including Jamila's more defiant and politicized view, Kureishi achieves a delicate balance.

Although most critical discussions of *The Buddha* focus on race, class is arguably equally important. Like *Great Expectations, The Buddha* is a novel of upward mobility and the aspirations of the young narrators provide a critique of social values. Both are outsiders trying to get in: for both there are divided loyalties, betrayals and disillusionment. In all Kureishi's work there is an emphasis on how race can affect class and vice versa. Migrants lose status on arrival in England, like Jeeta, a princess, who is seen as just another 'Paki' in a corner shop and looked down on by white Londoners. But Kureishi also shows that upper-class Indians, like Changez, can feel little solidarity with poor immigrants from India, whom they despise for failing to speak English (BS 210). Although racial considerations can affect social position, the class system is still hierarchical and the key to social mobility is still education. Like Pip in *Great Expectations*, Karim discovers that knowledge is intellectual capital which must be 'consciously acquired' (BS 178) in order to move on and up. Karim is angry at the lower-middle-class suburban culture which has allowed education to seem redundant: 'We were proud of never learning anything except the names of footballers, the personnel of rock groups and the lyrics of "I am the Walrus". What idiots we were!' (BS 178). Once he gets to London he discovers that, unlike the defeated lower middle class, the upper class has maintained its superiority: 'What infuriated me – what made me loathe both them and myself – was their confidence and knowledge' (BS 177). As Schoene argues, the suburbanites scramble after an identity but the upper class is still seen as traditionally English and impervious to post-imperial cosmopolitanism.[34]

Rita Felski argues that because *The Buddha* is 'usually interpreted through the lens of postcolonial theory' little attention has been paid to it as 'a novel about the shifting meanings of class in the 1960s and 1970s'. She suggests that 'being lower middle class is a singularly boring identity, possessing none of the radical chic that is sometimes ascribed to working-class roots.'[35] Typically seen as vulgar and reactionary by intellectuals, the 'petite bourgeoisie is peculiarly resistant to the romance of marginality'.[36] After examining George Orwell's treatment of the lower middle class in *A Clergyman's Daughter* (1935), *Keep the Aspidistra Flying* (1936) and *Coming Up for Air* (1939), she turns to *The Buddha* in order to ask: 'In what ways is the in-betweenness of the lower middle class at odds not only with the identity politics of gender and race but also with traditional ways of thinking about class?'[37]

■ The narrator's father is a 'badly paid and insignificant' clerk in the British civil service (BS 7), and his mother is a sales assistant in a shoe store. Lower-middle-classness is still a 'cage of umbrellas and steely regularity' (BS 26), marked by respectability, rigidity, and gray routine. There are the same guilt about money, anxiety about status, and fear of the neighbors' disapproval: the narrator wryly notes, '[M]y mother could never hang out the washing in the garden without combing her hair' (BS 188). The social life of the lower middle class is almost nonexistent, since the ubiquitous English pub is considered vulgar, working-class, and hence out-of-bounds. 'No one went out, there was nowhere to go, and Dad never socialized with anyone from the office. [...] Mum and Dad went to the pictures maybe once a year, and Dad always fell asleep; once they went to the theatre to see *West Side Story*' (BS 46). In many ways, the petit bourgeois structures of feeling mapped out in *The Buddha of Suburbia* are remarkably similar to those described by Orwell almost fifty years earlier.

Yet the face of lower-middle-class life is also undergoing a transformation. Kureishi's narrator, Karim Amir, is the child of an Indian father and English mother, 'a funny kind of Englishman, a new breed as it were, having emerged from two old histories' (BS 3). He is also bisexual, and he exhibits no anxiety or guilt as he embarks on a series of affairs with men and women. The sexual mores of suburbia are changing; the divorce of the narrator's parents and his father's affair with the socially ambitious Eva help precipitate Karim's own personal and social transformation. Furthermore, the new ideologies and lifestyles disseminated by the mass media are blurring the rigid distinctions between classes. The counter-cultures of the 1960s and 1970s are infiltrating the orderly homes of the lower middle class. Buddhism is emerging as a fad among the progressive adults in the suburbs, while the sounds of the Clash echo in teenage bedrooms around the country.

The Buddha of Suburbia is a story about the permeability of class divisions and the new possibilities of social mobility in postwar Britain. Karim eventually becomes a successful actor, escaping his suburban origins for a bohemian metropolitan world of artists and upper-middle-class intellectuals. But the novel also traces the tenacity and continuing power of class distinctions, as Kureishi's hero is constantly confronted with the differences between his background and that of his new friends. 'What infuriated me – what made me loathe both them and myself – was their confidence and knowledge. The easy talk of art, theatre, architecture, travel; the languages, the vocabulary, knowing the way round a whole culture – it was invaluable and irreplaceable capital' (BS 177).

Karim's cultural dislocation forces him to become a kind of class detective, hypersensitive to the complex and often confusing codes of class distinction. His new friends dress down, adopt working-class accents, and cultivate a local street sweeper, Heater, as an authentic voice of the proletariat. 'Heater was the only working-class person that most of them had met. So he became a sort of symbol for the masses and consequently received tickets to first nights and to the parties afterwards, having a busier social life than Cecil Beaton' (BS 175). Heater politely reciprocates by performing working-class life for his friends, talking about 'knife fights, Glasgow poverty and general loucheness and violence' (BS 176) before feeling free to broach the subjects that really interested him, Beethoven's late quartets and a textual problem in Huysmans.

Such instances of cross-class identification underscore the tenacity of class distinctions, the profound divisions between those who aspire upward and those whose status and cultural capital allow them to go slumming. Karim and his suburban friends are desperate to escape to London, lured by the fantasy of a glamorous, bohemian, metropolitan world. The intellectuals and artists who inhabit that culture have their own fantasy, of an authentic, gritty, working-class existence. But the lower middle class is no one's fantasy and no one's desire; it has no exchange value in the cultural marketplace. Thus Karim gradually learns to cover over his traces and hide his origins; he seeks, like Eva, 'to scour that suburban stigma' right off the body (BS 134). On the one hand, he is driven by his ambition and his 'loathing of the past' (BS 145); on the other hand, his new identity remains 'a second language, consciously acquired' (BS 178), perpetually reminding him of the class differences that he seeks to transcend. □

(Rita Felski, 'Nothing to Declare', 2000)[38]

Interestingly, the example of Heater shows that class, like race, is in part a performance. Nonetheless, like the 'racialised forms of power' discussed earlier, social and economic power exert a real influence.

As Felski notes, 'many of the traditional distinctions between the lower middle class and the working class are being eroded in a society where white-collar work is increasingly the norm'. The ranks of the lower middle class are swelling too with migrant groups 'who often create small family businesses'.[39] If the 'problem of the lower middle class' is central to understanding the industrialized west, then *The Buddha* goes some way to showing that class, like national identity, is a more complicated thing now, involving new elements.

The novel also represents different ideologies of class, from Terry's Socialist Worker Party (which appeals to Karim's resentment but which Eleanor calls ' "not a Party for black people" ' (BS 238)) to Auntie Jean's suburban conservatism. *The Buddha* itself celebrates peoples' ability to 'transform [themselves] by the bootlaces' (BS 31), which is an energizing concept but politically problematic. One of the final images in the filmed version of the novel is of Margaret Thatcher, in padded shoulders, rising up as the newly elected Prime Minister. As the great exponent of 'picking yourself up by your bootlaces' Thatcher seemed to many to be a radical. As we saw in chapter two, many Asian immigrants, like Nasser in *My Beautiful Laundrette*, thought she offered a way into British society: *The Buddha* is set in the 1970s, at the point where sexual liberation was sliding into economic laissez-faire. Eva starts out as a middle-aged hippie but ends up resolutely Thatcherite. It turns out to be a short step from self-awareness, yoga, ' "individual initiative and love of what you do" ' to contempt for ' "those people who live on sordid housing estates ... [who] expect others – the Government – to do everything for them" ' (BS 263). Eva's belief in self-fulfilment easily converts into Thatcherite individualism. *The Buddha*'s optimism about change seems to be based on a belief in the value of not knowing your place, but this is very different from espousing the survival of the fittest. The novel's investment in individualism is always tempered by an awareness of social and economic constraints; of how unevenly the odds are stacked. Although *The Buddha* follows Eva and her crew as they reinvent them-selves in the city, it also deals compassionately with those who, like Jean and Anwar, have difficulty with their laces. If the novel celebrates self-help, it also, through Jamila's commune, demonstrates the necessity for collective action. Even Karim is all for the 'equitable society' in theory – 'I knew we had to have it' (BS 218); it is just that he does not want to stay in south London eating nut rissoles with the comrades in order to achieve it.

In addition to race and class, the novel is also concerned with gender, sexual orientation and relations between the sexes. As we saw with *Laundrette* and *Sammy and Rosie*, sexuality and relations between the sexes are central to Kureishi's understanding of individual identity and society, so it is disappointing that there is very little discussion of this aspect of *The Buddha*. The postcolonial perspective has tended to obscure sexuality, as it has class.

But just as the novel has been credited with deconstructing a binarist discourse of black vs. white, it also subverts traditional gender roles. It is a woman who seeks political solutions and the men who are looking for love: Jamila is on the anti-racist march, while Kamila is futilely pursuing Eleanor. Indeed, the female characters are invariably stronger and more adaptable than the males, and the main agents of change. Karim envies Jammie for being 'powerful ... so in control and certain what to do about everything' (BS 55). Jamila outwits her father's attempt at patriarchal control, with her 'rebellion against rebellion' (BS 82), and arranges the marriage to suit herself. Changez attempts to whack her into submission but soon finds himself pleading to be allowed to go with her to the commune. The chauvinistic Changez discovers his feminine side 'wearing Jamila's pink silk dressing-gown ... He liked Jamila's clothes; he'd always have on one of her jumpers or shirts' (BS 182). At the commune, this 'fat, useless bum' learns how to cook, clean, look after children and in the process acquires a sense of purpose – ' "I'm going to make the most of my life now, *yaar*" ' (BS 222). Comically, after the birth of Jamila's daughter, Karim suspects that Changez is 'developing full female breasts' (BS 271). Meanwhile, Jeeta ignores Anwar's 'masterful advice' and transforms Paradise Stores from a run-down corner shop into a thriving business; her energy and determination are manifested in the growth of 'an iron nose like a hook with which she could lift heavy boxes of corned beef' (BS 208). Even Margaret, morosely performing the maternal role at the beginning of the novel, is transformed for the better when the 'three selfish men' (BS 20) leave her: she takes a new interest in herself and her house, and acquires a younger boyfriend. It is Eva who promotes Haroon's guru gigs, moves them all to London, finds Karim his first acting job and introduces him to painting and literature: 'Eva was unfolding the world for me. It was through her that I became interested in life' (BS 87). The well-connected Eleanor is Karim's next mentor, introducing him to a world of 'painters, novelists, lecturers', where he learns 'hard words and sophisticated ideas' and realizes that 'this language was the currency that bought you the best of what the world could offer' (BS 178). Indeed, men in the novel want knowledge and education from women, quite as much as they want sex; or rather, they want both. For Charlie, the United States is the land of intellectual opportunity, and smart New York women, 'with whom he discussed international politics, South American literature, dance, and the ability of alcohol to induce mystical states', are educating him (BS 248). Sex is 'recreational and informative' (BS 190) and women run the Access course.

The Buddha not only plays with traditional gender roles it deconstructs the binaries of homosexuality versus heterosexuality. Jamila has a child with Simon and also has a lesbian lover. Karim wants to sleep with boys *and* girls, feeling 'it would be heart-breaking to have to choose one or the other, like having to decide between the Beatles and the Rolling Stones' (BS 55). His main love is first Charlie and then Eleanor; he has a fling with Helen, later he wants to seduce Terry. The opening chapters show love as transgressive, in a way that parallels the mirror scene (with Nasser and his mistress on one side, the boys on the other) in *Laundrette*. Here Haroon castigates his son for being a ' "bum-banger" ' (BS 18) but Karim has seen his father bouncing on a garden bench with one-breasted Eva. Much of the novel's comedy, but also its sadness, lies in the treatment of sexuality; in particular Karim's failure to register just how much he is being taken for a ride.

Karim's desire for Charlie is clearly recognizable, even to Karim, as a form of envy: 'My love for him was unusual as love goes: it was not generous. I admired him more than anyone but I didn't wish him well. It was that I preferred him to me and wanted to be him. I coveted his talents, face, style. I wanted to wake up with them all transferred to me' (BS 15). This is more than simple envy of the popular boy; it is part of Karim's unacknowledged loathing of his Pakistani self. Once Karim stops hating himself, he falls out of love fast and completely: 'I realized I didn't love Charlie any more. I didn't care either for or about him' (BS 255). But although his love for Charlie is hardly generous, Karim is not the powerful one in the relationship. When Charlie comes in Karim's hand, Karim is ecstatic: 'it was, I swear, one of the pre-eminent moments of my earlyish life. There was dancing in my streets. My flags flew, my trumpets blew!' (BS 17). But Charlie avoids Karim's lips when he tries to kiss him. Karim does not see what the reader is allowed to see: that he has been used and Charlie doesn't give a damn.

Later erotic encounters take a similarly exploitative turn. If Karim's love for Charlie stems from his feeling of 'racial' inferiority, his love for Eleanor is tied up with class envy; the desire to be part of her haute bourgeois bohemian world. Here, again, Karim's love is not disinterested but he hardly deserves the public humiliation and rejection he suffers when Pyke reveals that for Eleanor it was only a ' "mercy fuck" ' (BS 245): 'The faces around him were looking at me and laughing. Why did they hate me so much? What had I done to them? Why wasn't I harder? Why did I feel so much?' (BS 244). And Pyke literally screws him, during the evening he spends with Pyke, Marlene and Eleanor, naively imaging himself the darling of the rich and famous: 'they accepted me and invited no one else and couldn't wait to make love to me' (BS 202). It is significant that on this occasion he recalls the night in Beckenham and how he went to Charlie 'for comfort' after witnessing his father's infidelity (BS 202). Here again he's been had. Although Karim narrates it as a comic episode – 'England's most interesting and radical theatre director was inserting his cock between my speaking lips' (BS 203) – later he begins 'to suspect [he]'d been seriously let down': 'That prick, which had fucked me up the arse while Marlene cheered us on as if we were all-in wrestlers – and while Eleanor fixed herself a drink – had virtually ruptured me' (BS 219).

Eleanor's rejection of Karim causes him to recall his humiliation at Helen's house, when he was abused by Helen's father: ' "We're with Enoch. If you put one of your black 'ands near my daughter I'll smash it with a 'ammer! With a 'ammer!" ' Instead of describing Karim's anger and hurt, Kureishi turns the episode into a comic set piece as the Great Dane pursues him down the garden path: 'The dog was in love with me – quick movements against my arse told me so' (BS 39–40). It is only much later, and very briefly, that he feels 'nauseous with anger and humiliation – none of the things I'd felt at the time' (BS 101). Helen and 'dog-cock' become inextricably connected (BS 68), so that Karim can only conceive of sex with Helen as 'a delicious moment of revenge' (BS 78). And Karim is still angrily harping on Hairy Back as he attempts to write a dignified farewell note to Eleanor:

■ And we pursued English roses as we pursued England; by possessing these prizes, this kindness and beauty, we stared defiantly into the eye of the Empire and all its self-regard – into the eye of Hairy Back, into the eye of the Great Fucking Dane. We became part of England and yet proudly stood outside it. But to be truly free we had to free ourselves of all bitterness and resentment, too. How was this possible when bitterness and resentment were generated afresh every day? □   (BS 227)

As we saw in *Sammy and Rosie*, Kureishi shows the relationship between white women and non-white men as complex: a way of gaining acceptance, a revenge against racism, and an attempt to transcend both.

Perhaps the one Karim loves (without ever seeming to know it) is Jamila. But having rubbed up against her in public lavatories since boyhood, she does not seem desirable in the way an unknown lover does; she is from the same side of the river, part of the world he is trying to get away from. Until he looks at her through a rival's eyes, she is veiled by familiarity: 'As Jamila sat there humming and reading, absorbed, with Changez's eyes also poring over her ... I felt this was Jamila's ultimate moment of herselfness. I, too, could have sat there like a fan watching an actress, like a lover watching his beloved' (BS 106). At the very end of the novel, Jamila is absent from the great gathering of friends and family and Karim still has to 'learn what the heart is'. Like the poor boy, Pip, in *Great Expectations*, disdaining the biddable Biddy and hankering after the unattainable Estella, Karim's sexual encounters only show him how far he stands outside. It is to his credit that when he attempts to seduce Terry, bitterness and resentment do not get the better of him: 'however much I wanted to humiliate Terry, I suddenly saw such humanity in his eyes, and in the way he tried to smile ... that I pulled away' (BS 241).

The novel's treatment of sexuality deepens and extends Kureishi's earlier explorations of 'sex as a focus of social, psychological, emotional, political energy ... and the dance that goes around it, all the seduction, betrayal, loyalty, failure, loneliness'.[40] Because sexuality is so central and so complex, it is (like race) capable of more than one interpretation. Critics have not paid much attention to this, but Max Vega-Ritter offers a psychoanalytical reading (translated here from French):

■ Individual identity in *The Buddha of Suburbia* is arranged around several axes: culture, Indianness/Englishness, gender differences, the development of the ego via its journey through the Oedipus Complex and the training of the artist. The narrator ironically announces his English identity in the very first line. Karim's link to his English identity is achieved via his mother as an intermediary. His relationship with his mother is mostly characterized by repulsion and escape, although it is also marked by his awareness of the suffering that he causes her. Karim prefers to identify with the Indianness of his father and with the struggle against the former colonialists. In his eyes, the English mother is synonymous with moral rigidity and social conformity, an absence of grace and naturalness. In short, she is the symbol of a despised identity. Karim abandons his mother to follow his father in his marital infidelity, which he almost shares since he is not insensitive to the sensual charm of Eva (BS 11).

The place next to the mother therefore remains left empty by his father. This place is, by implication, one of responsibility, faithfulness and law, the place of the man. This place remains deserted by the son or forbidden to him. To stay next to his mother would mean taking on the place and the responsibility abandoned by the father (BS 76). Karim therefore decides to follow the father, and even to confuse himself with him. In this way he chooses not to engage in a privileged relationship with his mother in order to follow the father and his mistress. Here, also, Karim is in a secondary position, that of a voyeur, since he is often a witness of the sexual frolics of the father and his mistress.

Although it is clear that Karim is sexually attracted to Eva, this does not set him against his father at any point. The latter treats Karim as an extension of himself. When the father gets angry after Karim fails his exams, the son shows the first signs of rebelling against him. Until then, there is no trace of jealousy or aggressiveness towards the man who is Eva's lover; on the contrary, the situation seems to stimulate a rush of heterosexual and homosexual desire in Karim. In fact, the excess of erotic passion thinly disguises the aggression or even hate. Karim, who throws himself on Charlie in a movement that resembles rape, shows a crazed desire to dispossess the other.

It is undoubtedly a matter of literally getting his hands on the superior beauty of the adolescent and the colour of his skin. Here, desire is also an expression of hatred of self or other. Interracial lust is not the only issue: there also seems to be an element of wanting to seize the power of the other. These acts are a transgression in the wrathful eyes of the father: the sexual aggression is indirectly directed towards the father.

When considering the fact that his father might marry Eva, Karim holds back from telling Charlie that they might have committed incest (BS 69). Here, the incest in question would be one between members of the same sex, a suggestion of incest between brothers that here echoes incest between father and son. The aggression towards Terry shows the same mix of an urge for power and desire for pleasure as the near-rape of Charlie.

The same act of destruction nevertheless gives rise to a veritable moment of ecstasy when Charlie ejaculates in Karim's hand. This moment is also a moment of triumph felt to strip Charlie. The ambiguity of the relationship with the male other submerges the aggression and the seizure of his phallus in a flood of emotional communion with the other.

But the erasure of borders is precisely one of the characteristics of the father figure. The strategy of the father figure aims to exercise seduction or the exchange of pleasure in the erasure of identities. This strategy does not seek, to any lesser extent, contact with strength, in order to absorb it in softness by way of osmosis. Father and son function together. When he makes love to Eleanor, Karim remembers his father and identifies with him ('Perhaps I was living out his dreams as I embraced Eleanor's flesh ... ' BS 207). Karim finally becomes aware of the possessive domination exerted over him by his father without his knowledge. Later, Karim rejoices to see him dominated by Eva, realizing that he has been a tyrant to him. In this way, he becomes aware of the weakness of his father but he also becomes disillusioned with his own thirst to do battle with his father. He starts to conceive of himself as having a separate existence from his father's being.

With the sado-masochistic fantasy scene, the paths of Karim and Charlie diverge definitively. In one sense, this scene is similar to the one featuring Karim with Terry. It is about the height of sexual violence, with its mix of pleasure and pain, activity and passivity. Karim 'fancied' Terry but also wanted to punish him. Charlie achieves the same mix but he does it to himself with Frankie as an intermediary.

In being aggressive with Terry, Karim discovers the depth of suffering, innocence, the need for love and the dignity of the other (BS 241). In attending the sado-masochism session, Karim discovers the pleasure and the vertigo of self-destruction. In the masochist ritual we can see the accomplishment of a cruelty whose true object remains out of bounds and veiled.

Charlie refused to recognize that he wanted Karim: during the masochistic ritual, he consents to it but it is because he is ready to sacrifice himself to cruelty, in order to accomplish it on himself via the other, in the absence of the father. Karim turns away from the masochistic ritual in a move that helps him to get over his fixation with the father.

The rituals and the sexual games take place in situations that are often observed. This first happens in the initial scene witnessed by Karim in Eva's garden. Eva is then a type of Amazon, at once mutilated and armed with only one breast. The two of them seem to have exchanged traditional gender roles: the Amazon shows her authority with a vigorous gesture, the father groans with pleasure seated on an uncomfortable bench.

Karim is therefore someone who sees that which he should not see. Fetishist observation will be the shape that Karim's future takes. With its rituals, the theatre will invade the life and even the intimacy of Karim. Similarly, the theatrical projections of the Indian identity of the protagonist are only glimpses that ward off the strong return of the threatening taboo.

This kind of fetishist observation is at the same time subjected to artistic development, which subverts it and changes it. Karim limps out of Eva's garden, as if wounded by an injury that represents an ironic relationship with himself and with the scene.

The nature of the bonds that attach the son to the father partly determine the bonds that Karim is able to have with women. His exuberant sexual energy seems to be most often a result of taboo, that of the father or the husband. Eleanor marks a change in attitude on the part of Karim in relation to women. He does not tolerate sharing her. He retains a humiliating memory of having been anally penetrated by his director (BS 219). In leaving Eleanor, Karim rejects a triangular relationship, in which a third person occupies the position of a kingly power. The homosexual relationship between Pyke and Karim echoes in an unmistakably reversed way that of Karim and Charlie, and the relationship of domination and affection in which the father held Karim captive at the beginning of his adolescence.

Under the flurry of sexual frolics there is an element of taboo that stimulates them. Its roots are in the law and the authority of the Father. But the latter appears struck by grotesque inauthenticity. In getting into the tree posture, symbol of a yoga practice that is meant to represent his new spiritual life, the father shows his genitals to the son and thus reveals what the ordinary paternal law endeavours to hide in its folds. This grotesque vision associates the contradictory with the irreconcilable: the Law and desire to show one's power. At any rate, the break-up of the couple and the father's moving to Eva's house are the actual evidence of the deviancy of the law in the eyes of Karim.

At the end, it seems that in the eyes of the narrator there are signs of kindness and moral value in the English mother. In a contradictory move, Karim identifies with this England at the same time as distancing himself from it. This image of the English mother is perhaps the only one to be truly loved (BS 227).

During this time, the *Buddha of Suburbia* is trying to re-create via Eva another legitimacy of the father as the layer-down of the Law. The announcement about Mum's new boyfriend having injected her with new life truly 'assassinated' Karim's dad (BS 281). He nevertheless appears to recover from this assassination since it is then that Eva and Dad decide to get married. The struggle with Englishness seems to have come to an end, perhaps with the establishment of a new Englishness embodied by Eva, an Englishness of drama and cross-cultural breeding. The narrator seems to suggest that parallel to Karim's attempts 'to locate himself and learn what the heart is' (BS 284), Dad has also chosen the place where he fits in. □

(Max Vega-Ritter, 'La Crise d'identité dans
The Buddha of Suburbia', 1997)[41]

I would argue that Karim's erotic encounter with Charlie is not a 'near-rape' and would question Vega-Ritter's assertion that Haroon's legitimacy as the 'layer-down of the Law' is re-created at the end of the novel, since Haroon's marriage to Eva seems more like helpless panic than finding his place. Moreover, it would seem that Karim is in love with his father and hates his mother; a pattern that is repeated with greater nakedness in *Intimacy*. Jay describes his mother as a 'lump of living death' (I 45) and writes with longing of his father: 'He loved kissing me. We kept one another company for years. He, more than anyone, was the person I wanted to marry' (I 42). Nonetheless, Vega-Ritter's reading usefully alerts us to the role of voyeurism, fetishism, and sexuality in the family.

The treatment of sexuality is often the occasion for humour: not only Karim's sexual adventures but also the comedy that arises out of his role as a voyeur. Karim's education might be summed up as 'look and learn': he is placed, like a character in a farce, behind sofas and hedges eyeballing the sexual antics of his father, Charlie, and Changez. The treatment of race too is often given a farcical twist: when Karim is 'fucked' by Hairy Back's Great Dane or when he is made to look like a 'turd in a bikini bottom' in Shadwell's play. It has been argued that the use of farce diminishes the novel's capacity to generate rage in the reader: we are allowed to laugh at events that should make us angry.[42] But it is also the comedy which stops *The Buddha* from ever being what Sukhdev Sandhu has called 'emergency literature'[43] – look how badly I'm being treated: help! Karim's comic narration prevents characters from becoming victims. Changez is attacked by National Front thugs but comedy turns the tables: 'They fled because Changez let off the siren of his Muslim warrior's call, which could be heard in Buenos Aires' (BS 224). Karim comments on the gangs 'beating Asians and shoving shit and burning rags through the letter boxes', so that Jamila takes up karate, but the tone soon becomes flippant: 'Jamila tried to recruit me to her cadre for training but I couldn't get up in the morning' (BS 56). Comedy also draws the reader in: as Karim notices in his role as Tariq in Pyke's play: 'I was a wretched and comic character. The other actors had the loaded lines, the many-syllabled political analysis, the flame-throwing attacks on pusillanimous Labour governments, but it was me the audience warmed to' (BS 220). It is humour that makes the reader warm to the novel.

One of the most pervasive comic effects in *The Buddha* is the use of the unnecessary detail. In Karim's account of how Jamila deals with racists, the humour is in the added simile: 'Jammie sprinted through the traffic before throwing the bastard off his bike and tugging out some of his hair, like someone weeding an overgrown garden' (BS 53). Another striking comic device is the frequent use of 'as if' similes (this was also a key stylistic feature of Dickens).[44] Haroon's domestic incompetence, for example, generates a stream of bizarre comparisons. Karim remembers that, when he was a toddler and his nappy needed changing, Haroon treated him 'as if I had the plague, he threw water at my legs while holding his nose with the other hand' (BS 26). Haroon 'handled a piece of bread as if it were a rare object he'd obtained on an archaeological dig' (BS 194). Eleanor's anger at Karim's sexual possessiveness derives its humour from an outlandish simile: 'she looked at me as if she wanted to press a hard grain of rice down the end of my penis' (BS 198); while Anwar's physical decline after his hunger strike is registered in an image of tragicomic aptness: 'he moved as if he had bags of sugar tied to his feet' (BS 79).

The 'as if' similes have more than just a comic function: they help to create the novel's distinctive ambience of possibility; they are a reminder of an alternative, hypothetical reality. Jeeta adapts successfully to new surroundings: 'it was as if Jamila had educated her in possibility' (BS 172). Excited by the new turn his life is about to take, Haroon kisses the family 'as if we'd recently been rescued from an earthquake' (BS 3). Similes of transformation multiply at moments of change or turning points in characters' lives. When Pyke unexpectedly asks Karim to join him, 'Terry looked at me as if I'd just announced I had a private income' (BS 163) and the whole cast stares 'as if I were a football match'. It is this sense of perpetual possibility which imbues the novel with its characteristic optimism and *brio*.

Similes generally make connections between things that are alike but in *The Buddha* they also do the reverse; they bring unlike things together, creating a comic effect but also reinforcing an awareness of disguise. At the guru gig, Carl and Marianne stand with 'the palms of their hands together in prayer and their heads bowed as if they were temple servants and not partners in the local TV rental firm of Rumbold & Toedrip' (BS 30). The 'as if' similes escalate during scenes of deception: 'Eleanor came over to Pyke; she came over to him quickly and passionately, as if he were of infinite value at that moment, as if she'd heard that he had a crucial message for her. She took his head in her hands as if it were a precious pot' (BS 203). With each simile the comedy, and the sense of betrayal, becomes more intense. Charlie's false manipulative charm is revealed through similes of unlike things: 'He knew how to look at you as if you were the only person who'd ever interested him' (BS 119). So, too, is his egotism: ' "I am suicidal," he announced grandly, as if he were pregnant' (BS 128). It seems fitting that much of the novel's distorting imagery should be attached to this latter-day Dorian Gray. Indeed, Oscar Wilde (1854–1900) and his *The Picture of Dorian Gray* (1890) are abiding influences on Kureishi (see chapter nine) and *The Buddha*'s emphasis on disguise could be seen as distinctively Wildean.

Towards the end of the novel, the 'as if' similes peter out and the vitality flags a little: after all the turbulence, the constant change, the characters take stock, and Karim himself becomes less wide-eyed, even disillusioned. The similes not only become less frequent but also less flamboyant, as they seem to foreclose on the future. Karim looks at his mother with her new boyfriend and feels disappointed: 'as if she'd let us down' by choosing an Englishman instead of an Indian (BS 270); and when Karim taunts Changez with Jamila's love for Joanna, Changez is 'uncomfortable. It was as if he wanted no more said. The subject was closed' (BS 273).

Several of the critical responses we have looked at consider *The Buddha* in terms of genre, in particular the picaresque: an episodic series of adventures with a trickster or rogue figure at the centre.[45] As a form this shares similarities with the *Bildungsroman*, the 'formation novel', which follows the development of the hero or heroine from childhood or adolescence into adulthood, in a troubled quest for identity. Whether critics call *The Buddha* a picaresque novel or a *Bildungsroman*, largely depends on the extent to which they see Karim as a rogue and how much they consider he actually *develops*: several critics use the terms interchangeably. Moore-Gilbert offers an interesting discussion of the novel as a *Bildungsroman*, and while he 'aligns' *The Buddha* with recent examples of the genre, such as *Absolute Beginners* (1959) by Colin MacInnes (1914–76),[46] he argues that Kureishi's fiction engages most extensively with *Kim* (1901) by Rudyard Kipling. He begins by drawing parallels: both protagonists have similar forenames, Kim and Karim; both texts are concerned with issues of 'pedigree'; both Kim and Karim are attractive to women; both constantly switch clothes; and like Kim, Karim is a spy (sent by the 'Party' to Pyke's house). Moore-Gilbert continues:

■ Perhaps most emphatic are the analogies between Kim's role as *chela* [follower and pupil] to the Lama (his principal father-figure) and Karim's service to his *guru* parent. Like the Lama, Haroon tends increasingly towards helplessness (even at the outset he relies on Karim to navigate him round London, and his disorientation with buses and telephones recalls the Lama's bafflement by train and telegraph). Like the Lama, Haroon is searching for enlightenment, which involves the attempt to educate his son morally (a pastiche of the Lama's instruction of Kim).

As is appropriate to the *Bildungsroman* genre, both Kim and Karim are involved in a process of inner growth and each suffers a series of crises which marks their evolution towards adulthood.[47] These entail bouts of severe depression, notably immediately after what appear to be each character's moments of greatest triumph. For both protagonists, such episodes centre on issues of identity … the conflict between different cultural affiliations. Thus, despite his disavowals of suburbia, it is remarkable how often Karim is drawn back to his roots, particularly after suffering setbacks. As with Kim, Karim's most important dilemma, however, concerns the competing claims of 'Indianness' and 'Englishness'. Whereas Kim is symbolically of mixed race (he is brought up by an Indian foster-mother), Karim is so literally. It could be argued that neither novel fully resolves the issues of cultural belonging which they raise and both end openly and ambiguously, with neither protagonist having either chosen decisively between the respective cultures to which they are affiliated or having found a fully satisfying synthesis of, or compromise between, them. □

(Bart Moore-Gilbert, *Hanif Kureishi*, 2001)[48]

Moore-Gilbert stresses that 'Kureishi's recourse to Kipling does not bespeak a desire simply to disavow colonial discourse' but seeks to 'recuperate and develop Kipling's interest in cross-cultural transactions', using *Kim* a precedent of cultural 'in-betweenness'.[49]

As Moore-Gilbert also points out, the *Bildungsroman* is a genre which presents identity 'as a developmental, unstable and shifting *process*, rather than a given and stable *product*'.[50] Susheila Nasta argues that Kureishi uses the traditional frame of the *Bildungsroman* but 'the form is subverted, re-angled, manipulated and appropriated for [his] own purposes'. The 'postcolonial and diasporic context' leads to the disruption of 'the seamless pattern of social integration typical of the genre'.[51]

According to Nasta this dictates the novel's open ending, which does not show the traditional pattern of trickster transforming into citizen: 'Karim appears at the close not, in fact, to be "going somewhere", but instead to be sitting on the fence, caught between a number of conflicting discourses.'[52] However, it is not the case that all *Bildungsromane* show a 'seamless pattern of social integration'; in particular, Pip at the end of *Great Expectations* is completely displaced: unable to go back home to the forge and no longer at ease with the gentlemanly life in London. Caught between conflicting discourses of class, the best Dickens can do for his protagonist is to pack him off to the colonies – Egypt, not India, but in the context of *The Buddha* nonetheless ironic.

Steven Connor, like Nasta, finds that *The Buddha* 'simultaneously summons and rebuffs the *Bildungsroman* with its typical equations between self and society, the growth of the individual and the cementing of social meaning'.[53] For Connor, *The Buddha* 'flaunts the contingency of its structure, replacing the slow, uncoiling dynamism of development with the sputtering, discontinuous energy of episodic renewal'.[54] But while Nasta would see this as symptomatic of the disaporic condition, Connor argues that the novel's ending tries to wrap things up, unconvincingly. According to Connor, the problem lies with the retrospective first-person narrative:

■ [This] makes it much harder to avoid drawing out significance and developing judgements on the experience offered. In the end, the novel lurches ... into a sort of summation, and ends, rather improbably, by representing the entire career of the narrator, along with its ramshackle, opportunistic narration, as a kind of sentimental education. 'I could think about the past and what I'd been through as I'd struggled to locate myself and learn what the heart is. Perhaps in the future I would live more deeply' (BS 283–4), declares Amir right at the end of the novel, in words whose offhand flatness scarcely succeeds in holding the novel from collapse into a routine kind of emotional piety. □
(Steven Connor, *The English Novel in History*, 1996)[55]

But the ending does not represent a sudden swerve: judging from Kureishi's original title – *The Streets of My Heart*[56] – it was always intended as a sentimental education. Connor concludes that *The Buddha* 'cannot altogether resist the lure of generality, and the desire to abstract and connect, even though this is to align it with some of the traditional ambitions of the novel from which it seems otherwise so ironically detached'.[57] But it could be argued that *The Buddha* is not as detached from the traditional novel as Connor believes. Once again *Great Expectations* is relevant here for, despite its use of a retrospective first-person narrative, Pip's life, like Karim's, is a 'mess' (BS 284) and

Dickens's struggle to conclude the narrative convincingly is manifest in the two very different endings he wrote for the novel, neither of which is actually conclusive.

In contrast to Connor, Alamgir Hashmi places the novel in the tradition of social realism. Hashmi spots the reference to 'Bromley High Street, next to the plaque that said H. G. Wells was born here' (BS 64) and goes on to argue that

> ■ Kureishi's design concentrates on the odd, the exotic, the typical, and the familiar according to the Wellsian laws of social probability. In fact, both H. G. Wells (1866–1946) and Kureishi are easily seen to evince an interest in the study of suburban drolls [oddballs], social mores, and people on the make, with a keen eye to their oddities and peculiarities.[58] □

Nasta, on the other hand, argues that

> ■ [w]ith Kureishi's novel, a literary genealogy can easily be traced back to earlier inscriptions by a number of male writers of a black and Asian Britain. Karim Amir is a professional actor, like Rushdie's Saladin [in *The Satanic Verses*], and furthermore, in a way similar to Selvon's 'boys' in *The Lonely Londoners*, he represents a picaresque anti-hero who navigates the city, reterritorializing and renaming its spaces. Kureishi also draws, like Selvon, on the use of iconoclasm, polyphony and parodic inversion as means of both appropriating and subverting commonly accepted stereotypes to comic effect. And, like Selvon's 'boys', too, Karim ... identifies himself first and foremost as a *Londoner*.[59] □

However, it should also be noted that Kureishi's style has very little in common with Rushdie's and his London is not, like Selvon's, a 'black' London.

The attempt to place *The Buddha* in a particular tradition has resulted in a whistle-stop tour of the western canon: Kipling, Wells, Colin MacInnes, Rushdie, Selvon, my own bid for Dickens, and the recourse of some French critics to their countrymen, Voltaire (1694–1778) and Molière (1622–73).[60] Kaleta compares *The Buddha* to 'initiation novels' by the English writers Henry Fielding (1707–54) and Evelyn Waugh (1902–66), and by the American authors F. Scott Fitzgerald (1896–1940), Mark Twain (1835–1910) and J. D. Salinger (born 1919).[61] This suggests, not just critics' own preoccupations, but what a fertile and rich text it is. It is also significant that few critics draw on non-western literature (apart from the migrant novelists, Rushdie and Selvon) in connection with Kureishi. Donald Weber argues that Kureishi is 'more helpfully situated as a striking variation on American "ethnic" writers, especially Philip Roth (born 1933), than as an example of "Black British" expression'.[62]

We could also add here that while most critics refer to the importance of pop music in *The Buddha*, Jörg Helbig claims that Karim listens almost exclusively to 'white' music and that his favourite music is 'by the most British of British pop bands, the Beatles'. Helbig notes that in the essay, 'Eight Arms to Hold You', Kureishi praised John Lennon as 'the central figure of the age' and Helbig argues that the use of the Beatles shows Kureishi's 'urge to dissolve ... any kind of borderlines, categories, and hierarchies'.[63] The Beatles were role models because they were lower-middle-class but had indisputably created great music. Moore-Gilbert suggests that for Kureishi pop music was the first 'global' cultural form, and he quotes Kureishi's claim that the Beatles 'spoke directly to the whole world'. According to Moore-Gilbert, Kureishi sees pop music as 'a template for the progressive processes of hybridisation and cross-fertilisation in which he is most interested'.[64] Pop's importance might also very obviously be attributed to the fact that it is *popular*, an accessible form that speaks to large numbers of people. All of Kureishi's work shares pop's imperative to reach its audience: it may be complex and capable of multiple interpretations but it is never wilfully obscure. If there is one pop figure whose influence pervades the novel, it is the leading avatar of transformation, the Bromley-born David Bowie, and one song above all that resonates on every page: 'Ch-Ch-Ch-Ch-Changes'.

Bowie scored the music for the four-part BBC TV version of *The Buddha* (1993), which was adapted from the novel by Kureishi himself and Roger Michell (who also directed). The series brilliantly transferred the book to the screen, despite the necessity to censor some of the more graphic sex scenes. Reviewers praised the evocation of the 1970s, captured through music and clothes; as Kureishi joked, 'the BBC is good at costume dramas'.[65] The series did not just excel at period detail: a wonderful cast fully realized the characters and, without resorting to voiceover, the adaptation managed to convey the inner confusion of its protagonist.[66]

After finishing the novel, Kureishi himself changed direction, and made the film of *London Kills Me*: 'When I began *The Buddha* I first started out being alone and with a subject, which was really race ... After writing the novel it just seemed natural to me to do my film that wasn't about race and to get out of the house.'[67] As this chapter has shown, critics rapidly responded to the main subject of *The Buddha*, but as we will see in the next chapter, they have been far less certain how to approach Kureishi's work when it is not about race.

CHAPTER FIVE

Dealer's Day: *London Kills Me* (1991)

K arim might sum up his life as a 'mess' but it is a successful mess. Clint (Justin Chadwick), the drug-dealing protagonist of *London Kills Me*, starts and ends his journey far worse off. As Kureishi commented: 'The boy in the *Buddha* is going somewhere – that's soap opera. But Clint winds up a waiter. That's reality.'[1] The film with which Kureishi made his debut as a director is set in a world of drugs, petty thievery, homelessness and prostitution, and centres on Clint, an emaciated addict who was sexually abused as a child, as he sets about finding a pair of shoes so he can get a job. But the film is anything but grim, documentary realism; this is partly because of Clint's optimism – the amazing survival of innocence – but also because of the soundtrack, which makes the film less like *Cathy Come Home* (the harrowing drama-documentary concerning homelessness directed by Ken Loach for the BBC in 1966) and more like the Beatles' *A Hard Day's Night* (1964). Unlike *Laundrette* and *Sammy and Rosie* there is no odd couple at the centre; instead there is a triangle: Clint is half in love with Muffdiver (Steven Mackintosh), 'the wonderful boy', and with the self-harming Sylvie (Emer McCourt). But *London Kills Me* does have echoes of Kureishi's previous work: the milieu shows his continued interest in 'the waste ground' of *Sammy and Rosie* (although the street life here is far from utopian). The comic scenes in Dr Bubba's (Roshan Seth) meditation centre are reminiscent of Haroon at the end of *The Buddha*, while the cynical, cool Muffdiver recalls Charlie from the same novel. Clint's Elvis-impersonating stepfather is a direct descendant of Bill in *The King and Me*. Like *Laundrette, London Kills Me* has elements of the gangster genre, which gives the narrative momentum. The film has a much narrower focus than the films Kureishi made with Frears, but although it does not explore ethnicity, Muffdiver's posse is a typically multiracial urban group. As Kureishi said: 'it's mostly about white kids. It seems to me progress to *assume* that we live in a mixed society. Before it was your job to say: "Oh, by the way, there are amazing people here who do live here and are part of Britain". Now we can integrate that into our work while not forgetting it.'[2]

London Kills Me is neither autobiographical nor concerned with race but it reflects Kureishi's continued fascination with London. It does not offer a panorama of London as a world city but a close-up of Notting Hill, then both down-at-heel and fashionable (and relatively unexplored on film), before it became the uniformly glamorous and white setting for the romantic comedy, *Notting Hill* (1999), directed by Roger Michell. *London Kills Me* also testifies to Kureishi's engagement with marginalized groups and the possibilities for change and transformation in the city. It explores alternative forms of family to the suburban Thatcherite model and, like *Laundrette* and *Sammy and Rosie*, it offers another ironic look at Thatcherite economics, this time in the guise of drug-dealing entrepreneurs. Again Kureishi's interest in popular culture, particularly music and fashion, give the film a distinctive style. In his introduction to *The Faber Book of Pop* and his essay on the Beatles, 'Eight Arms to Hold You', pop music features as a source of pleasure but also as a democratizing and subversive form of culture: 'the alternative history of our time told from the standpoint of popular music, which is as good a position as any to look from, since pop, intersecting with issues of class, race and particularly gender, has been at the centre of post-war culture' (F xix). *London Kills Me* is characteristic of Kureishi in its disavowal of the 'worthy' and the moralizing in favour of a comedy that shows us as 'being sad and pathetic people ... without just mocking us'.[3]

The most interesting discussion of this offbeat and almost unclassifiable film is by Philip Dodd in an interview with Kureishi:

■ Set around Ladbroke Grove in London's Notting Hill, the film focuses on a group of streetwise young drug dealers and is remarkable for its indifference to the dictum that drug films have to be grittily dour laments about lost souls and homelessness. I can think of no other film that takes such a subject and makes of it a tender comedy.

Like Isaac Julien's recent *Young Soul Rebels* (1991), *London Kills Me* is much absorbed with style and music. It is a film not only about London street kids and their lives, but made for them, working within their own idioms. Imagine Colin MacInnes' novel *Absolute Beginners* crossed with De Sica's *Bicycle Thieves* (1948) and Susan Seidelman's *Desperately Seeking Susan* (1985) – also a comedy about changing clothes and changing places – and you begin to have the feel of it. ...

... *London Kills Me* is a Working Title film, produced by Judy Hunt for £1.5 million and shot by Ed Lachman, the cinematographer for Jean-Luc Godard and Wim Wenders as well as for Susan Seidelman on *Desperately Seeking Susan*. ... The following is extracted from an interview that took place in London in August. We began by talking about how social problem films, from British documentaries of the 30s onwards, tend to make their subjects the objects of our sympathy and how films can be made that adopt the kids' point of view rather than the observers'.

Hanif Kureishi: There was a genre of films in the 80s – including Martin Scorsese's *After Hours* (1985) and Jonathan Demme's *Something Wild* (1986) – which showed what happens if you are a yuppie and you fall through the crust of money into the underworld, the world of the working class. They were versions, in a way, of the experience of the Americans in Vietnam: the good white man fallen among animals, except that this was in New York or Chicago or wherever. It seemed to me that you could get away from that way of looking at things if you stopped putting a frame around the action – the one thing you couldn't do was to start off with a journalist. Once the journalist goes in, you have the frame, which always seems to me to imply a sort of failure from the start.

I never saw this world of the kids of *London Kills Me* in that way. It's outside the world in which I live, but not outside my mental world. I recognised that the only way the film would work would be if you were involved in what was happening between these people – distancing in any way seemed beside the point.

Philip Dodd: As I watched, I kept thinking of Muffdiver's posse as Fagin's thieves in [Lionel Bart's musical *Oliver* (1960).] *Were they in your mind?*

Yes. Also I had seen a drawing that Malcolm McLaren made in 1973 of such street kids. Underneath it says, 'Dickens' London'. And the drawing could well be of The Sex Pistols: it's as if he found the boys and designed them according to his sketches.

When I was researching the film I would see these kids running around the streets of Notting Hill – dealing, being beaten up, getting into big fights, going to raves where they would make £1,000 from selling Ecstasy at £25 a shot. Sometimes some of the kids were being picked up by the police and put into police cells for two or three nights without anyone claiming them or the police sending them to the courts. And then you would pass someone from that other Notting Hill world – the affluent world of the media – or see Harold Pinter in a restaurant. Dickensian is not the right word, but it does conjure up the mixture of the rich and the poor, the idea of these worlds co-existing.

I remember you once said that there were enough stories in west London to keep you in work forever.

It always surprises me that people have to sack Waugh or Forster for stories – I bet it will be Huxley's turn next year – when all you have to do is look around London and see the extraordinary mix of people. Having an American, Ed Lachman, shoot the film was instructive. He saw how eccentric Notting Hill is, how eccentric people look. I can't think of many other places in London with its mix. I have also always liked *Performance* (1970), particularly the shots of Powis Square, as well as Colin MacInnes' novels. They are specifically about young people, fashion and music – things I felt hadn't been much represented, certainly not in the novel and not that often in films.

Clothes and style are certainly at the core of the movie. It's not merely that like some male Cinderella, Clint needs to find the right shoes so he can go to the ball, but that throughout the movie Clint and others dress and discard clothes at will. There's a wonderful scene in which Clint's Teddy boy stepfather dresses as Elvis Presley as he chases the posse from his homestead.

It's partly to do with the fact that we grew up, you and I, at a time when what people wore mattered a great deal. And I am very interested in the way people completely make and remake themselves all the time in the city. Muffdiver in the film imagines himself as a sort of gangster, a minor American drug criminal. His efforts are rather farcical because of the fantasies he has of that sort of life. The main character in my *Buddha of Suburbia* is rather like that, too: he becomes an actor, a profession of mutation; he plays Mowgli and then in another play he takes the part of an immigrant though this is a form of racism, of stereotyping. It is difficult for a person of colour to evade the definitions settled upon him.

One of the striking things about the movie is that it betrays no nostalgia for the lost roots of these kids, no sense that their identities are simply settled, and that without their families they are lost souls. In fact, the film seems to play with the idea of the posse as an alternative family, much as Young Soul Rebels *and* In Bed with Madonna (1991) *have 'pretend' families.*

The left has always fetishized roots. And the old left has a contempt for pop culture, for pop and the meanings it has embodied for people like us – it was always seen as just capitalism in another guise.

These young people are more involved in the present and future than in the past. Roots don't seem to be an absence in their lives. In a way a sort of family is formed in the film of the posse, a parody of Thatcher's idea of the family unit. Its members all have their own place – somebody makes the tea, there is a hierarchy – but they are not related by blood. That seems just arbitrary now.

The sequence which does try to deal with relationships in a biological family begins with Clint and the posse visiting Clint's mother and stepfather in the countryside. Yet this seemed the most fairytale part of the film with the posse wandering the fields like a band which has lost its Peter Pan.

... For *London Kills Me*, we did shoot some scenes where one of the posse did some speeches from *A Midsummer's Night Dream* and everyone was running around in the woods, but in the end we took it all out. It was a bit too bizarre, and in any case, I wanted the film to be like *A Hard Day's Night* or *Catch Us if You Can* (1965) – that film John Boorman made about The Dave Clark Five. I wanted it to be in some ways a take-off of those pop group films of the '60s or of The Monkees. Kids running around in that way rather than a sad film about being homeless.

But the movie is a historical film about several generations, told through style – about how each of them survives. There's Clint's macho Teddy boy stepfather with his Elvis obsession, who seems to have lived out that adage from Absolute Beginners *that Teds have left London to live in the provinces; there's the bohemian '60s group with their cowboy boots, wine bars and music; and there's the young with their raves.*

It's a way of looking at history that young people would immediately understand. They have a fantastic knowledge of the history of pop music and see the world through that: they see Harold Wilson as an adjunct to the Beatles.

So it's a deliberate attempt to write history in terms which the people in the film as well as those you want to watch it will recognise?

Yes, but it's also to do with having measured my own life out in pop music, in the way that the previous generation measure their lives out in terms of movies. Pop music affected me much more than films or litera-ture and it was always part of my cultural vocabulary – far more than any-thing more esoteric. I spent years pretending that one spent one's youth reading Dostoevsky, when in fact what I had really been doing was listen-ing to King Crimson. Since *The Buddha of Suburbia*, I have started to write about these things much more than before, when I was ashamed and wanted to seem as if I had more cultural ballast. Whereas in fact at the bottom of one's soul is Barclay James Harvest.

You seem reluctant to talk about the film's visual dynamic, yet at the centre is a visual idea: taking off and putting on a shoe. Where did the idea come from?

Two things. First there was a kid I knew, that I still know, who was an Ecstasy dealer. He was living in a squat and had borrowed this girl's shoes. We were sitting on the roof drinking a bottle of champagne he had stolen and this girl came up barefoot and said, 'Where's my fucking shoes?' She took them off him and then he was really stuck. The image stayed in my mind. [Although Kureishi does not refer to Harold Pinter's *The Caretaker* (1960), Clint's search for shoes is reminiscent of the pipe-dream of Davies, the tramp in that play, that if he had some boots he would go to Sidcup.]

I also like stories such as Maupassant's, or whoever, about necklaces or earrings or a particular jewel. The story of an object through film. And I wanted to do something much simpler than *My Beautiful Laundrette* or *Sammy and Rosie Get Laid*, in which politics and characters are com-bined. In *London Kills Me*, the characters aren't articulate in that way; they wouldn't speak for themselves or make any sort of statement on their own behalf.

But that's not to say these kids are passive victims.

When I was researching the film or hanging around meeting all these kids in the late '80s they were really energetic. Most of them didn't have established places to live or jobs – they had left their families and they were dealing – but they were real little go-ahead kids. They had sound systems for parties; some of them were doing magazines and selling little books; they were selling records and clothes and running raves. And, of course, the drug dealers were incredibly enterprising. They would go around with portable phones and bleepers; they would be hiring taxis to go to raves.

The whole thing seemed like a sort of parody of what Thatcher wanted. Here were all these kids who were quite badly educated, weren't housed and the State, the great Welfare State, had done very little for them; it couldn't even find them a room to live in. Yet they were living out the Thatcherite dream – they were on the street dealing really hard. So it was like a parody of what the yuppies were doing at the same time in the city.

In that sense, I suppose the film is about the waste: it is not a film that moralizes about waste, but these are people who have a lot of intelligence and energy and there is no place for them. One of the things that happens in the film is that Clint steals Muffdiver's money. I wanted to show that these relationships are poisoned by necessity and scarcity rather than pretending that feeling is foremost. You can pretend that is the case in bourgeois films, because there is a base there from which you can be in love. But if one of you is a junkie and other people are dealers then money is more important than the intimacy of sex.

I've gone back to the ending several times. Clint is presented with two possible solutions. He can disguise himself among the funereal black of the goths and escape London, like so many adolescent heroes before him. But instead he is incorporated; he dresses in a white shirt and smiles and smiles at the customers.

Let's remember that he gives up his relationships with Muffdiver, this wonderful boy, and with Sylvie, and his whole world of selling drugs, all to become a waiter. That is deeply worrying – an open question, rather like the end of *One Flew Over the Cuckoo's Nest* [originally a novel by Ken Kesey (born 1935), published 1962 and filmed 1975]. By deciding to do the right things – become a waiter – he has lost himself.

What happens to Clint is connected in some way with how Thatcher tried to straighten out England, to flatten it; Clint becoming a waiter is in a way like that. But the charm of England has always seemed to me that it is a sort of higgledy-piggledy, broken, crooked place. Since the war the one thing that Britain has been good at is producing pop music. This thing that Thatcher hates has actually made a great deal of money for this country – and in fact in the 60s and 70s the thing that prevented the country culturally from being taken over by America was the fact that we held our own in terms of pop music. The Who, The Kinks and, later on, The Sex Pistols, The Clash – the music seemed to me to be the centre of our identity and individuality. It was actually what was interesting about the place …

… There are some very funny sequences in the film, not least the one where the head of the Sufi centre, the sandal-clad Dr Bubba, meets the

local drug dealers. And structurally, the film seems to work as a comedy – the outcast is taken in. How deliberate is the choice of a comic idiom?

Comedy is not a suit you can put on, it's more a way of seeing the world. When I was a kid I wasn't sitting in the cinema watching Godard films, I was watching *Carry on Camping* (1969), *I'm All Right Jack* (1959). Every night I would come home from school, do my homework, have my tea and then watch these things [on TV] – *Steptoe and Son* (1962–65), *On the Buses* (1969–73). They are hilarious and they are very well observed, well written, well crafted. The worst thing you could be, it seemed to me, in the 80s as opposed to the 70s, was worthy. Worthy people had had it by the 80s – you couldn't be worthy even if you wanted to say serious things about racism. Ken Loach couldn't make the same films then that he had made before.

The danger with me and my work is that I will become, or already am, glib and flippant – that I will not be able to take the world seriously at all. What I have always wanted is a combination of feeling and serious-ness about the world: somehow the humour has always guarded the dig-nity of life ... □   (Philip Dodd, 'Requiem for a Rave', 1991)[4]

Kureishi goes on to say how much he learned from Stephen Frears in the previous two films and pays tribute to the cameraman, Ed Lachman, and the editor, Jon Gregory (who cuts Mike Leigh's films). Kureishi removed scenes with the characters talking about drugs but said: 'I regret not having some scenes showing what a good time you can have on drugs. I felt the film was rather unnecessarily anti-drugs; there should have been more of a "Say yes to drugs" to make you see why that world is so seductive.'[5] At the time, before *Trainspotting* (1996), audiences were unprepared to be seduced by smack users and squats.

For several reasons, not entirely connected to the film itself, the critical reception was generally poor. Kureishi's celebrity by this point was arguably the main reason the press mauled him. Kaleta provides a summary of initial reviews:

■ The popular critical reverence for Kureishi's status as an artist after his second film script gave way to the first critical rejection of his work in response to this next experiment. Kureishi had accepted the challenge of directing the film of his third screenplay, experimenting wearing two hats – that of writer and that of director. The critics nearly decapi-tated him twice.

Negative response dominated the reviews, although some of it was constructive, identifying the film's flaws. *Rolling Stone* magazine, how-ever, dismissed the film in a review of little more than one paragraph in length. The critic concluded, 'The directing debut of gifted screen-writer Hanif Kureishi is a crushing disappointment ... Stephen Frears made the characters come alive; Kureishi does not ... low in characterization, the film drowns in its own pretensions.'[6] In a British review, Kureishi's debut as a director was, once again, more chastised than were his efforts as writer, but his writing too was found lacking. 'Mainly it fails because it has precious little to say about characters who have precious little to say',[7] complained the critic.

Comparisons with the previous Kureishi/Frears collaborations were unflattering. 'Kureishi doesn't have Stephen Frears to hide behind any more ... London Kills Me pushes none of the right buttons',[8] wrote one reviewer. Some popular reviews of the film – and, more to the point, of Kureishi – extended beyond negative criticism to critical execution: 'Hanif Kureishi has declared that ... his directorial debut was made for the Saturday night Odeon crowd. Two men and a dog in an art house seem more likely ... Kureishi displays little cinematic sense ... This is a flim to be endured, like a migraine.'[9] ... ...

The negative response identified some cinematic problems. Kureishi was, at the time this film was made, and continues to be, in the process of developing a new perspective concerning the dynamics of literary and cinematic storytelling. But this film was seen as missing the mark, leaving Kureishi's searcher, in the words of one reviewer 'in Kureishi's moral limboland', merely wandering between film and literary conventions. According to the same reviewer, 'a vacuum surrounds this innocent abroad, which Kureishi needs to fill with a story which suits the emotional conflicts and comic mishaps that naturally spring from his Candide tales. Then he will have fully integrated his two disciplines, the literary and the cinematic.' ☐   (Kenneth Kaleta, Hanif Kureishi, 1998)[10]

As Kaleta points out, some critics blamed Kureishi's script, while others saw the film's weaknesses stemming from his inexperience as a director. Kaleta quotes Derek Malcolm: 'Kureishi is a good writer, though it could be argued that the louder he shouts, the less good he is. What he isn't yet is a good director, and London Kills Me bears all the signs of being pieced together to tell a wisp of a story in logical order rather than to make a film whose style mirrors its content with flair and dynamism.'[11] Kaleta sees parallels between London Kills Me and The Wizard of Oz (1939), with Clint's journey in his ruby-red boots down the winding Portobello Road a quest for 'Elsewhere' – the 'dream of finding happiness'.[12] He also offers a detailed discussion of the bathing scene with its direct allusion to Nicolas Roeg's cult film Performance.[13] But critics did not find that the different genres created a coherent film style. Kureishi himself has said that the difficulty was the burden of doing both things at once and not having a director with whom to thrash out ideas.[14]

Perhaps most significantly, Kaleta detects a 'cultural bias' in the critics' responses: 'An ominous undertow lurks in some negative reviews of London Kills Me – namely an apparent disapproval of the fact that Kureishi has dared to tell the story of a *white* street boy's experiences.'[15] Ranasinha also speculates about the extent to which this negative critical reception was due to the expectation that, as a 'minority' writer, Kureishi ought to deal with ethnicity. She argues that Kureishi contests the 'burden of representation' in *Laundrette* and *Sammy and Rosie*, and incorporates it as a theme in *Buddha*; in *London Kills Me* he goes one stage further and resists 'being confined to what is demarcated as the ethnic minority artist's terrain'.[16] However, she seems to suggest that 'although critics do tend to pigeonhole Kureishi as a minority artist, criticism of *London Kills Me* focused on Kureishi's lack of control as a *director*'. She concludes that 'the move from race was achieved with greater success in his novella and short stories in the late nineties'.[17]

Despite the generally poor critical reception, *London Kills Me* has had admirers. For Sukhdev Sandhu it is another testament to Kureishi's metrophilia, a celebration of the marginal and the 'messy':

■ One day, in *London Kills Me*, Clint's posse decide to leave the capital. They need a break, a day out. Clint himself has no job, no home and little money. He can't even steal the pair of shoes he needs to find paid work. He's scared that the drug-dealer, Mr. G, is going to pay him back for the previous night's failed business deal. So the posse leave for the countryside where they'll visit Clint's mother. They hope to escape the noise, the fumes, the endless pressure of city life. They want some fresh air, and they want to be revivified. They fail. As soon as they disembark from the bus onto the country lane they're 'a little bewildered, looking lost' (LKM 49). Clint's mum, Lily, isn't pleased to see them. Nor is her husband, Stone, who abuses them for being jobless 'slaves of sensation' (LKM 59). An argument breaks out. Clint starts tussling with his stepfather.

The posse return home. It's been a miserable, shitty day. But it has allowed Clint to come to a mushroom-fuelled insight about the kind of life he truly values. And it isn't one he'll find in the country where 'the people are sly and cunning and ignorant ... I know what I want to do. Get back to London and be with the only people for me, having adventures' (LKM 51).

It's a telling admission. Clint is hapless, dependent, and near the bottom of the capital's social and economic ladder. In this sense, London is killing him, grinding him down. But, for all that, Clint finds life in the capital preferable to the corrosive mean-mindedness of the countryside from which he's just fled. London, at least, is full of action, possibility, adrenalizing happenstance – it's good, it 'kills' him. □
(Sukhdev Sandhu, 'Pop Goes the Centre', 1999)[18]

And Sandhu is not the film's only admirer; most notably, Colin MacCabe considers it a 'very acute description of London in the early nineties'.[19] It is regrettable that so little critical attention has been paid to a film which captures an aspect of London life that is rarely seen. While *Laundrette* and *Sammy and Rosie* received considered reappraisal in the years following their first screenings, *London Kills Me* has been undeservedly neglected. With Kureishi's next book, which looks at Islamic fundamentalism, critics got back into their stride.

CHAPTER SIX

'Prince of Darkness Meets Princess of Porn': *The Black Album* (1995)

*L*ondon Kills Me and *The Black Album* might seem to have very little in common, except that the former epitomizes the values that Riaz and his posse in *The Black Album* are determined to resist as western decadence and self-destruction. After directing his first film, Kureishi adapted *The Buddha of Suburbia* for the BBC and *The Buddha* and *The Black Album* also show a marked contrast. As Schoene argues, *The Buddha* expressed Kureishi's faith in the 'individualistic escape from the confinement of "identity" ' while '*The Black Album* stresses the reality of cultural dislocation.' Karim makes a brief appearance in Kureishi's second novel but the 'herald of hybridity' has 'deteriorated into a glamorous celebrity' photographed by *Hello!* magazine (his ethnicity processed and marketed).[1] Shahid, the protagonist of this novel, is engaged in a desperate scramble for identity. Harsh political realities seem to have undermined Kureishi's belief in carnivalesque cultural performance: there is greater recognition of capitalism's capacity to co-opt and commodify, while communal identity exerts a stronger influence on the individual. *The Black Album*, even more than any other novel by Kureishi, has a specific historical context: namely, the furore that ensued after the publication of Salman Rushdie's *The Satanic Verses* (1988) and the *fatwa* issued by the Ayatollah Khomenei. The novel shows Shahid, a student at a college in north London, wavering between an affair with his postmodernist tutor, Deedee Osgood, and involvement with Riaz, the leader of a militant Islamic group, who plans to burn the blasphemous book. The novel is also set against the fall of the Berlin Wall with the consequent collapse of the Left. Less autobiographical than *The Buddha*, it is more directly political; a novel of ideas, or rather, clashing ideologies. Ultimately rejecting the stifling orthodoxies of Islam and Marxism, Shahid and Deedee speed towards Brighton for a breath of fresh air. Like the stories of Tania in *Laundrette* and Muffdiver and Sylvie in *London Kills Me*, Shahid's tale ends with a train ride: there are no certainties here, no final destination.

In an interview with Maya Jaggi, Kureishi explained his motivation for writing the novel. As Jaggi points out, neither Rushdie nor *The Satanic Verses* is mentioned in *The Black Album* but there are references to 'the author of *Midnight's Children*'. Kureishi told Jaggi: 'The book was never intended to be about Salman or the Rushdie affair. I wanted it to be about the issues that interested me at the time of the fatwa. But the interest started because this thing happened to my friend.' Jaggi points out that Kureishi was one of the first to speak out against Ayatollah Khomeini's death threat; and that although he describes himself as from 'a Muslim background, but not in a religious sense', he approached the 'fundamentalists' with sympathy. Kureishi told Jaggi:

■ I started going to the mosque in Whitechapel, hanging around with them. I wondered why normal blokes got to the point where they wanted to see an author killed. I tried to be fair. I really liked the kids – I still see them. I felt sympathetic; they seemed lost, and fundamentalism gave them a sense of place, of belonging. So many were unemployed, and had friends involved in drugs; religion kept them out of trouble. □

Jaggi suggests that the novel shows Muslim fundamentalism as a means of resisting racism. Shahid had wanted to join the British National Party ('I would have filled in the forms – if they have forms'): thinking: 'why can't I be a racist like everyone else?' Kureishi, whose school friends were skinheads, saw himself as white when growing up, and says: 'I wanted a picture of a bloke going mad with an identity crisis. He was so fucked up he wanted to join the National Front. His father has died, his brother's a junkie, he's looking for something. That was the springboard for joining the fundamentalist group.'

According to Jaggi, the publishers had the novel scrutinized by advisers. Kureishi said:

■ I was careful not to do anything blasphemous – I wouldn't want to. And it's quite different to Rushdie's book. He wrote a book about religion; mine's about what people might do in its name. I'm not interested in the spiritual, but in religion as ideology, as a system of authority, a kind of business. It's important we ask questions: what are they doing with their money, with young people? It would be a disaster for everyone – including Muslims – if we couldn't write about religion, or ourselves. It would be playing into the hands of people who think badly of Islam, who say it's so volatile and insular and intolerant, Muslims will go nuts. Those I've met aren't like that at all .... I didn't want to write a book that took sides. I'm interested in all sides of the argument. □

According to Kureishi, Shahid opts for an open-minded provisionality: 'He makes an effort to join their community, but he can't fit in.'

Jaggi goes on to argue that through Dr Brownlow, the cuckolded Marxist-Leninist who has been 'stuttering since Eastern Europe began collapsing', and Rugman Rudder, a Labour councillor, Kureishi exposes what he refers to as the appeasing 'ideological contortions' of some on the left, or of politicians who try to 'help the Asian community out of weird liberal decency'.

Although Jaggi complains that the novel does not satirize the ostensible liberals who insisted that 'they' obey 'our' laws or 'go back to where they come from', Kureishi agreed that 'You could see the racism coming out. To claim that there was a tradition in this country of unsullied free speech which these Muslims fucked up is a simplistic idea.' Jaggi concludes with Kureishi's belief that many British Muslims see the fatwa as a 'terrible mistake. It's been very bad propaganda for Islam. It's allowed it to be represented as something it doesn't have to be, with Muslims labelled as fanatics and book-burners.'[2]

In the light of some criticisms of the novel, it is worth noting here that Kureishi intended to represent the 'fundamentalists' with sympathy and to show how the rise in militant Islam amongst the young in the west is in part a defence against racism and alienation. As in previous works of Kureishi, there is also the issue of whether he is seen by the media as an 'insider', but he makes it clear that he writes as a liberal individualist and not as a spokesperson for the British Asian Muslim community. But above all, *The Black Album* raised the question of a writer's responsibility to combat negative stereotyping, especially during a time of rising Muslimophobia. Jaggi concludes her article on *The Black Album* by noting that the novel does not sufficiently challenge the representation of Muslims as fanatics and book-burners.

Drawing on Tariq Modood's delineation of 'cultural racism' against Muslims in Britain, Ranasinha gives a useful context in which to look at Kureishi's representations of British Asian Muslims:

■ Modood defines cultural racism as the forms of prejudice that exclude and racialize culturally different ethnic minorities. As Modood suggests, Britain's shifting racialized boundaries are beginning to include certain culturally assimilated South Asian and African-Caribbean (middle-class) values, but continue to exclude and racialize culturally 'different' Asians, Arabs, and non-white Muslims.[3] Modood demonstrates that Britain's South Asian Muslims, particularly its Pakistani and Bangladeshi communities, are the most alienated, 'socially deprived and racially harassed group'.[4] Modood examines why Muslims are portrayed as a 'radical assault upon British values, a threat to the state and an enemy to good race relations'.[5] He suggests cultural racism is particularly aggressive towards minorities 'sufficiently numerous to reproduce [themselves] as a community'. It is hostile to communities with a distinctive and cohesive value system, which can be perceived as an alternative, and possible challenge, to the 'norm' and to those who wish to maintain and assert their cultural distinctiveness in public (for example, visible markers such as wearing the veil).[6] British Asian Muslims are perceived as the minority most resistant to assimilation. British Muslims' mass protests against Rushdie's *The Satanic Verses* provided a focal point for anti-Muslim racism. A recent Commission for Racial Equality survey revealed that the younger Muslims in the group were acutely aware of the stereotypes of Islam that prevail in British society, and were at pains to emphasize the positive aspects of their religion and culture.[7] Modood makes the important point that discourses that see Muslims as a problem or a threat are not confined to an extreme fringe, popular prejudice or the right wing ... [T]hey can be implicit or explicit in both élite and progressive discourses. ☐

(Ruvani Ranasinha, *Hanif Kureishi*, 2002)[8]

It could be argued that this contemporary form of cultural racism is more pernicious than old-fashioned colour prejudice because it is both more pervasive and less easily recognized; not a crude matter of 'we don't like blacks' but of seeing certain values, assumed to belong to particular communities, as incompatible with British liberal democracy.

In an interview with Colin MacCabe, Kureishi was asked by a member of the audience why there could not 'be a comfortable accommodation between the British Muslims and the rest of the society, given that there are now one million Muslims, and most of them are not fundamentalists'. Kureishi positioned himself as a liberal who is critical of aspects of Islam, especially 'fundamentalism', which he referred to earlier in the interview as a fear of mixing: 'it's an attempt to create a purity. It's to say we're not really living in England at all.'[9] He went on to speak about the conversation about Islam that needs to take place within the Muslim community:

■ [T]here are parts of Islam ... that, if you take them seriously, are still neo-fascist. And it is a very, very unpleasant religion in all sorts of ways. I know you can't say that and you're not supposed to think that, but it's true.

And so is Christianity. You have to jettison those bits, you know, in order to live in this country. It seems to me that the basis of our living in England, of our living in England together, is liberalism. And liberalism and certain parts of Islam don't go together at all.

And I think as Muslims we've got to thrash this out and talk about this seriously, and really see what it is that we want to do with the religion. I mean, a religion isn't only something that you just swallow whole. It is a pick and choose thing too. I mean, there are bits of it you emphasise, bits of it you still use, bits of it that you're not interested in, that are redundant, and so on. And I think all Muslims have to come to terms with that, because an old religion in the modern world is a strange thing. And that religion has to evolve too. ☐

(Hanif Kureishi interview with Colin MacCabe, 1999)[10]

These comments would seem to confirm that Kureishi sees aspects of Islam as incompatible with liberalism. Ranasinha argues that in *The Black Album*, Kureishi 'uncritically reflects and embodies rather than questions [the dominant majority's] predominant fears, prejudices and perceptions of devout British Muslims as "fundamentalists", constructed as particularly threatening in the West. His caricatures further objectify this already objectified group, whilst reinscribing dominant liberalism as the norm.'[11]

As part of her argument, Ranasinha gives a brief summary of the plot, highlighting the polarities that are set up in the novel between liberal individualism and fundamentalism:

■ The insistent juxtaposition between Shahid's sexual life with Deedee and his encounter with the 'rave' scene of 1989, and the Islamic group 'forbidden to kiss or touch' is overdone (BA 126). Shahid wavers between intimacy and sexual experimentation with Deedee and helping in anti-racist vigils and typing Riaz's religious tracts. Finally, the Muslim students burn a copy of Salman Rushdie's *The Satanic Verses* on campus,which precipitates his decision to leave the group. Deedee speaks out against the book-burning and calls the police. The group plan to teach her a 'lesson', when they discover Shahid's own act of blasphemy in rewriting Riaz's religious writings as an erotic epic. Chad (Riaz's henchman) and Sadiq assault Shahid for having 'deceived and spat on his own people' (BA 266). At the last moment, Shahid's wastrel brother Chilli [*sic*] (a familiar Kureishi creation, a brash, materialistic arch-Thatcherite) saves Shahid and ejects the posse. The group moves on to 'other business', Chad is badly burnt by firebombing a bookshop that sells *The Satanic Verses*. The novel ends with Shahid and Deedee escaping the aftermath of the book-burning and firebombing on a weekend trip to the countryside 'until it stops being fun' (BA 276). □

(Ruvani Ranasinha, *Hanif Kureishi*, 2002)[12]

Mistakenly, Ranasinha refers to 'the first-person narrator' but the novel is told in the third person.[13] It is an important difference. Ranasinha sees the novel as being biased in favour of liberal individualism but the use of a third-person narrator suggests the distance between Kureishi and his protagonist. As Kureishi said to Kenneth Kaleta: '*The Black Album* is a more objective novel [than *Buddha*]. ... Obviously it's about Shahid, his experience in his life, but it's not from his point of view in that way, not from inside his mind. It's a cooler book emotionally.'[14]

Although Kureishi stated that he did not intend to write a book that took sides, Ranasinha argues that 'in this novel the "debate" is so weighted against the Islamists that Shahid's liberal individualism and decision to leave the "paranoid" Islamic group is unequivocally presented as enlightened self-interest (BA 258)'. She then draws on the

Russian theorist Mikhail Bakhtin (1895–1975), whose book *Problems of Dostoevsky's Poetics* (1929) contrasted the 'dialogic' interplay of various characters' voices in the novels of Dostoevsky (1821–81) with the 'monological' subordination of characters to the single viewpoint of the author in the works of Tolstoy (1828–1910). Similarly, Ranasinha distinguishes between *The Buddha* and *Sammy and Rosie*, which she calls ' "dialogic", making the reader provide the closure, in contrast [*The Black Album*] is "monologic", less complex and nuanced and therefore weaker'.[15] The various perspectives and multiple subplots, Ranasinha argues, are all marshalled to articulate the novel's central conflict: between liberalism and fundamentalism. Despite the evident sympathy for characters such as Chad, a former drug addict, who embraces Islam as a positive Asian identity ('No more Paki. Me a Muslim', BA128), Ranasinha claims that Kureishi '*invents* a polarity between Islamic fundamentalism and detached liberal individualism' because he ignores 'the range of different forms of Islam that are not extreme or aggressive'.[16] By failing to show the shades of opinion within the Muslim community, he constructs a 'monolithic portrait of the Islamic believers' and one which 'rehearses stereotypes of Muslims as intrinsically violent'. As the 'posse's political activism soon "inevitably" descends into extremism – book-burning, the firebombing of shops and assault', she argues that Kureishi does little to counter the hysterical anti-Muslim prejudice that surfaced at the time of the fatwa.[17]

According to Ranasinha, even the dialogue – the debates that take place in the novel concerning free speech versus censorship, or the value of literature – are rigged in favour of the liberal individualist position. Developing the distinction between 'monologic' and 'dialogic' texts, she characterizes *The Black Album* in terms of Shohat and Stam's 'pseudo-polyphonic discourse', which allows the disempowered to speak but only in a way that marginalizes their voices:

■ Polyphony does not consist in the mere appearance of a given group but rather in the fostering of a textual setting where the group's voice can be heard with its full force and resonance.[18] Kureishi makes no effort to talk about Islam, fundamentalism or separatism (already highly charged terms in Britain) except in a caricatured way, sometimes implicitly eliding the desire to adopt distinct cultural values with separatism. The text proliferates binary polarities between anti-intellectualism and the free inquiry of rational Western liberal thought: Riaz exhorts Shahid to 'dismiss questions – Just believe in the truth! These intellectuals just tie themselves up in knots' (BA 175). Riaz describes their Marxist lecturer Brownlow's attitude to Islam as symptomatic of the 'smug intellectual atmosphere of Western civilisation ... [and the desire] to dominate others with your particular morality, which has ... gone hand-in-hand with fascist imperialism' (BA 98–9). Yet despite this critique, the text ultimately reinforces the 'superiority' of Western ideologies identified with the freedom of sexual expression and polarized against the 'irrationality' of Islam. □

(Ruvani Ranasinha, *Hanif Kureishi*, 2002)[19]

Ranasinha argues that the bias in the novel emerges clearly in mainstream responses and she concludes her argument by pointing to the unreliability of authorial intentions:

■ Reviewers tend to reinscribe the clichés in Kureishi's portrayals. The *Daily Express* describes the main objects of satire as the 'politically correct' and the 'ghastly Muslim fundamentalists'.[20] The *Sunday Times* review of *Black Album* refers to the '*scary* fanaticism' of British-born Muslims.[21] One might expect *The Times*'s usually conservative stance on drugs to surface, but even this is jettisoned when hedonism is defined in opposition to what is perceived as even more threatening, fundamentalism. This kind of response underscores the way in which Kureishi is able to exploit a liberal distrust of fundamentalism to privilege hedonism. Critics also reinforce some of the polarities that Kureishi 'produces'. Donald Weber in the *Massachusetts Review* describes Shahid as 'torn between the appeal of religious orthodoxy and the claims of personal imagination'. He rejects 'fanatic anti-intellectualism in the name of the capricious, fluid, playful [read Western] imagination'. Here Kureishi is presented as a subversive crusader against 'uninterrogated religious and cultural pieties'. His 'instinctive impulse to take on the poison of both Thatcherism and Islam' is emphasized and commended. This is an example of a recurrent tendency to interpret Kureishi's work in terms of his own self-conscious presentation. Kureishi as the liberal artist in society, asserting his right to artistic freedom, bravely defying the censoring '*policing* efforts of ... worried Pakistani emigrants in London'.[22] The ease with which Kureishi's creative portrayals lend themselves to stereotypes, despite his stated wish 'to be fair' and approach the Muslim fundamentalists with sympathy, indicates the penetration of dominant representations and illustrates that textual complexities cannot be contained within authorial intentions. □

(Ruvani Ranasinha, *Hanif Kureishi*, 2002)[23]

It is a persuasive argument and Ranasinha is right to point out that an author's intentions are no guarantee of the outcome. It might be added here, however, that the characterization of Brownlow is savagely satirical and the scene in which he collapses in tears at the thought of the Beatles' 'Revolution' while calling the working class ' "fucking greedy, myopic c-cunts" ' (BA 202) hardly presents a convincing portrait of 'superiority'. As Brownlow recognizes, it is the Left that is ideologically bankrupt and religion that has been resurrected. Nor is sexual freedom presented unequivocally. Shahid ponders Riaz's belief that without a 'fixed morality ... love was impossible. Otherwise, people merely rented one another for a period. ... And moved on. And on' (BA 199). The end of the novel shows Shahid choosing to be with Deedee until it stops being 'fun', but even to a liberal reader this may sound a little flimsy.

Frederick M. Holmes stresses the ambivalence in Kureishi's treatment of liberalism, of London as a postmodern playground, and of the value of pleasure, all of which Ranasinha takes to be unequivocally endorsed:

■ In the end, Shahid chooses Deedee over Riaz, but the ephemerality and indefiniteness of what she stands for as a postmodernist seems to undercut the value of his choice. Kureishi, like Rushdie, celebrates the hybrid combinations of peoples and cultures that result from the postmodern erosion of boundaries and definitions, but both writers are cognizant, too, that what is sacrificed in such a fluid world is stability and enduring purpose. For example, although Kureishi has said that what he 'liked about [Shahid and Deedee's] relationship was the provisionality of it,'[24] it lacks any *raison d'être* beyond the fleeting pleasures of the moment. At the novel's conclusion, Deedee and Shahid agree, in a sort of compact, to stay together ' "[u]ntil it stops being fun" ' (BA 287). 'That shouldn't take long,' I scrawled in the margin of my copy of the novel. However necessary 'fun' is, it is hardly the sole basis for a lasting partnership ... At bottom, Deedee is a hedonist, who, in response to Shahid's question of whether the goal of life is just pleasure, asks rhetorically, ' "What else is there?" ' (BA 119). Shahid, clearly, is troubled by the apparent absence in their relationship of higher values, which he recognized in Islam, for all that religion proved untenable for him (BA 251). □

(Frederick M. Holmes, 'The Postcolonial Subject Divided between East and West', 2001)[25]

All interpretations depend on the locality of the reader. Ranasinha focuses on the stereotyping of Asian Muslims, while Holmes is preoccupied with the weaknesses of the liberal individualist. In an interview with Adnan Ashraf, Kureishi said, according to Ashraf, that he had 'received a letter from Saudi Arabia wherein a reader commended [Kureishi] for unveiling the wickedness of the West'.[26]

In contrast to Ranasinha, Moore-Gilbert argues that *The Black Album* programmatically counters many stereotypes about 'fundamentalism'. He begins by noting the sympathetic characterisation of Riaz and continues:

■ Shahid's visit to the mosque leads to his recognition of the hybrid nature of Islam's adherents, rebutting the widespread conception that the religion is a monolithic (and essentially non-western) formation: 'Men of so many types and nationalities – Tunisians, Indians, Algerians,

Scots, French ... gathered there ... Here race and class barriers had been suspended' (BA 109). The Islamophobia expressed in a variety of registers, from the aristocratic Jump to the working-class racists on the 'sink' estate, is challenged by many aspects of Kureishi's depiction of Riaz's group. Its desire for social justice, its hostility to the unrestrained capitalism of the Thatcher era, the second chance in life which it offers characters as diverse as Chad and Strapper, are all represented positively. Equally, the group is seen favourably in comparison with the extreme assimilationism represented by the 'arch-Thatcherite' (BA 72) Chili, the dissolute yuppie who is only partially redeemed by his courageous confrontation with Chad at the end of the novel. Finally, the degree of real threat posed by Riaz's group is put into perspective by the novel's references to the violence of the extreme Right and the campaign of urban terror waged by the IRA, whose disruptions to the life of the capital in the 1980s punctuate the narrative. The arson attack on the bookshop is, by comparison, a relatively minor incident which, as is suggested by the wound which Chad receives, is primarily *self*-destructive. □

(Bart Moore-Gilbert, *Hanif Kureishi*, 2001)[27]

Moreover, Moore-Gilbert goes on to note that Chad's extremism is explained in terms of his

■ early life-experience in Britain. Brought up in the country by white foster-parents who are determined to extirpate every trace of his roots, Chad's turn to 'fundamentalism' is presented as an understandable, if overstated, attempt to recover legitimate parts of his cultural identity ... If Chad is a soul 'lost in translation' (BA 89), the most ironic lesson of his trajectory is that it is precisely the intolerance of the host society towards its 'Others' which generates the physical and ideological resistance that the dominant ethnicity most abhors and fears.[28] □

Later in his discussion, Moore-Gilbert concedes that the absence of moderate Muslims, and the 'Orientalist' stereotype of Islam as superstition (in the passages relating to the divinely-inscribed aubergine), mean that the novel manifests 'ideological confusion'.[29] It should be added here, however, that the aubergine episode was based on a real event.[30]

Moore-Gilbert not only sees the novel as counteracting many stereotypes of Islamic fundamentalism; he also argues that it is very critical of western radicalism. He discusses the relationship between Deedee and Shahid from the perspective of 'colonial discourse analysis', pioneered by Edward Said (1935–2003) in his ground-breaking study, *Orientalism* (1978), in which Said showed how writing about and research into the Orient has always been an essential part of Europe's imperial project. Moore-Gilbert argues: 'Kureishi is much preoccupied by the continuing purchase in contemporary Britain of negative and dichotomising attitudes towards cultures of non-western origin which were formed in the colonial period.' In *The Black Album* Jump, who sees Islam as a threat to the west, represents an extreme form of modern 'Orientalism'. The debates in the novel about Deedee's course on colonial literature show that such hostile attitudes have their roots in much of the canon of English literature, as Said argued in *Orientalism*.[31] Moore-Gilbert continues:

■ *The Black Album* extends Kureishi's critique of radical forms of metropolitan anti-racism by a more specific focus on the relationship between western feminism and the struggles of the racially oppressed, a topic which is by comparison less explicit in *Sammy and Rosie* ... [T]here is an unmistakable whiff of the female colonial missionary about Deedee. For instance, amongst the three college students who are lodgers in her home are two young British-Asian women whom Deedee sees herself as having 'liberated' from an oppressive and obscurantist home environment. In this context Deedee's feminism is clearly vulnerable to the charge of ethnocentrism brought by Chad: 'Would I dare to hide a member of Osgood's family in my house and fill her with propaganda? If I did, what accusations? Terrorist! Fanatic! Lunatic! We can never win. The imperialist idea hasn't died' (BA 191).[32]

The problem is again apparent in Deedee's conduct as a teacher. At one point, Shahid passes 'the hut in which she was teaching "her" girls, a class of black women fashion students. One of them was, somewhat embarrassedly, standing on a chair. The others were giggling and clapping. Deedee was also laughing and pointing at the woman's shoes' (BA, 184). The location (a 'hut'), the 'spectacle' which the black student is making of herself at her teacher's behest, the emphatic use of the possessive adjective – all contribute to making this scene a parodic reinscription of a common trope in colonial discourse, the gaze of the coloniser on the 'manners and customs' of the subject peoples.[33]

Deedee's relationship with Shahid raises similar issues ... ... Thus, although Shahid is never simply the silent and passive object of her attention, Deedee instigates the liaison and there is an inescapable sense that she is abusing her position of power, as she herself seems to acknowledge implicitly in her anxiety that the relationship should not be discovered at college. The unequal power relations are particularly evident early in their affair, when Shahid often feels coerced by a mentor who behaves towards him in a manner reminiscent of Riaz ... : 'But he didn't like being slotted into her plans, as if he were being hired for a job, the specifications of which she had prepared already' (BA 102). Sadiq's comment that 'she is having it away with two Rastamen' (BA 190) may be simply a slur to alienate Shahid from Deedee, but there is no evidence to contradict the supposition that Shahid's ethnicity is a crucial factor in Deedee's choice of him as a sexual partner, especially when she waxes lyrical about his 'café-au-lait' skin. As Tahira complains: 'Our people have always been sexual objects for the whites' (BA 190).

Deedee increasingly sees it as her mission to save Shahid from the fate that his attraction to Riaz's community represents in her eyes. To this extent, *The Black Album* can be approached in terms of Spivak's analysis of the discourse surrounding the prohibition of *sati* in nineteenth-century India which was organised, she suggests, around the trope of '[w]hite men saving brown women from brown men'.[34] By contrast, Deedee can be understood as the 'benevolent' white woman who intervenes to save the brown man from his fellows. This rearranges the terms of the colonial trope without disturbing the racialised power relations which underpin it. Moreover, Kureishi stresses that it is only by placing Shahid in the subject-position of oppressed victim (which he strenuously resists) that the 'benevolence' of figures like Deedee ... can operate. The coercive nature of her 'benevolence' is particularly evident in Deedee's insistence on Shahid's unequivocal rejection of Riaz, which entails the rejection of potentially crucial parts of his identity. Damagingly for Deedee, this links her to much more obviously racist figures like Chad's foster-mother.

Kureishi's anxieties about Deedee's politics reach a climax with her attempt to disrupt Riaz's book-burning protest by calling in the police. Certain kinds of western feminism, it seems, may be no less absolutist – and no less unwilling to resort to force and censorship, in support of supposedly 'universal' values (from the effects of which, ironically, feminists have complained that they have suffered historically quite as much as any other 'minority' formation), than the 'fundamentalism' she opposes. As Sadiq complains: 'Our voices suppressed by Osgood types with the colonial mentality. To her we coolies not cool' (BA 181). As such responses suggest, as much as other kinds of western radicalism, metropolitan feminism's desire to help give voice to or liberate the oppressed may reinscribe power relations which preserve the authority of the ethnic centre. □

(Bart Moore-Gilbert, *Hanif Kureishi*, 2001)[35]

In Moore-Gilbert's reading, which stresses the sympathetic characterization of the fundamentalists and the flaws in Western feminism, Shahid's wavering between Deedee and Riaz becomes far less clear-cut.

Bronwyn T. Williams has a different focus: not whether the novel reinscribes stereotypes of Muslims as fundamentalists or critiques western radicalism, but Shahid's identity crisis. Williams first distinguishes between postcolonial migrant writers, such as Salman Rushdie and Buchi Emecheta (born 1944), and Black British writers, such as Kureishi and Caryl Phillips (born 1958): 'They are not writing as the postindependence or postcolonial subject displaced in Britain; they are writing as the British subject in a postcolonial world trying to contest and displace the dominant narrative of nation.' This generational split emerges in the difference between the experience of Shahid, born in Britain, and his father and uncles' concern with Pakistan. So for Shahid, 'the argument that matters is happening on the streets of London over what form of identity he and his fellow students will construct in a Britain that refuses to recognize them as embodiments of its culture'.[36] For Williams, *The Black Album* is primarily about transnational cultural connections, the fluidity of identifications; how to restage national narratives without being incorporated or marginalized. Williams describes the 'competing, discontinuous, and fragmented stories' of Chili, Riaz, Deedee, Chad and Brownlow in relation to Shahid's longing for a stable cultural identity, showing how 'he is drawn to and torn among all of the people who touch his life':

■ Yet Shahid discovers through the course of events that he is always-already all of these people and none of them. He cannot place himself with certainty – and more important without questioning – within any of the narratives that the other characters inhabit. He cannot give himself to either the pure faith required by Riaz or the pure skepticism required by Deedee. 'The problem was, when he was with his friends their story compelled him. But when he walked out, like someone leaving a cinema, he found the world to be more subtle and inexplicable' (BA 110). When he accompanies Deedee to fashionable coffee houses, he can't help realizing that he is the only dark face. When he goes to Tower Hamlets with Chad to try to help Pakistani and Indian families under threat of violence, he is rejected both by those residents and by the White working-class English families with whom he tries to reason. Near the novel's end, Shahid tries to find the agency of faith in the postmodern moment. 'There was no fixed self; surely our several selves melted and mutated daily? There had to be innumerable ways of being in the world. He would spread himself out, in his work and in love, following his curiosity' (BA 228).

Even as Shahid grapples with positioning himself in a postmodern and postcolonial Britain, so the Britain he inhabits is a shifting stage itself. There is no stable culture for him to see. The rewriting of the metropolis and the creation of new narrativzes continues from day to day as he sees when he visits a mosque in London. [Here Williams quotes (BA 109) also quoted by Moore-Gilbert above.]

Not only have class and race barriers been suspended within the mosque, but so have cultural and national identities. The Islam that is represented by the men in the mosque is as shifting a sign as the emblems of the state in the uniforms of Underground and Post Office workers. There is not a simple definable culture that can be identified within this mix. There are only the multiple narratives of the multiple voices that re-position the subjects in ways that not only disrupt the homogenous mythology of the dominant culture, but necessitate a way of considering the narratives that, as Chakrabarty[37] urges, go beyond the limits of the nation/state to allow us to begin to comprehend what is being said. □

(Bronwyn T. Williams, 'A State of Perpetual Wandering', 1999)[38]

In this reading, *The Black Album* is an attempt to 'hybridize the discourse' of the dominant culture, 'to reconfigure the concept of all cultural identities as fluid and heterogeneous'.[39]

For Maria Degabriele, too, the novel is primarily about identity. In 'Prince of Darkness Meets Princess of Porn', she explores the web of pop allusions in *The Black Album* in order to discuss Kureishi's representation of (plural and partial) sexual and political identities. Degabriele compares Shahid's dilemma to Saladin Chamcha's in Rushdie's *The Satanic Verses*, being pulled between a fragmented, postmodern sense of self and the certainties offered by an Islamic identity. Pop is one of the 'defining locations' of postmodernity and *The Black Album* is 'about the repressed text of pop music' – Prince's 'Black Album' which 'has in fact no title, no name or illustration. It is a chromatic reversal of, and a tribute to, the Beatles' "White Album" '.[40] Emphasizing the importance of play and the comic in Kureishi (and Rushdie), Degabriele explores the significance of Prince and Madonna in relation to Shahid and Deedee:

■ The whole Rushdie Affair has highlighted issues around the power of popular culture, or the political effects of the popularisation of cultural icons that are considered sacred. In response to Shahid's love of novels, Chad says 'There's more to life than entertaining ourselves!' (BA 21). He refuses to see the connection between art and life. However, it is precisely through Shahid's interest in pop culture that he and Deedee Osgood, his teacher, meet and seduce each other. They share the same musical and cultural taste. She has pictures of Prince, Madonna and Oscar Wilde pinned over her desk, and she encourages Shahid to talk about Prince. He says Prince is [in fact Deedee says this, and Shahid agrees]

> half black and half white, half man, half woman, half size, feminine but macho too. His work contains and extends the history of black American music, Little Richard, James Brown, Sly Stone, Hendrix. (BA 21)

It is through their mutual interpretations of such cultural icons as emblematic of the practice of explicit liberation politics that Shahid and Deedee begin their affair. The Islamic brothers, especially Chad, insist that Shahid's lack of commitment to Islam is the result of his listening to too much pop music, especially Prince, and his desire for Deedee Osgood and indulgence in all forms of Western popular culture. The brothers try to steer Shahid away from Deedee, and Chad says 'Get clean! Gimme those Prince records!' (BA 66).

Some of the characteristics of, and people's reactions to, both Prince and Madonna can be mapped onto Shahid and Deedee. All four perform and politicise their sexuality. Like Prince, Shahid identifies as 'half black and half white ... feminine but macho too' (BA 25). He enjoys Deedee making-up his face. She does this to the sound of Madonna's song 'What are you looking at?' from her CD, *Vogue*.[41] They have sex and simulate pornography. Like Madonna, Deedee, in the narrator's words, turns herself into pornography for Shahid. However, she does so 'without losing her soul' (BA 99). It is a sublime combination of mimicry of pornography and eros ... Deedee's 'groupies' are devoted, 'dressing as she did and studying her as if she were Madonna' (BA 167), continuing this chain of simulation. In representing herself as male desire, Deedee also performs representation and sex as politics. Shahid sees Deedee as a street-wise woman who turns both academic and bedroom culture into exciting popular culture. This parallels the way Shahid eventually finds his identity reflected in popular culture as fragmented.

Shahid and Deedee interpret and celebrate pornography as part of pop culture. It is part of the whole culture of simulation. Even though the tropes of pornography circulate publicly, they are performed or consumed privately. The Islamicists also interpret pornography as part of pop culture. And they denounce all pop culture as equivalent to pornography. For them to describe something as pornographic is a profound insult. However, it is in between these two positions that *The Black Album* explores fragmented, multiple identities ... ... [Degabriele goes on to discuss how the Islamicists see Deedee as quintessentially white and repressive.]

The Muslim brothers find ... popular music [dangerous], claiming that it corrupts and thus leads to amorality and to drugs, and so to complete destruction. But they also fear the flattening, or deculturing effect of Western imperialism. And this is where more ambivalence surfaces. They fully understand what is going on but will not admit any criticism of or deviation from their own orthodoxy. In his argument against the Western mass media, Akbar S. Ahmed says that many Muslims react to self-styled radical scholars in a paranoid and hysterical way, seeing the West as a force whose sole purpose is to dominate, subvert, and subjugate them. This sort of occidentalism derives almost entirely from movies, television, and the tabloid press which portray stereotypes. One such stereotype is of 'western women as characterized with their legs wide open, waiting for sex on car bonnets.'[42] This is the sort of stereotype through which Deedee is interpreted by the Islamic brotherhood. Kureishi does not shy away from or merely react to such stereotypes. For example, Deedee tells Shahid that she likes to masturbate while reading *Crash* (1973), [the novel by J. G. Ballard (born 1930)] that depicts precisely the above (BA 98). However, Deedee's performance of pornography is, like Ballard's, a simulation, so that it both is and is not pornography.

Kureishi (like Ballard) probes the meanings and experiences of pornography as an expression of postmodernity. It is in the blurring of the boundaries between fact and fiction, eros and the sacred, that desire is located. So too in *The Black Album* it is in the blurring of the boundaries between the 'fact' of the sexual encounter between Shahid and Deedee, and the 'fictions' of pop culture that their desire is located. The sexual relationship between Shahid and Deedee is very political. They both push experience until it overflows, like popular culture itself, with its promise of 'something more,'[43] especially in [the] context of 'gender-benders' like Prince and the explicit iconography of Madonna. □

(Maria Degabriele, 'Prince of Darkness Meets Princess of Porn', 1999)[44]

Degabriele sees the conflict in *The Black Album* stemming from the incompatibility between fundamentalism and postmodernism, with the novel affirming fluid identities as Deedee announces at the end of the novel that 'she'd got tickets for the Prince concert' (BA 229). Kureishi himself contrasts the scene in which Chad dresses Shahid in a pure white salwar with the way Shahid and Deedee dress up: 'Deedee becomes a guy who wears make-up. Shahid becomes a woman. If you're a Mulsim you can't play with your identity in that way.'[45] As in *The Buddha*, it is play, transformation and the reinvention of identity that is privileged, although it should be added that the debate about the value of pop versus high culture in *The Black Album* is not unequivocal: '[Shahid] intended to embark on the migraine reads. Turgenev, Proust, Barthes, Kundera ... He didn't always appreciate being played Madonna in class ... or offered a lecture on the history of funk as if it were somehow more "him" than *Fathers and Sons*' (BA 112).

Frederick M. Holmes also explores the competing claims of a 'mon-grelized condition' of the self and society, and a 'totalizing religious faith'. But in his examination of *The Black Album* as an intertext of Rushdie's *The Satanic Verses*, he makes an interesting contrast between their different forms:

■ the curious split between the narrative content of *The Black Album* (which could be labeled postcolonialist and postmodernist) and the narrative form (which, unlike that of *The Satanic Verses*, is linear, unself-conscious realism). Whereas Kureishi's screenplays (particularly *Sammy and Rosie Get Laid*) are formally fragmented, elliptical and, in places, surrealistic, in *The Black Album* he relies on a traditional set of narrative methods which, by their nature, presuppose a stability and coherence denied by contemporary culture, as Kureishi himself presents it. In a context in which Kureishi confounds existing definitions and categories of all kinds, the capacity of an undramatized narrator to convey an authoritative, objectively accurate, seamless representation of this turbulent, multiform new reality is never called into question. □

(Frederick M. Holmes, 'The Postcolonial Subject Divided between East and West', 2001)[46]

As noted earlier in this chapter, Holmes is alert to the novel's ambivalence about the postmodern condition and the contradictions within
liberalism, and he connects this to Kureishi's choice of a traditional,
rather than a postmodernist, novelistic form. Before turning to his conclusion, we can look first at Holmes's comparison between Riaz and
Shahid in *The Black Album* and Mahound (a fictionalized version of
Muhammad) and Salman the Persian in Rushdie's *The Satanic Verses*:

■ Although Riaz would not consciously elevate himself to the level of
the Prophet vouchsafed the revelation of Allah's purpose, he is, in fact,
treated by his followers with the unswerving devotion due to a divinely
inspired sage. He writes religious poetry, and Shahid acts as his secre-
tary, just as Salman the Persian does for Mahound. Both scribes alter the
received texts, demonstrating (in Bakhtin's terms) the impossibility of
monologism and the inevitability of dialogism. Their motives differ,
though. Underlying Salman's alterations is an anxious desire to test the
authenticity of Mahound's pronouncements. When Mahound does not
notice the changes made to what he has dictated, Salman skeptically
concludes that Mahound's claim that he is God's Messenger is bogus.

In contrast, Shahid's more radical revisions of Riaz's poems are
inspired by a more positive wish to celebrate areas outside of Riaz's
experience ... Because 'religion [cannot] admit the comic' (BA 161),
Shahid contemplates leaving a pornographic magazine open in Riaz's
room as a practical joke. And because orthodox Muslim teaching
proscribes eroticism, Shahid explores it poetically in rewriting Riaz's sexually puritanical poetry. □

(Frederick M. Holmes, 'The Postcolonial Subject Divided
between East and West', 2001)[47]

Holmes goes on to argue that, for Kureishi as for Rushdie, the narratives
that emerge from religious and literary activity have no special authority, and he quotes Kureishi's comment that *The Black Album* 'is
concerned with stories ... Just as Riaz, as it were, reinvents Islam to suit
him, ... Shahid is doing the same when he rewrites Riaz's poems ... The
point is that life is reinterpreted all the time as we live it.'[48] This
postmodernist rejection of master narratives or totalizing and absolute
explanations makes Kureishi's choice of a traditional novelistic
form surprising but Holmes explains this choice through reference
to Jameson's claim that 'postmodernism is the cultural logic of late
capitalism':[49]

■ Liberatory slogans such as the one displayed in Deedee's office at
the college ('All limitations are prisons') are easily appropriated by
corporations. Think of Nike's 'Just Do It!' in this regard. Although Shahid
sees the moral vacuity of his brother Chili's brand-name consumerism

('his suits were Boss, his underwear Calvin Klein, his actor Pacino' (BA 47)), the supposedly more progressive, alternative lifestyle he adopts with Deedee nevertheless involves a good deal of rather aimless shopping. Kureishi's love for 'inner London,' where 'there is fluidity and possibilities are unlimited,'[50] is not unambiguous, then, since it is apparently accompanied by a frustrated desire for solidity and significant purpose. This dissatisfaction perhaps led him to seek a compensatory stability in the aesthetic realm. Such a hypothesis would account for the conservative, rather old-fashioned novelistic form of *The Black Album*. As James Saynor states, Kureishi 'seems more attuned to the 18th-century English picaresque and to the style of 20th-century raconteurs like Kingsley Amis (1922–95) than to any literary idiom closer to the international cutting edge. (Shahid likes *Midnight's Children*, but it gives him a pain in the head (BA 40).)'[51]

... Finally, despite the fact that Kureishi's protagonist is a budding author, his novel lacks the metafictional dimension supplied by the narrator's overt commentary in *The Satanic Verses*. As Marlena Corcoran shows,[52] this fictional self-consciousness has the effect of applying to *The Satanic Verses* itself the questions about textual authority that are raised about sacred scripture within the narrative strand centered on Mahound. The absence from *The Black Album* of such fictional self-scrutiny regarding the authority of its own representations is a curious blind spot in an otherwise postmodernist novel. □

(Frederick M. Holmes, 'The Postcolonial Subject Divided between East and West', 2001)[53]

According to Holmes, *The Black Album* is 'less interesting generically as a *Künstlerroman* [an 'artist novel' in which the central character is a writer, painter, composer, etc.] than it might have been' but it is convincing 'as a novel of ideas' which manages not to flatten the characters into 'one-dimensional stereotypes'.[54]

In taking up 'the brown man's burden' (BA 5), in order to show the ironies inherent in the liberal position and the appeal of fundamentalism to a besieged community, Kureishi incurred a mixed critical response: some critics consider that *The Black Album* reinscribes stereotypes and others that it challenges them. In many ways, this is an intensified reprise of the debate that surfaced after *My Beautiful Laundrette* and in *The Buddha*. Given the hysterical anti-Muslim feeling in Britain after the Rushdie affair, even those critics who eschewed the demand for 'positive images' might have been happier if Kureishi had thrown in a chain-smoking Islamic feminist or a moderate Muslim scholar. Otherwise, to adapt Tracey's criticism of Karim's portrayal of Anwar: ' "Your picture is what white people already think of us. That we're funny, with strange habits and weird customs and then you have Chad and Riaz burning books." ' But the justification for showing this would be that *not* to do so is a form of censorship and ultimately insulting to the majority of moderate Muslims. A writer cannot show everything, and Kureishi clearly considered he had more to say on militant Islam as a form of identity politics, and as a means of resisting both capitalism and racism, when he adapted his short story, 'My Son the Fanatic', into his next film.

CHAPTER SEVEN

Taxi Driver in Bradford: *My Son the Fanatic* (1997)

The film of *My Son the Fanatic* focuses on Parvez, a Pakistani immigrant scraping a living as a taxi driver, and his British-born son, Farid, who rejects his father's attempts to assimilate and opts for a separatist, Islamic identity. Based on a short story, which appeared first in the *New Yorker* (1994) before being collected in *Love in a Blue Time*, Kureishi's screenplay was directed by Udayan Prasad for the BBC. Kureishi worked closely with Prasad and considered that the collaboration was fruitful. Although Prasad is not a Muslim, Kureishi felt that the film should have an Asian director.[1] In *The Black Album*, Muslim fundamentalism was shown 'filling a space where Marxism and capitalism had failed to take hold'.[2] Shahid and Deedee choose hedonism over either of the orthodoxies of Marxism or Islam, but *My Son the Fanatic* recognizes the need for a better philosophy than capitalist laissez-faire and having fun. Moreover, both the story and the film register the irony of the liberal position more dramatically than *The Black Album*. The paradox is that sceptical liberalism can be fanatical in its denunciation of fundamentalism. When Parvez tries to beat the fanaticism out of his son, it is clear that liberalism needs not only to question itself but also to rethink its relation to deeply held religious beliefs.

Although, like earlier works, *My Son the Fanatic* is concerned with the difficulties faced by immigrants and with Islam, it is the first of Kureishi's films to be set outside London, in a provincial city. Kureishi's interest in the Asian community in the north of England is clear from his earlier essay, 'Bradford' (1986), which several critics use as a context for analysing the film.[3] *My Son the Fanatic* is also the first work to reverse the point of view from sons to fathers: not teenagers rebelling against restrictive elders, but puritanical sons rejecting the liberalism of their fathers.

Ranasinha offers a summary of the plot:

■ [The film] extends the short story's conflict between the quasi-liberal, westernized Pakistani taxi-driver Parvez (Om Puri), who loves Scotch,

119

jazz and bacon-butties, and his ... son Farid's new-found religious zeal. Farid (Akbar Kurtha) abandons his white fiancée, accountancy career, guitar and cricket playing to embrace a fundamentalist sect of Islam. He invites a *maulvi* [an expert in Islamic law] from Lahore, with whose help the young acolytes launch a demonstration against local sex-workers that erupts into violence. (These wider, escalating tensions provide the momentum necessary for the film medium.) This is further complicated as Parvez has begun a love affair with one of the sex-workers, Bettina (Rachel Griffiths), his confidante over his concerns about Farid. Their unfolding relationship, set against the backdrop of their twilight world on the fringe of society (and scrutinized by the enclosed Asian community), is the strongest part of the film: moving, tender, yet without sentimentality. Farid's assault on Bettina at the demonstration provokes Parvez to lash out at Farid inciting him to leave home. Parvez's wife Minoo (Gopi Desai) – who despite her occasional fiery outbursts remains a stereotype of a traditional, devoted South Asian wife – conveniently leaves for Lahore and Parvez is now free (although the film's conclusion is ambiguous) to pursue (what is always privileged in Kureishi's work) his transgressive, inter-racial relationship with Bettina. In contrast to the short story, the film is centrally concerned with the way Parvez's life is thrown into crisis, which forces him to rethink how he wants to live, and begin anew. ☐   (Ruvani Ranasinha, *Hanif Kureishi*, 2002)[4]

In the following extract from 'Sex and Secularity', Kureishi's introduction to his *Collected Screenplays 1* (2002), he discusses the rise of militant Islam as a response to the west and his own relation to these 'fighting couples':

■ Fundamentalist Islam is an ideology that began to flourish in a conspicuous age of plenty in the West, and in a time of media expansion. Everyone could see, via satellite and video, not only how wealthy the West was, but how sexualised it had become. (All 'sex and secularity over there, yaar', as I heard it put.) This was particularly shocking for countries that were still feudal. If you were in any sense a Third Worlder, you could either envy Western ideals and aspire to them, or you could envy and reject them. Either way, you could only make a life in relation to them. The new Islam is as recent as postmodernism.

... ... I have often been asked how it's possible for someone like me to carry two quite different world-views within, of Islam and the West: not, of course, that I do. Once my uncle said to me with some suspicion: 'You're not a Christian, are you?' 'No,' I said. 'I'm an atheist.' 'So am I,' he replied. 'But I am still Muslim.' 'A Muslim atheist?' I said, 'It sounds odd.' He said: 'Not as odd as being nothing, an unbeliever.'

Like a lot of queries put to writers, this question about how to put different things together is a representative one. We all have built-in and contrasting attitudes, represented by the different sexes of our parents, each of whom would have a different background and psychic history. Parents always disagree about which ideals they believe their children should pursue. A child is a cocktail of its parent's desires. Being a child at all involves resolving, or synthesising, at least two different worlds, outlooks and positions.

If it becomes too difficult to hold disparate material within, if this feels too 'mad' or becomes a 'clash', one way of coping would be to reject one entirely, perhaps by forgetting it. Another way is to be at war with it internally, trying to evacuate it, but never succeeding, an attempt Farid makes in *My Son the Fanatic*. All he does is constantly reinstate an electric tension between differences – differences that his father can bear and even enjoy, as he listens to Louis Armstrong and speaks Urdu. My father, who had similar tastes to the character played by Om Puri, never lived in Pakistan. But like a lot of middle-class Indians, he was educated by both mullahs and nuns, and developed an aversion to both. He came to love Nat King Cole and Louis Armstrong, the music of black American former slaves. It is this kind of complexity that the fundamentalist has to reject.

Like the racist, the fundamentalist works only with fantasy. For instance, there are those who like to consider the West to be only materialistic and the East only religious. The fundamentalist's idea of the West, like the racist's idea of his victim, is immune to argument or contact with reality. (Every self-confessed fundamentalist I have met was anti-Semitic.) This fantasy of the Other is always sexual, too. The West is recreated as a godless orgiastic stew of immoral copulation. If the black person has been demonised by the white, in turn the white is now being demonised by the militant Muslim. These fighting couples can't leave one another alone.

These disassociations are eternal human strategies and they are banal. What a fiction writer can do is show the historical forms they take at different times: how they are lived out day by day by particular individuals. And if we cannot prevent individuals believing whatever they like about others – putting their fantasies into them – we can at least prevent these prejudices becoming institutionalised or an acceptable part of the culture. □   (Hanif Kureishi, 'Sex and Secularity', 2002)[5]

It is worth noting that Kureishi does not see Muslim fundamentalism as an old faith clashing with modernity but as a recent phenomenon, as recent as postmodernism and a defence against it. Several critics refer to the scene in which the *maulvi* is shown watching cartoons on television as a way of mocking his superficiality or making him look childish, but this scene also places militant Islam in a postmodernist context.

Although *My Son the Fanatic* recognizes more fully the contradictions within liberalism than *The Black Album* does, Kureishi does not show moderate Muslim believers, only 'Muslim atheists' and fundamentalists.

The possibility that this will reinscribe a negative view of the Muslim community is the subject of much of the academic response to the film. It also seems worth stressing (in the light of hostile criticisms made of the film) that Kureishi sees fundamentalism and racism as mirror images of each other: both diminish or even demonize the Other. The crucial difference is that racism (in the West) and economic disadvantage (both in the West and the so-called 'Third World') are seen as creating the conditions for fundamentalism. This emerges clearly in the following extract, taken from 'The Road Exactly', the introduction Kureishi wrote specifically for *My Son the Fanatic*:

■ It must not be forgotten ... that the backgrounds to the lives of these young people includes colonialism – being made to feel inferior in your own country. And then, in Britain, racism; again, being made to feel inferior in your own country. My father's generation came to Britain full of hope and expectation. It would be an adventure, it would be difficult, but it would be worth it.

However, the settling in, with all the compromises and losses that that implies, has been more complicated and taken longer than anyone could imagine. Yet all along it was taken for granted that 'belonging', which means, in a sense, not having to notice where you are, and, more importantly, not being seen as different, would happen eventually. Where it hasn't, there is, in the children and grandchildren of the great post-war wave of immigrants, considerable anger and disillusionment. With some exceptions, Asians are still at the bottom of the pile; more likely to suffer from unemployment, poor housing, discrimination and ill-health. In a sense it hasn't worked out. The 'West' was a dream that didn't come true. But one cannot go home again. One is stuck.

Clearly this affects people in different ways. But without a doubt it is constraining, limiting, degrading, to be a victim in your own country. If you feel excluded it might be tempting to exclude others. The fundamentalists liked to reject the usual liberal pieties, sometimes for histrionic reasons. But their enemies – gays, Jews, the media, unsubmissive women, writers – were important to them. Their idea of themselves was based, like the MCC, or like any provincial snob, on who they excluded. [The MCC, the Marylebone Cricket Club, was the body that controlled English cricket until 1969 and remains highly influential.] Not only that, the central tenets of the West – democracy, pluralism, tolerance, which many people in Islamic countries, Muslim and non-Muslim alike, are struggling for – could be treated as a joke. For those whose lives had been negated by colonialism and racism such notions could only seem a luxury and of no benefit to them; they were a kind of hypocrisy. □

(Hanif Kureishi, 'The Road Exactly', 1997)[6]

Again, in the light of criticisms of the film for showing Islam in opposition to the West, it is clear that Kureishi accepts that many Muslims believe in democracy and tolerance; it is only fundamentalists who see the West as the enemy, and they have reason for doing so.

Moore-Gilbert draws on differences between the story, the screenplay and the film itself in order to explore Kureishi's 'reconsideration of the problems posed by *The Black Album's* treatment of similar issues'.[7] Most significantly, his account of the film stresses the importance of economic deprivation, where other critics tend to ignore class as a motive for separatism:

■ The introduction of these new characters [Minoo, the Fingerhuts, the *maulvi* from Lahore, Fizzie and Herr Schitz] entails a marked expansion of the meanings of the short story. For example, the Bradford settings are used to reconsider broad questions of social deprivation in a manner reminiscent of Kureishi's earlier work. (This perhaps marks a return to the more explicit focus on class issues of Kureishi's early plays.) Some scenes in the script, many of which are not used in the film itself, clearly recall the decayed urban-scapes of the first three films. Many of these issues coalesce around the character of Schitz, the German entrepreneur. On the one hand, he provides a point of comparison with Parvez, reminding the audience that there are different kinds of economic migrant, whose reception by the 'host' society varies according to the migrant's national origin, class and ethnic identity. Schitz enjoys a quite different reception in the working men's club from Parvez. As a developer of shopping centres in this former industrial city, Schitz's presence signals an accelerating shift in British economic life from traditional industries to a service economy, a reorientation which is in part the product of globalisation. Generally identified in the film script simply as 'The German', Schitz represents the growing influence on Britain of Europe, in which a newly united Germany is the economic dynamo and, as such, a potentially oppressive force.

Perhaps the most significant change of emphasis between short story and film script involves the representation of the relationship between father and son and their respective value systems. In the story Ali largely conforms to the stereotypical vision of Muslim 'fundamentalists', being cold, militant, humourless and judgemental ... In some ways the critique of Islam is even sharper in the film, primarily because of the introduction of the Pakistani *maulvi*. Hypocritical and parasitical, the *maulvi* nonetheless succeeds in galvanising Farid and his friends into direct action against the prostitutes. The vigilantes' violence against the under-age hooker and Farid's own assault on Bettina during the riot lend support to Parvez's disavowal of the seemingly simplistic convictions of Farid's circle, which are further evident in its anti-semitism. As in the novels, gender issues are used to emphasise the regressive nature of the *maulvi*'s religious beliefs. Minoo increasingly takes on the role of servant in her own home after the cleric's arrival, even being required to eat apart from her husband.

However, the treatment of Islam in *My Son the Fanatic* is much more nuanced than all this might suggest and significantly extends *The Black Album* in this respect. In the film script, Farid is drawn in a more complex and sympathetic manner than Ali in the original tale and greater insight is provided into the reasons for his turn to religion. In the first place (though this aspect of the script does not survive into the film), religion provides Farid with an escape route from a lifestyle which earlier threatened to destroy him. (Compare Chad in *The Black Album*; it is Farid's experiments with the drug scene which bring him into contact with Madelaine, making the relationship between the taxi-driver's son and the Police Inspector's daughter more immediately credible in the script than in the film itself.) Secondly, Farid's turning to religion is a credible rebellion against a parent who has anticipated more conventional forms of dissent, such as a career in pop music, by actively encouraging them. Thirdly, Farid's turn to Islam can be understood as a reaction against Parvez's extramarital relationship (of which he has intimations much earlier in the script than in the film itself) and is thus an expression of solidarity with his mother.

As a consequence, there are also major differences between tale and film in terms of their cultural/political meanings. In his introduction to the film script ... Kureishi links the growing appeal of militant brands of Islam to the fact that large numbers of British-Asians continue to exist at the bottom of British society. Parvez's humiliation at 'Manningham's' club is indicative of the hostility of the 'host' culture, which requires him to carry a wooden club for self-protection at work. (The horrifying violence against British-Asian cab drivers is a powerful theme in the essay 'Bradford', which provides *My Son the Fanatic* with many of its details.) In this context, Islam is seen as a legitimate locus of resistance, communal self-help and solidarity. As the older Muslim whom Parvez meets at the mosque argues: 'But ... these young people – they're not afraid of the truth. They stand up for things. We never did that' (MSF 58).

Equally, the moral appeal of Islam is represented more sympathetically in the film script than the original short story. The recurrence of the street of whores as a backdrop in the film, the decadence of the hotel-room scene involving Schitz and Bettina and the orgiastic party to celebrate the acquisition of the businessman's new premises (much more graphically treated in the script than in the final film) are all signs of the decadence which understandably alarms the *maulvi*'s disciples ... Farid's abandonment of his accountancy studies signals his refusal to be part of an economic system in which humans, too, are simply commodities to be bought and sold. Bettina herself recognises the legitimacy of his search for a more spiritual way of living: 'Who can blame the young for believing in something beside money?' (MSF 53).

Moreover, in the film of *My Son the Fanatic* Parvez is a much more ambivalent representative of liberalism – and thus a less convincing critic of his son's 'fundamentalism' – than in the short story. Parvez is perhaps the most complex and sympathetic character in the film ... In part, of course, Parvez's humanity derives precisely from his contradictions and confusions, which are abundant. To begin with, his seemingly liberal attitudes in fact co-exist with unreconstructed conceptions of family roles. He expects unquestioning obedience from his wife, who even before the arrival of the *maulvi* sometimes behaves like a servant – for example, cleaning Parvez's shoes after his first excursion with Bettina – about whom, of course, Parvez never tells Minoo the full truth ... In fact, the film script makes much more of Minoo's resentment and frustration at the limitations of her life prior to the *maulvi*'s appearance than the film itself. In this context, there is a crucial difference between the script and the film. The latter chooses not to include the scene in which a drunken Parvez attempts to rape his wife. From this point on, in the script at least, Minoo's attitudes harden and her return to a strict form of Islam is seen as a form of self-protection.

Parvez is equally patriarchal towards his son, opportunistically citing the Koran to enforce his authority. Perhaps most ironically, his attitude towards Farid's engagement with Madelaine is based on a traditionalist conception of paternal rights. Threatening to 'break open his face until he obeys' (MSF 30), Parvez complains: 'You go to [others] secretly when I have hand-picked Miss Fingerhut!' (MSF 38). The limitations of his liberalism are equally clear in Parvez's early investigations into his son's increasingly erratic behaviour. During his attempt to establish Farid's 'normality', Parvez expresses the same kind of homophobia as Haroon in *The Buddha*: 'He used to love his clothes ... I was worried he'd gone homo' (MSF 35).

Like Amjad in *Borderline* and Nasser in *Laundrette*, Parvez sees Britain rosily as a place of opportunity, the pursuit of which requires cultural 'roots' to be torn up. As he says to Minoo: 'You're not in the village now, this is England. We have to fit in' (LBT 125). Indeed, Parvez has a blandly affirmative view of the status quo, despite its obvious inequalities. Thus, his attitude towards prostitution is that it is a reflection of 'human nature' (MSF 77), rather than a social problem; and, although exploited himself, Parvez happily takes on the role of pimp for Schitz and his colleagues. As Farid points out, the realities of discrimination mean that in daily life Parvez must rely on obsequiousness to survive. His father's unctuous attitude toward Inspector Fingerhut (in the script, though not the film, Parvez boasts of his police contacts to boost his prestige) and his compliance with Schitz, who consistently patronises Parvez as ' "his" little man' – and even on one occasion assaults him – understandably strengthen Farid's determination not to follow the same path.

Ironically, Parvez's liberal ideals leave him one of the most bereft and isolated figures in Kureishi's recent work, abandoned by both son and wife and alienated from former friends like Fizzy. From one perspective, the sacrifices he has been prepared to make for his beliefs bespeak a nobility of soul which reinforces the authority of his liberal perspectives.

Yet they also bespeak an inability to compromise (or 'fanaticism') which is comparable to his opponents'. As in the ending of *The Black Album*, Parvez's predicament exemplifies Kureishi's conviction of the difficulties of inhabiting the 'in-between' state of cultural hybridity that Farid rails against. Ground between the hostility and indifference of the 'host' society on the one hand and the surly certainties of the *maulvi*'s followers on the other, Parvez is in the end as pathetic as he is tragic. As this might suggest, in contrast to the evasive end of *The Black Album, My Son the Fanatic* is more nuanced and obviously troubled in its treatment of the issues raised by 'the politics of recognition'[8] [a term used to explore the political challenge posed by liberal multiculturalism: the demand of some minority groups, not for individual rights, but for recognition of their rights as communities].[9] □

(Bart Moore-Gilbert, *Hanif Kureishi*, 2001)

Like Moore-Gilbert, Ranasinha begins with an appreciation of Kureishi's more nuanced representation of Islamic fundamentalism in *My Son the Fanatic*.

■ The link between exclusion and Farid's desire to discover his Islamic identity is dramatized more effectively in this filmic text than in *Black Album*. We witness Farid's movement from potential integration (in his engagement to his white girlfriend) to separatism and fundamentalism. The film opens with Farid and his parents at Madeleine's [sic] home at a strained celebration of their engagement. The subtle tensions of this scene are superbly realized. Kureishi's ability to distil the seeds of Farid's subsequent transformation into a single vignette is an example of his particular strength as a screenwriter. In the directions, *'Parvez is both terrified and ecstatic to be there'* (MSF 3). (Although this is not present in the film, Kureishi's text articulates Parvez's resentment that after 'All the years I've lived here, not one single Englishman has invited me to his house' (MSF 65)). *'Farid is cringing ... embarrassed and repelled'* by both his father's attempts to ingratiate himself with Madeleine's snobbish middle-class parents (police chief Inspector Fingerhut and his wife), and by the latter's thinly veiled contempt and displeasure over the match (MSF 6–7). Later Farid refers to this incident when he explains why he broke off his engagement. Farid comments: 'Surely you grasped how ashamed I was, seeing you toadying to Fingerhut. ... Do you think his men care about racial attacks? And couldn't you see how much he hated his daughter being with me, and how repellent ... he found you?' Parvez, incredulous and unable to respond, *'stares at him in shock'* (MSF 68). In this instance, Farid confronts the insidious forms of racism that his father is prepared to overlook. But, on the whole, the dialogues between the two tend to define Parvez as an enlightened, down-to-earth voice of reason, realistic and humane, in contrast to his deluded, indoctrinated and self-righteous son. Significantly, in his preface, Kureishi insists that the young Islamists he interviewed 'were not stupid; many were very intelligent' (MSF, p. viii). Despite this assurance, his 'fundamentalist' Muslim characters never express themselves in anything but clichés, as if to suggest they are simply enunciating internalized propaganda. In Kureishi's screenplay, Farid argues: 'This is the true alternative to empty living from day to day ... in the capitalist dominated world we are suffering from!' (MSF 69) ... ...

... Unlike *Black Album*, where the 'debate' was heavily weighted against the Islamists, *My Son* does not raise Farid's arguments simply to dismiss them. There is a complex irony in the final confrontation between father and son: there is literal 'truth' in Farid's accusations and yet Parvez's incredulous expression suggests he cannot recognize himself as a 'dirty ... pimp who organizes sexual parties' (MSF 117). The audience is presented with irreconcilable 'truths' ...

... The articulation of dissension within the mosque undoes monolithic conceptions of the religious community. One older member voices the intergenerational conflicts within the mosque and the elders' ambivalent response to the younger group:

> These boys are not welcome. They are always arguing with the elders. They think everyone but them is corrupt and foolish. ... They are always fighting for radical actions on many subjects. It is irritating us all here, yaar. But they have something these young people – they're not afraid of the truth. They stand up for things. We never did that. □
> (MSF 58) (Ruvani Ranasinha, *Hanif Kureishi*, 2002)[10]

Most persuasively, Ranasinha sees the film as undermining the simplistic dichotomy found in *The Black Album* between fundamentalism and liberalism through its 'broader critique of patriarchy'.[11] However, backtracking from this reading, she concludes her discussion by suggesting that, despite the effort to avoid popular misconceptions about Muslims, Kureishi does in fact reinforce stereotypes:

■ This work is more nuanced than *Black Album* in that the critique of Muslim men is part of a wider indictment of patriarchal abuse. The misogyny of the Muslim men's brutal harassment of the sex-workers is targeted. The women accuse the Islamists of beating up a 15-year-old member of their group, although Farid denies this. Patriarchal double standards are explored in the hypocrisy of Parvez's fellow taxi-driver Rashid (not one of the fundamentalist group), previously seen (in the original script) groping the women, who then assaults one of them during the demonstration. The film engages only superficially with the oppression of women within the Muslim community: patriarchal attitudes are alluded to in Farid's comment: 'Many [women] lack belief, and therefore reason' (MSF 69). The gender segregation in their home after the *maulvi*'s visit is an example highlighted by many reviewers. In reviewer's shorthand, the *Financial Times* focuses on the impact of the *maulvi*'s visit: 'messianic misogyny bans [banishes] mum to the kitchen' and ignores Kureishi's more subtle, ambivalent take on this.[12] The directions portray the previously isolated Minoo with '*young women in the hijab cooking for the troops outside ... in a comfortable chair, with her feet up, chats to the women, enjoying their company, and the hustle and bustle*' (MSF 106). Another scene makes the significant point that Minoo has not benefited from her husband's westernization: 'If I'd been given your freedom ... think what I would have done ... I would have studied. I would have gone everywhere. And talked ... talked' (MSF 23–4). This is not present in the film version. This suggests that some of the complexity of Kureishi's script is lost in the adaptation.

Rather than limit himself to the liberalism/fundamentalism debate, in *My Son*, Kureishi seems to be interested in examining the sex-workers as an ambivalent site of female exploitation and empowerment, although it is the former that is most convincing. The portrayals of the male clients are trenchant critiques of forms of masculinity. The scenes are explicit and searing. Through Parvez's car mirror we see Bettina's expressionless face beyond disgust while a client reaches orgasm. Bettina is portrayed as defiant and unafraid of her client Schitz, she verbally challenges the way he crudely objectifies her, but the bruises on her back tell another story. Characteristically, Kureishi neither sentimentalizes nor victimizes the women. In the scene of the 'sexual' party Schitz organizes with Parvez's help, Kureishi's directions underline his concern to suggest the shifting power dynamics in these kinds of encounters: '*The two Strippers start trying to undress the Men. One Sikh Businessman has his shirt off and his trousers down. Another man is resisting, as the Stripper sits on his chest and tries pulling his shirt off. The unselfconscious women seem to attack the Men, pulling at them, humiliating them*' (MSF 100). This element is not foregrounded in the film version. This idea is explicitly examined [in] and stems from Kureishi's earlier essay 'Wild Women, Wild Men', a factual account of Zarina and Qumar who made money as 'Pakistani Muslims who stripped and did a lesbian double-act' (MBL 147). Kureishi emphasizes the 'anarchic' element of their show. He observes [that], though the Asian male audience came to see the women, part of the act was to round on the men, 'not to turn them on – to humiliate them and frighten them' (MBL 150). Altogether, the density and complexity of *My Son* spills over its own frame, making this a richer work than *Black Album*. □

(Ruvani Ranasinha, Hanif Kureishi, 2002)[13]

Nonetheless, Ranasinha goes on to argue that because Kureishi only explores 'fundamentalist' forms of Islam, he suggests that religion is the problem and secularity is the solution. Moreover, by setting up an 'irresolvable opposition between community and individual ... there is no representation of the communal that is not fundamentalist'. She goes on to explore how Homi Bhabha's theories of 'subaltern' or marginalized secularism provide a way out of the trap that pits liberal individualism against religious communalism. Bhabha shows how the term 'secularism' can be used in an imperialistic sense in order to characterize migrant communities as 'backward' and 'fundamentalist'; and in a way that fails to recognize that the 'secularism of the privileged' bears no relation to the secularism of the marginalized. Ranasinha argues that *My Son the Fanatic* exemplifies what Bhabha calls the 'limitations of "liberal" secularism' because it does not '*keep faith* with those communities and individuals who have been … excluded from the egalitarian and tolerant values of liberal individualism'.[14]

Although Ranasinha says in her discussion of *The Black Album* and *My Son the Fanatic* that she is 'not suggesting that Kureishi distorts "real" Muslims or fails to provide positive images of a marginalized group',[15] her complaint is that he does not show moderate Muslim believers (in other words, he does not show a positive view of Islam). Ranasinha also claims that Kureishi's earlier films created controversy but his work on Muslim fundamentalists has been uncontested by black critics. However, Maya Jaggi argues that Kureishi fails to 'challenge' the representation of Muslims as 'fanatics and book-burners',[16] while Professor Akbar Ahmed complains of the 'tired stereotypes' of the Muslim community in *My Son the Fanatic*.[17] Harvey Thompson, in an otherwise favourable review, sees the treatment of fundamentalism as the film's main weakness and regrets the caricaturing of Islamic extremists as 'frenzied, almost clownish'.[18] In contrast to Ranasinha, I would argue that academics were, in general, supportive of Kureishi's refusal to produce 'cheering fictions' and positive stereotypes of British Asians in *Laundrette* and *Sammy and Rosie*, but they seem far more disturbed by his refusal to provide positive images of devout British Muslims. In a climate of rising Islamophobia, there is considerable unease about representations of homophobia or misogyny in the Muslim community. Ranasinha believes that the popular hysteria against Muslims makes it imperative to challenge negative views; Kureishi has argued that this should not preclude debate about the negative elements in fundamentalism.

Perhaps because so much time has been spent on the politics of representation, little critical attention has been given to the cinematic qualities of *My Son the Fanatic*. But Sukhdev Sandhu, in an otherwise negative response to Kureishi's midlife works which we will consider in the next chapter, pays a brief tribute to the film:

■ The cinematography is fantastic too. Just as Blackpool was revivified in *Bhaji on the Beach* (1993), here Alan Almond photographs Bradford so

extraordinarily that, unlike the grittily wholemeal Northern landscapes painted by Ken Loach or *The Full Monty* (1997), the city heaves with the visceral dread and sexy menace of 1930s German Expressionist films. □
(Sukhdev Sandhu, untitled review, 1999)[19]

It is not just Bradford which is revivified. Two scenes take place outside the city that is fraught with racial tensions and violence. Bettina takes Parvez to the hills around Bradford, which remind him of where he grew up; for both of them it is an escape, somewhere they can be themselves in a way that is impossible in the tight-knit, provincial city. In Fizzy's restaurant, Bettina is despised as a low-class female; in the working-man's club, Parvez is despised as a 'Paki'. The scenes in the Yorkshire countryside are a breath of fresh air and strikingly original: a setting long associated with the Brontës appears misty and tropical. Multiculturalism has been seen as an urban phenomenon and the countryside the last bastion of Englishness: here, for the first time in British film, cultural hybridity is located in a rural landscape.[20] A form of reverse colonization, perhaps, and also an appropriate background for the odd couple, Bettina and Parvez. As Parvez says hesitantly: 'Friendship is ... good, Minoo. I think it can be found ... in the funniest places.'[21]

Finally, we can return to Moore-Gilbert's appreciation of *My Son the Fanatic* and its engagement with Martin Scorsese's *Taxi Driver*:

■ The transition from short story to film is partly mediated by means of an extended engagement with Martin Scorsese's *Taxi Driver* (1976), a film much admired by Chili in *The Black Album* and which his brother Shahid watches in the hope that it will prepare him for life in London. (In *The Buddha*, Karim attends a season of Scorsese's films at the ICA.) Most obviously, Parvez and Travis Bickle (Robert de Niro) share the same job and both are isolated figures, alienated from their workmates. The principal female role in both films is a prostitute with whom the male lead falls in love and whom he seeks to redeem. Certain characters and incidents in *My Son the Fanatic* have their precedents in Scorsese's work. For example, both films feature an angry hooker who appears at intervals and, early on in each, a prostitute and client have sex in the rear of the cab, causing the respective drivers great concern about their upholstery.

Three of Scorsese's central themes recur in *My Son the Fanatic*. Firstly, *Taxi Driver* emphasises the racial divisions of New York, the city in which it is set. Travis's colleagues are reluctant to drive in Harlem, which Dough-Boy describes as 'fucking Mau-Mau land'. At one point Travis is surrounded by a gang of black youths who attack his car (this perhaps also provides the precedent for *Laundrette*, when Johnny's gang ambush Salim's vehicle). At another moment, Travis picks up a fare (played by Scorsese himself) who is on his way to kill his wife for having an affair with a 'nigger' (compare Parvez and Bettina). Secondly, Scorsese's film is preoccupied by questions of belonging. Travis is a Vietnam veteran who has returned to a city where his sense of displacement generates paranoid tendencies. Thirdly, *Taxi Driver* is also concerned with moral fanaticism. Like Farid rather than Parvez, Travis is disgusted by the degeneracy of New York. In his eyes, it is 'like an open sewer' and he hopes that someone 'will flush it right down the fucking toilet'. Travis, too, sees the sex industry as the most striking symbol of corruption. Those who work in it (Easy apart) are 'scum of the earth' and his 'cleansing' mission is directed at them.

The influence of *Taxi Driver* on *My Son the Fanatic* is also evident at the level of style. Their respective depictions of New York and Bradford are largely naturalistic, with the 'mean streets' of each location foregrounded (more so in Kureishi's script, perhaps, than the film). However, this is counterbalanced by an eye for the beauty of urbanscapes in each work. When Parvez drives at night, his city is often made hauntingly lovely by the distorting lens of his rain-swept windscreen. (Travis's night drives produce similar effects, making *Taxi Driver*, too, a kind of nocturne.) In both works, the sound-track is critically important. However, whereas Scorsese relies on an at times enervatingly moody and downbeat jazz track, Kureishi draws on a range of genres (including jazz – Parvez is obsessed by Louis Armstrong), in the manner of *London Kills Me*, reflecting the more varied tonal palette of *My Son the Fanatic* compared with *Taxi Driver*.

Despite the serious issues it addresses, *My Son the Fanatic* is a much more tender, human and humorous film than the portentously sombre *Taxi Driver*, perhaps ultimately because of the different national, social and cultural contexts in which each work is situated. There is genuine comedy in the scene where Parvez discovers the *maulvi* surreptitiously watching TV cartoons, and in his anxious search for evidence of his son's substance abuse. Even as their relationship declines, there are moments of real poignancy between Parvez and Minoo, for example when he beguiles her into laughing at his imitation of the *maulvi*. Such touches help to make *My Son the Fanatic* possibly the most satisfying and complex of Kureishi's films at the aesthetic and psychological levels and the most nuanced and penetrating in its cultural politics. Less sentimental than *Laundrette*, less fractured than *Sammy and Rosie*, more engaging than *London Kills Me*, *My Son the Fanatic* thoroughly vindicated Kureishi's return to scriptwriting. □

(Bart Moore-Gilbert, *Hanif Kureishi*, 2001)[22]

The film has all the qualities of Kureishi's best work: the humour and humanity, the ability to surprise and yet be credible, the exploration of complex human lives in a particular historical moment. It shows what culture can do: 'if both racism and fundamentalism are diminishers of life – reducing others to abstractions – the effort of culture must be to keep others alive by describing and celebrating their intricacy, by seeing that this is not only of value but a necessity'.[23] As Parvez says poignantly to his son: 'There are many ways of being a good man.'[24]

My Son the Fanatic offers another version of the odd couple, used in *Sammy and Rosie* and *Laundrette*, and also points to Kureishi's middle-period meditations on adultery, and falling out of love. 'My Son the Fanatic' was included in *Love in a Blue Time* because it is a story about a man in love with a woman who is not his wife.[25] Like many of the characters discussed in the following chapter, Parvez is caught between family and the hope of satisfaction with another: 'What else is there for me, yaar, but sitting behind the wheel without tenderness? That's it for me, is it, until I drop dead, and not another human touch?' (MSF 112). Kureishi's midlife work shows a continued interest in desire but a diminished concern with the complications of class and race.

CHAPTER EIGHT

'Should I Stay or Should I Go?': *Love in a Blue Time* (1997), *Intimacy* (1998), *Sleep with Me* (1999) and *Midnight All Day* (1999)

In these middle works, Kureishi abandons the picaresque and begins, as Karim would say, to 'search the inner room' (BS 3). Where earlier work had explored class, race, fucking and farce, as his protagonists zigzagged across London looking for trouble, these are more often introverted tales, confessional monologues, writing from the couch. As Jay says: 'Freud was our new father, as we turned inwards' (I 54). This change in direction may, in part, have resulted from the fact that Kureishi considered he had said all he wanted to (for the moment) on class and race, while at the same time his view of life seems to have darkened. Earlier works have been considered through the lens of postcolonial theory; critics tend to view this work in the context of the 'male testimonial', and literature which explores new forms of masculinity in a post-feminist era. In his own life, he was preoccupied by the difficulties of relationships and his fictional exploration of emotional upheaval can be seen as part of a widespread change in domestic values: 'a new restlessness' (I 100). If, despite the restiveness, there is an overall impression of stasis and claustrophobia, it is because many of the characters seem trapped by domesticity, torn between the desire to go and the responsibility to stay. These characters exist in a narrower social context than in his earlier fictions, with few found on sink estates or run-down squats. Although they are not all affluent media types, many resemble those whom Karim turns away from in disgust in *The Buddha*: 'I saw how much was enervated and useless in them. What passion or desire or hunger did they have as they lounged in their London living-rooms?' (B 225). There is still desire but it is often morbid, perceived by the characters themselves as sickness. And London here is no longer a playground, a theatre, a place of opportunity, but 'a city of love vampires, turning from person to person, hunting the one who will make a difference' (LBT 142).

Despite the change in tone, these stories continue Kureishi's preoccupation with what kind of values we want to live by in our personal lives. In *The Buddha*, the son watches with horror and fascination as his father leaves his mother; in these stories it is more often the father watching the devastation caused to his wife and sons as he walks out on them. There are both continuities and substantial shifts between the early and middle works, then, but perhaps the most profound change is that Kureishi used to be perceived as radical and subversive, writing from a subaltern perspective, but is now more often considered to belong to the dominant group: male, middle-class and middle-aged. Kureishi himself, however, sees his midlife work differently: not as a chronicle of domestic misery, but as a challenge to emotional orthodoxies. *Intimacy*, he said, transgressed 'the Koran of the middle classes'; by portraying a man walking out on his partner, he had violated 'a sacred taboo'.[1]

According to Kureishi, his focus on relationships rather than society is a reflection of the 'politically torpid' times, but he also maintains that there is still a political dimension:

■ If our age seems 'unideological' compared to the period between the mid-1960s and mid-1980s; if Britain seems pleasantly hedonistic and politically torpid, it might be because politics has moved inside, into the body. The politics of personal relationships, of private need, of gender, marriage, sexuality, the place of children, have replaced that of society, which seems uncontrollable. □

(Hanif Kureishi, 'Filming *Intimacy*', 2002)[2]

In addition, Kureishi has said that not only is there 'less social stuff' in his work now but that he is also aiming for more experimental forms and a more economical use of language:

■ I think that often does happen to artists: you become very interested in economy, doing things as economically as you can, and the wrong word, or too many words, offends you. I think you look for new styles. I am much more interested in a piece of writing that is broken up, fragmented, unfinished ... You show it to people and they tell you that you can't publish it as it is not 'written' yet. But it is the fact that it is *not* written that interests me. Then, to follow through, you may be moving away from the public. I guess my writing has always been quite conventional. I start at the beginning and move all the way through – just like the novels I read as I grew up – or the way I thought they worked. But now I am much more interested in the experimental, not for its own sake but because I like the look of the words on the page in that way – the gaps, the unfinished bits ... It is quite difficult, particularly when you are an established writer, to decide how far you can go in terms of your relationship with the audience. I liked *Intimacy* being a rough book in that sense; the cruelty, the fragmentation, the lack of smoothing out or over. People have said the book is so cruel and horrible, the people in it are so nasty and I say 'well, that's what it's like.' I wanted the book to be an experience. If I wrote a book now about a relationship that split up ten years ago, it would probably be overworked and too thought-out. I wanted to capture the roughness. The style you use has to reflect what is going on in the mind at the time of writing. □

(Kureishi interview with Nahem Yousaf, 2002)[3]

Perhaps it was this 'roughness' which contributed to the perception that *Intimacy* was not a novel but a public exposure of private misery.

The question raised here about 'how far you can go with your reader' is an interesting one, which arguably has greater relevance for a self-consciously autobiographical writer such as Kureishi. Readers' and critics' involvement in Kureishi's work is often deeply personal. In 'The Body', the writer Adam is ironic about his biographer's belief that he knows the writer's life better than Adam himself. While this may be an illusion common to biographers, it also seems to indicate the kind of investment that readers have made in Kureishi as an author. Amitava Kumar's memoir, *Bombay London New York* (2002), has a chapter called 'My Hanif Kureishi Life'. For Sukhdev Sandhu, Kureishi is almost a fallen idol. In the days of *Laundrette* and *The Buddha* Kureishi was 'mainlining the energies of metropolitan youth'; he had 'assumed almost iconic status for many second-generation Asians in this country' who saw 'their own ambitions and wanderlust embodied by Kureishi's characters'. It was as if he was writing Sandhu's life as well, or his life as he wanted it to be. But Sandhu lambasts Kureishi for slipping into sociologese, didacticism and sluggish prose with *Intimacy*. Sandhu is so enraged he does not know whether to condemn Kureishi's middle works for the supposed 'sea change' from optimism and the possibilities of transformation to stagnation and self-recrimination, or to crucify him for 'rehash[ing] the same themes he's been peddling for years' of 'running from domesticity, lusting after an ill-defined sense of change'.[4] It is clear from the intensity of Sandhu's response that only a writer who had meant so much could have disappointed him so bitterly. It perhaps also shows how readers want writers to keep giving them more of what they got before; not necessarily the same themes but the same affirmations.

The main controversy in the press reviews of these middle works stemmed from the widespread belief that Kureishi had used elements of his own life, or rather the lives of those connected with him, without integrity. These texts, in particular *Intimacy*, have been read as directly autobiographical, mirror images of his own relationships. The basic autobiographical facts are summarized by Moore-Gilbert:

> ■ in 1993, Kureishi became the father of twins and the following year turned forty. He became increasingly unhappy in his personal life and in 1995 began a relationship with Monique Proudlove, with whom he had a son in 1998. The acrimonious parting from the mother of his twin boys and partner of seven years, Tracey Scoffield, received a lot of unfavourable media coverage which, it could be argued, unfairly influenced the reception of much of his subsequent work.[5] □

It is with this background in mind that we can look at the reviews of these books before going on to the more considered responses of both Moore-Gilbert and Ranasinha.

But first it might be useful to think about the relationship between life and literature, since this has been the most controversial aspect of these middle works. Auto/biographical fiction, particularly the use of other people as fictional models, has always provoked a heated response. Dickens never seems to have understood that his friends would object to seeing themselves, as they thought, travestied in the pages of his latest bestseller. Serial publication even allowed readers to object at the time, hence the change in characterization of Miss Mowcher in *David Copperfield* (1849–50) from villainous, to doughty, dwarf, after the real-life source threatened to sue Dickens for libel. James Joyce, despite the modernist mantra of impersonality, was a relentlessly auto/biographical writer, whose friends dreaded the moment he took out his notebook. Nora Barnacle, reading about her life with Joyce in 'The Dead' (1907), which later became the concluding story in *Dubliners* (1914), was understandably hurt and angry that the intimacies of their relationship were on public display, but few would now wish the story had not been written. Despite the pain that may have been caused to individuals, *David Copperfield* and *Dubliners*, to name but two auto/biographically inspired fictions, have survived as classics. Perhaps it is not possible to make judgements about whether writers should use the lives around them in a way that makes those lives uncomfortably visible; however, despite the obvious alibi – 'it's fiction, stupid' – writers who do so must acknowledge that they are in a privileged position, with the power to trap others in their descriptions.

Closer to home, Kureishi has said he was influenced by the confessional monologue, which achieved its contemporary prominence first in America with works by J. D. Salinger, Sylvia Plath (1932–63), Philip Roth and Saul Bellow (born 1915).[6] If nothing else, Roth's *I Married a Communist* (1998), in part a response to his ex-wife's memoir, Claire Bloom's *Leaving a Doll's House* (1996); and Bellow's *Ravelstein* (2000), suggest that the genre has a distinguished pedigree. The blurring of autobiography and fiction emerges as a preoccupation in these stories: ' "Why did you take parts of me and put them in a book?" ' asks one of the characters of her former lover in 'That Was Then' (MAD 74). 'Sucking Stones', from the same collection, portrays a successful novelist as smug and calculating, interested in others only as material. Indeed, an anxiety about this kind of exploitation has often been evident in Kureishi's work. When Changez forbids Karim ' "to enter me by the back door and portray me in your play" ' (BS 185), the language suggests that this is a form of violation. Moreover, Karim recognizes that, having used Changez, 'there would be debts to pay' (BS 231). The payment exacted from Kureishi after the publication of *Intimacy* took the form of vitriolic attacks from the press and public criticism from some members of his family.

LOVE IN A BLUE TIME

The ten stories in this collection are about desire, love and hate; several involve the break-up of relationships. 'Lately' shows Lisa deciding to leave Rocco in order to live: ' "to learn to sing and dance. To paint. To row on the river. To play guitars and drums. I can't wait to begin my life!" ' (LBT 172). In the last story, flies infest the homes of loveless couples but the misery is smothered by silence. There is bitterness and betrayal: in 'D'Accord Baby', for example, a male character seeks revenge on his wife's lover by sleeping with his daughter. According to Jenny Turner in the *Independent*, 'there are few sights in the world less appealing than the sort of men Kureishi writes about in this book'. The title story portrays the rich, ageing bohemian lecher, Roy, and the poor alcoholic 'genius maudit', Jimmy. As Kureishi acknowledges: 'There are few creatures more despised than middle-aged men with strong desires, and desire renews itself each day, returning like a recurring illness, crying out, more life, more!' (LBT 144).

According to Turner, the most disturbing story is 'The Tale of a Turd' in which a 44-year-old roué, at dinner with the parents of his 18-year-old girlfriend, boasts: 'I've been injecting my little girl. It breaks my heart but I've got, maybe, two years with her before she sees I can't be helped and she will pass beyond me into worlds I cannot enter.' For Turner, this is like Milton's Satan: the unforgivable sin is the agony of despair. But yet she finds it hard to sympathize with a man whose bitterness is like the 'useless floating waste' evoked by the title. Turner says that she searched the stories for some evidence of self-awareness, or real interest in one's children or wife, but in vain. She concludes that the protagonists' greed, myopia and narcissism are entirely 'unredeemed'. Turner concludes, however, that the polished and technically competent writing makes this book full of unpleasantly shallow characters seem curiously pleasant to read.[7]

Much of the pleasure of reading this collection, as Dr Robbie Clipper Sethi points out, is due to Kureishi's characteristic wit: 'For years women had fallen at Jimmy's feet; now he collapsed at theirs' (LBT 9). Roy suggests, 'it's easy to underestimate how casual and reassuring married love can be. You can talk about other things while you're doing it' (LBT 23). But the wit is sour: in 'Nightlight' a divorced character recalls trying to be 'the sort of man she might countenance. He wept at every opportunity, and communicated with animals whenever he found them' (LBT 141). Clipper Sethi also finds, in 'Nightlight', 'a portrayal of loneliness and desire, surrounding a scene straight from Kureishi's absurdist theater, in which an unnamed man leaves his wife of ten years, picking up the television on his way out, because he must take something, and his computer is attached to too many wires' (LBT 143). Moreover, not all the stories are about marital break-ups. According to Clipper Sethi, 'With your Tongue Down my Throat' 'develops the best of Kureishi's take on Pakistani and English youth culture' and 'We're not Jews' shows 'the prejudice against Pakistanis in England and an English woman who has married outside of her English working-class origins'. 'My Son the Fanatic' 'offers Ali as Kureishi's Muslim "Eli the Fanatic" (1959), after Philip Roth's story about the difference between secular and fully practicing members of a diasporic religion'. Given the variety of stories, Clipper Sethi concludes that the collection 'is a treat'.[8]

It is interesting to note that, unusually for Kureishi, two of the stories in this collection have literary models: the reworking of Roth in 'My Son the Fanatic' and the recourse to Chekhov's 'The Duel' in 'Lately'; while 'Nightlight' and 'The Flies' both carry epigraphs (from Robert Louis Stevenson (1850–94) and Italo Calvino (born 1923), respectively). This gives Love in a Blue Time a greater feeling of literariness than any of his previous prose. Indeed, Andrew Gallix refers to 'The Flies' in terms of the Austrian modernist author Franz Kafka (1883–1924) meeting the American 'Beat' writer William Burroughs (1914–97) through the French existentialist philosopher, novelist and playwright Jean-Paul Sartre (1905–80), with a little of the American postmodernist William H. Gass (born 1924) 'thrown in for good measure'.[9] At the same time as the impression of 'roughness', of not being 'overworked', of which Kureishi speaks in the interview quoted above, there is a contrasting sense of these stories as self-consciously constructed literary texts.

Most reviewers concentrate on what they perceive to be Kureishi's dissection of the hollowness of conventional relationships. Charles

Taylor, although not wholly enthusiastic, praises Kureishi for being contemporary and cool. He speculates that it is Kureishi's affinity for pop music that allows him to evoke a period though its style, in a way that makes the work of other contemporary British writers look old hat. As Taylor suggests, Kureishi can size up those who succeeded in the Thatcher era in one paragraph:

■ He had lived through an age when men and women with energy and ruthlessness but without much ability or persistence excelled. And even though most of them had gone under, their ignorance had confused Roy, making him wonder whether the things he had striven to learn, and thought of as 'culture,' were irrelevant. Everything was supposed to be the same: commercials, Beethoven's late quartets, pop records, shopfronts, Freud, multi-coloured hair. Greatness, comparison, value, depth: gone, gone, gone. Anything could give some pleasure; he saw that. But not everything provided the sustenance of a deeper understanding. □ (LBT 16)

But Taylor concludes that the way in which Kureishi 'reduces character to a few nasty brushstrokes' in this paragraph epitomizes the collection's weakness.[10]

In addition to the commercialization of culture that Charles Taylor notes, these stories also take place against a backdrop of moral uncertainty. Roy, for example, 'no longer had any clue what social or political obligations he had, nor much idea where such ideas should come from' (LBT 9). It is one of the ironies of the collection that the characters flounder in cultural, moral and political relativism, where in earlier works so much energy came from kicking against the established rules and categories.

While reviews in England and the USA have been mixed, the response in Europe has been more appreciative. One measure of a work's value may be its capacity to inspire other artists. In June 2003, the Italian Institute in London staged an exhibition of paintings by the Italian-born artist, Serena Nono (born 1964), based on the story 'Nightlight' in *Love in a Blue Time*, in which a couple who meet by chance spend Wednesday afternoons making love without talking. The same story and the novella *Intimacy* were the inspiration for Patrice Chereau's film *Intimacy* (2001), which starred Kerry Fox and Mark Rylance, and won the Golden Bear award at that year's Berlin Film Festival. However, since Kureishi did not actually write the screenplay, we will focus on *Intimacy*, the book.[11]

INTIMACY

The most controversial of these middle works has undoubtedly been *Intimacy*, the story of a disgruntled screenwriter, Jay, who decides one night to leave his partner, Susan, and his children, partly in the hope of being with his younger girlfriend, Nina. Kureishi has said in an interview that he feels the book has been misunderstood because it has been read as a memoir rather than a novel:

> ■ I think some reviewers were caught up in the furore around *Intimacy* and so haven't yet looked fairly and squarely at the book. Nor have they yet taken into consideration the fact that I was aware I was playing a literary game. I consciously wrote *Intimacy* in the form of a confession and was also aware that it might be read as 'Hanif Kureishi telling the truth about a relationship break-up.' That too is a literary construct: it is artificial. All of one's work is autobiographical to the extent that it reflects one's interests. But the book hasn't yet been read as a move in a literary game which is quite disappointing. It operates as a construct – written in the first person, constructed as a confession – and this is the basis on which it should begin to be evaluated. I wanted a book people could play with in that way. It is a text, not me. I am not the text. □
> (Hanif Kureishi interview with Nahem Yousaf, 2002)[12]

But first we had better take a brief sampling of those reviews in which Kureishi was most definitely seen as the text and look at one example of the outrage caused by the infamous 'fuck-and-freezing-sea' sentence. David Sexton, in the *Evening Standard*, categorized *Intimacy* as a flagrant example of the fashion for misogyny, displayed also in John Updike's *Toward the End of Time* (1997), Howard Jacobson's *No More Mister Nice Guy* (1998) and Tim Parks's *Europa* (1997). He notes that misogyny is nothing new but argues that 'these novels are different. They are written by men who did not appear previously to hate women at all. On the contrary. They are sexy novelists. But they are sexy novelists who have aged and have stopped bothering to mask their underlying feelings.' Sexton singles out Kureishi as the worst offender of the four, observing that *Intimacy* has been highly controversial. Kureishi's family complained that he misrepresented them; and his former partner, Tracey Scoffield, confirmed that the book is about their relationship. According to Scoffield, to call *Intimacy* a novel is 'total hypocrisy. You may as well call it a fish.' Sexton also maintains that Kureishi has betrayed men in general; all those who are not like him, or his alter ego, Jay. Sexton asserts that the misogynistic attitudes expressed in the novel are endorsed by the author. He cites as examples Jay's abuse of his mother as 'inert and obese … a lump of living death', and his reference to his partner's 'fat, red weeping face'. Sexton considers that Jay is still pathetically hankering after the 1960s and 1970s, when he imagined he belonged 'to other young people, and to some sort of oppositional movement', but to Sexton, Jay is simply obsessed with sex. 'The world is a skirt I want to lift up', Jay says, which Sexton regards as a 'jerk's creed'. Sexton strongly objects to Jay's assertion that 'There are some fucks for which a person would have their partner and children drown in a freezing sea.' However, Sexton fails to observe that this statement is carefully non-gender-specific and therefore cannot be regarded as misogyny.

Finally, Sexton argues that although a good novel can be written about a bad man, the problem with *Intimacy* is that it has been seen by women as representative of all men. Her refers to Julie Myerson's review in the *Mail on Sunday*, which praised it as 'by far the most astute and painful dissection of male sexual restlessness that I've read'. This provokes Sexton to assert that men should state emphatically that 'Hanif Kureishi, *ce n'est pas moi* [he isn't me].'[13]

It might seem from Sexton's review that what he most dislikes is not misogyny in itself but the possibility that he might be mistaken for a misogynist. Jay is one character, in whom some men may recognize certain aspects of themselves, but he is not representative of all men. Ironically, this recalls earlier debates about Kureishi's ability to 'speak for' British Asians. But just as he then disavowed any intention of speaking on behalf of others; he is not, with due respect to Sexton, attempting now to 'speak for' men. Sexton's review also exposes the way this novel provoked intensely personal responses, which virtually precluded any possibility of rational debate.

Women readers have in general been more sympathetic to *Intimacy* than male reviewers, and not necessarily because they prefer misogyny to be out in the open. Like Julie Myerson in the *Mail on Sunday*, Suzanne Moore in the *Guardian* has applauded the novel as an example of 'male honesty',[14] while Sylvia Brownrigg in *The Village Voice* sees it as exposing misogyny and the dilemmas of a generation. She considers that Jay's selfishness and hostility are brutally exposed, and she particularly relishes the scene in which he masturbates into his wife's underwear while fantasizing about his girlfriend. According to Brownrigg, Susan is an 'obviously blameless woman' and Jay's view of her is distorted by dislike. She quotes Kureishi's belief that falling out of love is as much an illusion as falling in love; that hate can be as 'intoxicating' as desire. Apparently, Kureishi at one time considered calling the novel *Animosity*.

Brownrigg goes on to speculate whether the novel can be considered misogynist. She concludes that it could only seem so if Jay's hatred of Susan is taken as a 'general animus against women'. She contrasts Kureishi's clear-eyed view of men walking out on women with Nick Hornby's reassuring but less realistic nice guys who wind up doing the right thing. She quotes Jay's dilemma: 'Are you an optimistic man because you ran away or are you a coward because you ran away? Who would decide?' And concludes that these are the male doubts of

Kureishi's generation.[15] Similarly, Polly Rance has argued: 'No one comes out of this novel looking worse than the protagonist himself. This is a book of unnerving honesty; disturbing, powerful and intensely personal, a novel that runs on the aggressive energy of self-loathing.'[16]

But there are some discordant notes in the female choir, perhaps most notably by Laura Cumming, who describes *Intimacy* as pathological. According to Cumming's review in the *Guardian*, Susan is a put-upon wife, written off in the novel as a 'bitch', and Cumming is not convinced of the narrator's integrity. Jay writes: 'I want an absolute honesty that doesn't merely involve saying how awful one is.' But this sentence only exposes the novel's 'bad faith', according to Cumming, since Jay's self-reproach is invariably bound up with self-congratulation. Jay's references to his Beethoven CDs and the 'volume of Strindberg' he had been reading strike Cumming as cultural posturing, and she scoffs at his parting shot at Susan: 'If she has any flair she will slash my Vivienne Westwood jacket.' Instead of genuine sadness about leaving, Cumming finds only bathos. She considers *Intimacy* to be a lazy book: the attacks on Thatcher have been done before, while the sexual adventures are narrated without vitality. She disagrees with every proposition in the novel and utterly refutes the possibility, suggested by the references to Sartre, that Jay's act is an attempt to achieve existential freedom.[17]

Since the initial furore, there has been time for a more considered evaluation. Moore-Gilbert suggests that a useful context in which to examine *Intimacy* might be that of the 'male testimonial', and he cites *Fever Pitch* (1992) by Nick Hornby (born 1957), *Cock and Bull* (1992) by Will Self (born 1961), *Man and Boy* (1999) by Tony Parsons (born 1955) and *Mr Commitment* (2000) by Mike Gayle (born 1970) as other examples of fictional explorations of contemporary masculinity in crisis. Moore-Gilbert also argues that '*Intimacy* draws heavily on the conventions of feminist testimonial and fiction', in particular *The Golden Notebook* (1962) by Doris Lessing (born 1919), which he believes 'was obviously on Kureishi's mind'.[18] Although Moore-Gilbert provides a detailed comparison between the two works, Kureishi has said that 'Doris Lessing had no influence on me.'[19] The most convincing aspect of Moore-Gilbert's argument is his emphasis on the 'counter-perspective' which comes from Susan. As he says, she emerges from Jay's account as 'anything but the monster he claims she is'. He continues:

■ [S]he provides one of the most penetrating critiques of the attitudes informing Jay's behaviour although, interestingly, its terms of reference are not gender-specific. As he recalls:

She talks of a Thatcherism of the soul that imagines that people are not dependent on one another. In love, these days, it is a free market;

browse and buy, pick and choose, rent and reject, as you like. There's no sexual and social security; everyone has to take care of themselves, or not. Fulfilment, self-expression and 'creativity' are the only values. (I 52–3) □   (Bart Moore-Gilbert, *Hanif Kureishi*, 2001)[20]

Accordingly, for Moore-Gilbert, the jury is out on whether Kureishi is guilty of misogyny or not. He finds evidence in *Intimacy* that it is a critique of patriarchy but, equally, there are symptoms of the hostility to feminism that Susan Faludi exposed in *Backlash* (1991). He concludes:

■ *Intimacy* might thus be taken as partial corroboration of certain 'post-feminist' works, such as Susan Faludi's *Stiffed* and Ros Coward's *Sacred Cows* (both 1999), which diverge significantly from their authors' earlier work in criticising feminism from the point of view of its failure to register sufficiently some of the consequences of the Women's Movement's successes for contemporary men. □
(Bart Moore-Gilbert, *Hanif Kureishi*, 2001)[21]

Ranasinha agrees that Susan emerges from the text as a likeable character but finds Nina less convincing, little more than a 'shadowy figure of male fantasy ... eager to meet all Jay's sexual demands'.[22] Like Moore-Gilbert, she argues that 'Kureishi's ironic distance makes *Intimacy* ambivalent reading', with Jay constructed as both 'villain' ('selfish, cruel and immature') and 'hero' ('courageous enough to leave', 'to defy bourgeois morality').[23] Observing that Jay is positioned as part of the 'new restlessness' (I 100), she goes on to ask : 'To what extent is Kureishi's work a justification of "older" forms of male selfishness, need for freedom and avoidance of commitment, repackaged as "a new restlessness" and "new" masculinity?':

■ Kureishi's novella and stories both parody and exonerate his 'privileged and spoilt' derailed generation: the 'inheritors of the freedoms won by our seditious elders in the late sixties' (I 53). Kureishi invokes post-sixties freedoms to give a socio-political framework and philosophy for self-indulgence. Defined in contrast to their predecessors, this generation is not constrained by social or religious scruples. Jay declares: 'I am of a generation that believes in the necessity of satisfying oneself' (I 60) ... 'All of me, along with the age, stood against compulsion' (I 69). Kureishi defines the contradictions of this generation of 'new' men shaped by feminism and sexual politics. Displaced from the dominant role their fathers occupied, 'where the man had the power and had to be protective' (I 43), they are intimidated by female strength and resentful of women's refusal to fulfil all their sexual demands. Nurtured on therapy, psychoanalysis and 'the ungovernable desires of the unconscious' (I 74) – 'Freud was our new father, as we turned inwards' (I 54) – they are in touch with their feelings to the point of self-obsession. We see flashes of a male backlash against feminists: mocking references to the 'screeching of feminists' and 'she thinks she's a feminist, but she's just bad-tempered' (I 79) ... Kureishi maps relationships between a confused generation of men and their more capable and pragmatic female partners, which may appear to reflect female empowerment, but actually constrains women, allowing their male partners to be wayward and immature. Moreover, in *Intimacy* Susan's capabilities are used to demonize her. □

(Ruvani Ranasinha, *Hanif Kureishi*, 2002)[24]

Ranasinha goes on to argue that Kureishi 'privilege[s] Jay's individualism'. Although we are allowed to see an alternative morality to the narrator's in his friend, Asif's, acceptance of obligations and responsibilities, 'ultimately Asif's disapproval of "the modern way" implies that he articulates values of an outdated era (I 100)'. In answer to her question about how 'new' is this crisis in masculinity, Ranasinha responds: 'Kureishi's ability to give one couple's failed relationship such resonance gives his work contemporary relevance.'[25] Her comment on the novel's reception is also pertinent: where once Kureishi was accused of using his cultural background without integrity, he is now accused of indulging in 'marital revenge rhetoric'; where once he was on trial for 'internalized racism', the charge is now 'misogyny'.[26]

Indeed, most critical readings of *Intimacy* are political, and/or biographical, rather than aesthetic. This makes Amitava Kumar's interpretation particularly interesting. He does not simply respond to the novel but explores its complex effect on the reader:

■ Kureishi's prose in the book was lucid and elegant. Jay was a mixture of doubt and desire. As a result, the clarity of the writing produced a strange effect, a tense sense of disquiet ... [O]n that night, he wanted to record what he was feeling as he went through his separation, because he desired 'an absolute honesty that doesn't merely involve saying how awful one is.' In other words, he wanted to achieve an intimacy with himself at the very moment he had become certain that he had lost every shred of it with his wife. Perhaps the tension that the reader experienced while reading the novella was that it mirrored the disturbing closeness that lies between the intimacy of love and, on the other hand, the intimacy of the act of infidelity. □

(Amitava Kumar, *Bombay London New York*, 2002)[27]

The reader's ambivalence towards the novella enacts the ambivalence of intimacy itself, as we both seek it and draw away from it in equal measure. Kumar argues that 'Kureishi's elaboration of the idea of sexuality and desire is that it comes into play in his work not as nostalgic, return-to-sixties rebellion against bourgeois norms but as a way of coming to grips with the contemporary landscape that is mined with politics.' For Kumar, 'Kureishi's lucid lesson is that our desires, even when they are opposed to our more austere orders, are inextricably bound in conflict ... . [It is not] a case of choosing between promiscuity and commitment. Rather, we learn our choices are threatened by, and even drawn toward, their opposites.'[28]

SLEEP WITH ME

Set over the course of a summer weekend in the country, Kureishi's first play for 15 years (directed by Anthony Page for the National Theatre) could almost be called a dramatization of *Intimacy*. Although the central characters have different names, now Stephen and Julie, they undergo the same dilemmas. There are also additional characters: the au pair, Lorraine, Stephen's former lover, Sophie, and her old leftie husband, Barrie; and two friends, Charles, and media mogul, Russell.

The critical reception was hostile. Michael Billington in the *Guardian* found the characters a 'dislikeable bunch', whose sell-out to success and emotional confusion left him cold. The characters of Barrie and Sophie (a teacher and social worker), who live 'outside the media goldfish bowl' are written off as stereotypes. The play's treatment of relationships is scathingly dismissed as Mills and Boon; for example, when Stephen's mistress tells him, 'You like being loved ... but you are afraid to love back.' And when Barry complains about his wife's infidelity, 'He touched the parts of you I thought were mine', Billington is reminded of 'a peculiarly potent lager'. He concludes that the characters' tendency to dissolve in tears belongs in a Barbara Cartland novel.[29] Paul Taylor, in the *Independent*, was equally unimpressed. Noting the similarities to the novel *Intimacy*, he suggests that the Chekhovian device of gathering a group in the country 'would appear to be a response to the charges of solipsism which the novel invited'. He assumes that the dramatic form was intended to be more objective, to include a wider range of perspectives; but he considers that Kureishi fails because, unlike Chekhov, he is incapable of 'impartial compassion'. For example, Taylor finds the wife to be neurotic, bossy and wholly unappealing. He cites her belief that 'the family is the point you can live from' but he concludes that she makes this sound like someone offering a 'straitjacket' as a means of 'self-development'.[30]

Although the reviews of *Sleep with Me* were almost uniformly negative, audiences seemed to enjoy it, particularly the farcical elements and the witty one-liners. Before the production, Kureishi described the play to Moore-Gilbert as 'Joe Orton meets Chekhov' (the playwrights whose early influence on Kureishi we looked at in chapter one) and Moore-Gilbert suggests that the reason for the play's failure is that these influences 'work against each other'. As he says: '[s]uch tensions are most obvious in the area of characterisation, where the tendency of ... Orton towards caricature conflicts with the emphasis on psychological depth and moral complexity in Chekhov'.[31] Moore-Gilbert concludes his discussion with Robert's remark in 'Midnight All Day': 'the theatre is not a profession you can turn to at will' (MAD 46).[32] It should be added, however, that Kureishi is returning to the theatre in 2004 with a play called *When the Night Begins*.

MIDNIGHT ALL DAY

The title for this collection of ten stories perhaps recalls *Good Morning, Midnight* (1939) by Jean Rhys (1894–1979) – itself a quotation from the poet Emily Dickinson (1830–86) – and, like much of Jean Rhys, it is not a book you would read in bed to cheer yourself up. One story, 'Four Blue Chairs', celebrates a new love, and one, 'Penis' (like the shaggy bog story, 'The Tale of a Turd', in *Love in a Blue Time*), is a surreal fable; but the other eight are tales of adultery, separation, or difficult relationships. There is no celebration of love across racial and class barriers, as in so much of Kureishi's earlier work, but a sense of 'love as the exchange of problems' (MAD 178).

Like *Love in a Blue Time* and *Intimacy*, reviews of this collection have focused mainly on Kureishi's portrayal of masculinity, although Paul Binding finds the female characters warm and convincing. Binding begins his review in the *Independent* with a quotation from 'Morning in the Bowl of Night': 'From a certain point of view the world was ashes. You could also convert it to dust by burning away all hope, appetite, desire. But to live was, in some sense, to believe in the future. You couldn't keep returning to the same dirty place' (MAD 203). Binding notes that Kureishi's male protagonists are 'subtly differentiated' but that they share an awareness of the causes, both cultural and individual, of the dilemmas from which they are nonetheless unable to escape. Although they are intelligent and sensitive, they have difficulty dealing with the complications brought about by sexual desire. Binding observes that nearly all the stories are about separations or new relationships, and he singles out 'That Was Then' as a particularly subtle exploration of the complications of desire. He also applauds the sensitivity with which Kureishi represents his female protagonists; particularly in 'Girl' and 'Sucking Stones'. In the latter, a frustrated writer and single mother, Marcia, hopes for encouragement from a famous novelist, who is only interested in her as material. Marcia decides to give up writing, hoping that 'after a time there might be new things'.[33]

Binding praises Kureishi's disciplined prose, 'reminiscent of the French tradition', but James Hopkin is less convinced. He considers that the stories are too introspective and unleavened by humour; and that the attempt to achieve simplicity sometimes results in the merely simplistic. The main problem for Hopkin is Kureishi's inability to capture profound themes of love and loss in 'slick pop prose'. He observes that there are very few metaphors or similes in the book and suggests that this may be symptomatic of Kureishi's alienated view, which registers only fragmentation instead of likeness. Hopkin concludes that Kureishi's work is now 'miniaturist' rather than 'minimalist'.[34]

But the critic who misses Kureishi's 'bodyrocking brio' most is Sukhdev Sandhu, who deplores the subject matter and the style in equal measure:

■ Where once Kureishi's heroes were scrambling towards material and creative prosperity, they now tend to dwell on the right side of affluence. Squatting and communal living have been replaced by luxury pads and invitations to private parties at the ICA. They run film production companies, lecture on human rights in the States, write zeitgeisty novels. They holiday in the Hamptons. They eat humous and florentines. When they feel intellectually undernourished they turn to Nietzsche and Pascal rather than to Kerouac and Eldridge Cleaver. And when they feel a bit rotten, as they often do, they like to compare themselves to figures in paintings by Lucian Freud. Like anorexic film stars and rock musicians writing their not-so-difficult fourth album, it appears that Kureishi's characters are suffering from a low-key form of Paradise Syndrome.

Relationships have become the main source of angst. Some, like Marcia in 'Sucking Stones', who has regular assignations with a Bulgarian former Olympic cyclist in his shabby bedsit, are stuck in company they're not sure they want to keep any longer. Others, like Rob, a successful working-class actor from South London, are distraught that their partners are about to leave them. Infidelity is rife. Husbands scramble to hold onto wives. Ex-wives hiss at the men who abandoned them. Ex-girlfriends do their best to drag their former partners into bed. Those who are in relationships nurse dark fears about the future.

Sex used to offer joys of Lucullan excess in Kureishi's work. Wishing to counterblast what he believed to be the state-sponsored repression of the 1980s, the original title for *Sammy and Rosie Get Laid* was 'The Fuck'. Sex was joy, intentionally gratuitous. However bizarre and squalid, it was a form of liberation. No longer. In place of unfettered sexual activity there is only bruised pensiveness. Characters see themselves as too old to be bohemian. Though they're rich and adulated, they worry incessantly about the greying hair behind their ears, their failing eyesight. They feel estranged from themselves as much as from others. Where they used to be dazed and confused by the vertiginous possibilities for self-transformation London offered, now they wander the capital perplexed by what's happened to their lives and how they have become so congealed. The titles of the short stories – 'Strangers When We Meet', 'That Was Then', 'Morning in the Bowl of Night' – catch the mood of crepuscular resentment.

'It has come to this,' says one of the characters self-reproachfully. The reader of *Midnight All Day* might be tempted to say the same. The book represents – along with *Love in a Blue Time* (1997) and *Intimacy* (1998) – the third instalment in the ongoing decline of a once vital writer. The problem resides not so much in the cosseted and unlikable characters, nor in the stagnation of the stories, but in Kureishi's inability to exploit his form. Short stories require a metonymic imagination, a desire to distil experience. Kureishi, however, thrives on aggregation and accumulation. He is essentially a metropolitan writer and the urban aesthetic, as Jonathan Raban has argued, is noun-orientated, always striving to catalogue the density of new information that the city spews out. Kureishi's soft-porn rites-of-passage movies and novels involve multiple pile-ups of disparate characters and social worlds. Such constant hustling – upwards! onwards! – is not well suited to the short story.

For a book which dwells on the fraughtness of human relationships and the difficulties of communicating, it seems odd that everyone is able to express their confusion in meticulous sentences. Rob, the narrator of 'Strangers When We Meet', accidentally bumps into the husband of the woman he has been seeing for a year. They discuss, he says later, 'the emptying out; the fear of living; the creation of a wasteland; the denigration of value and meaning' (MAD 26). Idling in a friend's apartment in Paris to which he has escaped with his pregnant lover – this is in the title story – Ian explains his decline in relation to Thatcherism: 'Following her, they had moved to the right and ended up in the centre. Their left politics had ended up as social tolerance and lack of deference' (MAD 168). These lunges towards portentousness are greedy and inelegant. They are so simplistic that one is tempted to assume that Kureishi is being ironic. In 'Meeting, At Last', Eric asks his wife's lover to tell him what he thinks about deception: 'Your demeanour suggests that it doesn't matter, either. Are you that cynical? This is important. Look at the century! ... I work in television news. I know what goes on. Your cruelty is the same thing. Think of the Jews' (MAD 150).

The attempts to yoke the priapic to the political in the style of Roth or Updike also fail on linguistic grounds. Kureishi is not a prose writer of any distinction. For all their grousing and despair none of his characters is capable of producing the 'jeroboams of self-absorption' found in *American Pastoral* (1997). They explicate rather than illuminate. One announces that 'When I am depressed I shut everything down, living in a tiny part of myself, in my sexuality or ambition to be an actor. Otherwise, I kill myself off' (MAD 15). Another declaims: 'Falling in love was simple; one had only to yield. Digesting another person, however, and sustaining a love, was bloody work, and not a soft job' MAD 98). But this bloodiness never crosses over into the words. The idiomatic, suited-and-booted dialogue of his early work has disappeared. Prim, medium-lengthed, stiff-backed, shorn of excess, his prose – as well as his characterisation – lacks warmth.

Like his characters, Kureishi seems to have reached an impasse. All the bodyrocking brio of old has waned. His work is sapped and weary. It hasn't even the passion or swagger to merit the accusations of misan-thropy and misogyny that have recently been hurled at him. □

(Sukhdev Sandhu, 'Paradise Syndrome', 2000)[35]

The distinction between the 'metonymic imagination' (the process of association) required for the short story form, and the urban novel's aes-thetic of aggregation and accumulation, is a telling one. Certainly Kureishi is a master of the exuberant pile-up, but Sandhu underesti-mates Kureishi's ability to 'distil experience'. As I suggested at the begin-ning of this chapter, Sandhu wants Kureishi to continue ever upwards! onwards! but in these stories he is looking resolutely inwards and back-wards. In 'The Umbrella', for example, Roger is a lecturer on human rights who is returning his sons to his ex-wife at the house they used to live in together. As he considers their separation, he cannot 'resolve competing claims: those of freedom – his freedom – to live and develop as he liked, against the right of his family to have his dependable pres-ence' (MAD 186). The story also connects domestic conflict to battle zones in the wider world, in order to relate the sexual and the political, the public and private aspects of life. Roger cannot understand war: 'The hatred he witnessed puzzled him still. It was atavistic but abstract; mostly the people did not know one another. It had made him aware of how people clung to their antipathies, and used them to maintain an impor-tant distance' (MAD 189). He concludes that 'after all the political analy-sis and talk of rights, ... people had to grasp the necessity of loving one another; and if that was too much, they had to let one another alone' (MAD 189). But this 'banality' is immediately undermined as he finds himself in a furious, petty and humiliating fight with his wife over an umbrella. He is astonished at the depth of his uncontrollable hatred: 'He had had psychotherapy; he took tranquillisers ... . None of the ideas he had about life would make this feeling go away' (MAD 190). He pushes his wife, she punches him and the boys scream: it's a small, atavistic skir-mish with little hope of resolution. The best Roger can think of is to tell himself 'not to mind' (MAD 192). The story is hatred distilled; the umbrella is a phallic symbol, a potential weapon, a moral umbrella on which Roger attempts to balance the rival claims of duty and desire.

Kureishi's middle works, then, look back to the emotional dilemmas of *The Buddha*: ' "Should people pursue their own happiness at the expense of others? Or should they be unhappy so others can be happy?" ' (BS 76). Haroon's questions are still unanswered, but the words that echo longest here are the father's admonition to the son in *Intimacy*: ' "Don't be cruel, boy" ' (I 42). These stories also look forward to 'The Body' and *Gabriel's Gift*, where for the first time in Kureishi, it is no longer assumed that marriage is bourgeois idiocy. *Gabriel's Gift* even celebrates a couple getting back together.

CHAPTER NINE

Cheerful Fictions: *Gabriel's Gift* (2001) and *The Body and Seven Stories* (2002)

After the 'intentionally horrible'[1] subject matter of Kureishi's middle period, his recent work has been seen as a return to more cheerful fictions. While the mood is more upbeat than in *Love in a Blue Time*, *Intimacy* and *Midnight All Day*, both *Gabriel's Gift* and *The Body and Seven Stories* are short pieces (the novella, 'The Body', makes up half the book) and, like the middle works, they have a fairly restricted canvas. For the most part these are stories about families and personal relationships. The preoccupation with what values we live by, evident from the earliest works, is still central but there is little sign here of a return to political and racial questions. Kureishi seems to have lost faith, or lost interest, in the 1970s agenda which saw literature as an agent for political or social change. Now he is more likely to talk of literature's role in considering the 'human condition'[2] than in examining the 'Condition of England'. Nonetheless, part of the appeal of *Gabriel's Gift* is that it is a story of youthful struggle, as in *The Buddha*, rather than of 'the enervated and useless' (BS 225) London media types who seem so unappealing in his middle works. Gabriel belongs to the middle class, 'almost' (GG 10), and is going somewhere. *Gabriel's Gift* begins with the break-up of a relationship, with the teenage son, Gabriel, like Karim in *The Buddha*, becoming a go-between and support to his incompetent father. As in *The Buddha*, there is emotional betrayal, but unlike the middle works there is optimism about the possibilities for change and renewal, at least on a personal level. Like Karim, finding himself through acting, Gabriel has a gift, for film-making; the fathers in both novels find meaning in teaching (music, here, rather than mysticism), and in the end Gabriel's parents, Rex and Christine, get back together. The book ends with a marriage. *Gabriel's Gift*, although not a first-person narrative, is imbued with the energy and brio of its adolescent protagonist who wants parties, dissipation and women (GG 154), and looks on London both as his playground and as a place in which to succeed: 'Here

anything could be achieved! You only had to wish high enough!'
(GG 154). It is not surprising to find that Karim and Charlie from the
The Buddha have cameo roles.

Gabriel's Gift, unusually for Kureishi, employs elements of fantasy
and the surreal. On the opening page Gabriel sees leaves fluttering back
up to the trees 'before turning green again', and daffodils wink at him
(GG 1). When Gabriel copies a picture of a pair of boots (presumably by
Van Gogh), which then turn into real boots, it is almost as if we are in a
magical realist novel. Also, Gabriel has a twin brother, who died aged
two and a half: 'the dead brother, alive inside the living half, had
become a magic, and wiser, boy – Gabriel's daemon or personal spirit'
(GG 19). But Gabriel's mess[ing] with magic' (GG 19) turns out to be a
way of talking about the artistic gift, while Gabriel's double self becomes
a metaphor for his emerging identity. Perhaps more tellingly, there is an
element of willed optimism in how the happy ending is achieved. In The
Buddha, the lower-middle-class schoolboys go down on their knees
before a photo of David Bowie, 'praying to be made into pop stars and
for release from a lifetime as a motor mechanic' (BS 68), but in Gabriel's
Gift a Bowie-like character, Lester Jones, actually appears in the novel,
encouraging Gabriel in his artistic ambitions and giving him a valuable
picture. The closest the boys in The Buddha ever get to Bowie is to dress
up like him; in Gabriel's Gift it is as if Bowie descends, dressed in silver,
and waves his magic wand. The young artist's fragile self-belief is
strengthened when Lester tells Gabriel: ' "You're talented, … I'm telling
you – and now you know for ever. Hear my voice and carry these words
wherever you go" ' (GG 50).

If there is an element of whimsy in Gabriel's Gift, it does not detract
from the sharp realism of the novel's evocation of place. We are soon
back in Kureishi's London, with Gabriel, like Karim before him, a keen
observer of the changing face of the city. As he walks to the fashionable
new bar where his mother is working as a waitress, he notes:

■ The city was no longer home to immigrants only from the former
colonies, plus a few others: every race was present, living side by side
without, most of the time, killing one another. It held together, this new
international city called London – just about – without being unnecessarily anarchic or corrupt. There was, however, little chance of being understood in any shop. Dad once said, 'The last time I visited the barber's I
came out with a bowl of couscous, half a gram of Charlie and a number
two crop. I only went in for a shave!'
    Their neighbourhood was changing. Only that morning a man had been
walking down the road with a mouldy mattress on his head, which you
knew he was going to sleep on; other men shoved supermarket trolleys
up the street, looking for discarded junk to sell; and there were still
those whose idea of dressing up was to shave or put their teeth in.

However, there lived, next door, pallid television types with builders always shaking their heads on the front step. If you weren't stabbed on the way, you could find an accurate acupuncturist on the corner, or rent a movie with subtitles. In the latest restaurants there was nothing pronounceable on the menu and, it was said, people were taking dictionaries with them to dinner. In the delis, queens in pinnies provided obscure soups for smart supper parties. Even ten years ago it was difficult to get a decent cup of coffee in this town. Now people threw a fit if the milk wasn't skimmed to within a centimetre of its life and the coffee not picked on their preferred square foot of Arabia. □   (GG 8)

One could argue that since the narration is from Gabriel's point of view, it is not altogether convincing that these observations, or the language in which they are expressed, are those of a 15-year-old. The registering of gentrification cheek-by-jowl with abject poverty and of London's new immigrants are quintessentially Kureishi observations. There is even a reference to *London Kills Me* as Gabriel plays with a possible film scenario called 'Dealer's Day':

■ In the last few days he had been drawing the story-board for a short film. He and his father had been watching Carol Reed's *Oliver!*, which, when Gabriel was younger, had been one of his favourites. The 'Dodger' had been his original punk hero. ... Gabriel had thought it was still possible to make a film about the parts of London that most people never saw. □   (GG 14)

In *The Body*, too, Kureishi's love affair with London continues as the narrator tells us: 'although I have lived in London since I was a student, when I open my front door today I am still excited by the thought of what I might see or hear, and by who I might run into and be made to think about' (B 6). John Clement Ball has referred to Kureishi's London as a 'semi-detached metropolis',[3] and London seems increasingly detached from the rest of England here:

■ London seems no longer part of Britain – in my view a dreary, narrow place full of fields, boarded-up shops and cities trying to imitate London – but has developed into a semi-independent city-state, like New York, and has begun to come to terms with the importance of gratification. On the other hand, ... it was impossible to get to the end of the street without people stopping you to ask for money. □   (B 6)

The Body also references Kureishi's earlier novels, with the narrator turning out to have connections with characters in *The Black Album*: 'I had been to a club once, in the early 1990s, to see Prince, with my son and the college lecturer who seemed to be educating him (in bed), Deedee Osgood' (B 57–8). And the references to Bowie and Prince are indicative of Kureishi's continued interest in popular culture, particularly music. As he explains:

■ Music was our common culture in the 1960s and 1970s. The only thing we talked about was pop and in those days it was exciting and new – there was Hendrix and the Rolling Stones and so on, and a whole culture that went with it: the drugs, the parties, the clothes, the sexuality, even politics. □

But he seems less enthusiastic about contemporary pop music: '[it] has more power now, but only in terms of selling things'.[4] Indeed the narrator of *The Body* views most forms of cultural and social life with 'semi-senile' incomprehension:

■ I no longer believe or hope that book knowledge will satisfy or even entertain me, and if I watch TV for too long I begin to feel hollow. How out of the world I already believe myself to be! I am no longer familiar with the pop stars, actors or serials on TV. I'm never sure who the pornographic boy and girl bodies belong to. It is like trying to take part in a conversation of which I can grasp only a fraction. As for the politicians, I can barely make out which side they are on. □   (B 5)

But then things change (always a magic word in Kureishi's fiction), when Adam becomes almost literally a new man by trying on a younger body. Like *Gabriel's Gift*, 'The Body' perhaps represents a frustration with realism and a desire to try on different fictional genres. Since there is little interest in the medical or mechanical aspects of brains being implanted into recently deceased bodies, 'The Body' does not read like science fiction but rather allegory or fable.

The device allows Kureishi to push his exploration of the possibilities of transformation to the limit and to test further the concept of authenticity, the possibilities of new personae. Where changing social identity in *The Buddha* was explored through clothes, 'The Body' asks to what extent the self is corporeal or mental. As the narrator says: ' "The identity theorists are going to be busy worrying about this one" ' (B 40). Regrettably, reviewers have not busied themselves with this at all. But it does seem that although the fable depends on the concept of mind–body dualism, this is also undermined. Adam's desires, thoughts and memories survive the transplant intact so that he seems recognizably the same in every respect but the physical, which might seem to suggest a separation between mind and body. But he is also aware of a 'ghost or shadow-soul' inside him: ' "I can feel things, perhaps memories, of the man who was here first. Perhaps the physical body has a soul. There's a phrase of Freud's that might apply here: the bodily ego" ' (B 45).

Curiously, despite the extreme form of transformation in 'The Body', the concept of the identity here seems more fixed and incapable of change than in earlier works: 'Nothing has cured me of myself, of the self I cling to. If you asked me, I would probably say that my problems are myself; my life is my dilemmas ...' (B 5). 'As you age, the source of your convolutedly self-stymieing behaviour seems almost beyond reach in the past; why, now, would you want to untangle it?' (B 7). Whatever the self is, and whatever lengths you might go to renew yourself, reinvention seems impossible. At the end of the story, Adam has succeeded only in becoming a nowhere man: a 'stranger on the earth, a nobody with nothing, belonging nowhere, a body alone' (B 126).

GABRIEL'S GIFT

In an interview with Robert McCrum, Kureishi explains the inspiration for the novel:

> ■ David Bowie asked me to write a book for him to illustrate, and we both assumed that this would be a kid's book. But as the book developed it became more of an adult book. And then the Bowie figure crept in and became part of the story. ... It's about fathers and sons, which is something that's always interested me, and also about sons being perhaps more talented than their fathers. It's about separation between mothers and fathers, which is always traumatic. It's about people being able to change their lives. □
>
> (Hanif Kureishi interview with Robert McCrum, 'I got out of the suburbs but did they get out of me?', 2001)[5]

Kureishi goes on to say that he wanted to write a 'sweeter' book than the melancholy *Love in a Blue Time, Midnight All Day* and *Intimacy*. This return to a more optimistic view is underlined by the ending, the most positive in any Kureishi novel, as Gabriel calls out: ' "Turn over! And – action!" ' (GG 178). Even at the conclusion of *The Buddha*, everything is still a 'mess' and there is considerable ambivalence about the way art is turned into a commodity, but the end of *Gabriel's Gift* is unsullied by money power or the marketing of ethnicity. Gabriel is about to make his first film: 'this was the only kind of magic Gabriel wanted, a shared dream, turning stories into pictures. Soon the images would be on film; not long afterwards, others would be able to see what he had been carrying in his mind, these past few months, and he wouldn't be alone anymore' (GG 178). *Gabriel's Gift* is an affirmation of the value of art: as self-expression, communication, vocation and consolation. If art can be ranged on a continuum from art-for-art's sake to agit-prop (where Kureishi began), this novel most definitely celebrates art as magic.

Most critics seem to have welcomed Kureishi's return to a more humorous vein. Alex Clark, in the *Guardian*, sees Kureishi's funny side emerging after the fictions about middle age, although he has reservations about the dialogue and, occasionally, the prose style. Clark likens the 'caperish' *Gabriel's Gift* to Kureishi's earlier novels and points out that Charlie Hero and Karim Amir from *The Buddha of Suburbia*, and Deedee Osgood from *The Black Album*, appear as caricatures. According to Clark, the break-up of Gabriel's parents, Christine and Rex, is narrated with a gentle sensibility and with relish for its comic potential, evident as Christine calls out: ' "When you're gone, Rex, we'll know exactly what to do. Our souls will soar. You're the ballast in our balloon, mate." ' But Clark also finds some of the dialogue unconvincing, for example, when Rex asserts his heterosexuality by asking: ' "Have I ever taken such a turn with teapots or any such fancy, nancy objects?" '.[6]

Alex Clark goes on to praise the comedy, the 'confident sketches of an entire generation of semi-talented has-beens', and the potential tragedy in Gabriel's collusion with his parents' childish antics, but concludes that the novel is 'curiously jumbled' and never fully engages with its subject: 'As Gabriel realizes early on, "art is what you do when other people leave the room"; for Kureishi the performer, the room is never quite vacated'. One could add other examples of somewhat uncertain dialogue. Hannah, the East European immigrant, who is learning English by watching soap operas and frequently has difficulty with even simple syntax (' "Those clothes – to me give." ' (GG 22)), reveals an astonishing vocabulary when asked to imagine her ideal menu: ' "Ice-cream … and burgers. Pigs' trotters. Pies. Rabbit stew. Jam, And … " ' (GG 10).

The *Telegraph* reviewer, Katie Owen, also considers *Gabriel's Gift* an engaging look at adulthood through the eyes of a child. Unlike Alex Clark, she considers the 'plain style' and 'often very funny images' to be 'pitch-perfect'. But she has reservations about Kureishi's treatment of the creative imagination. Gabriel's 'gift' is for visual art and screenwriting, and the novel suggests that by devoting himself to his art he will have a better life than his father, who squandered his talent. But Owen considers that this theme is expressed in surprisingly clichéd terms: 'the imagination is like a fire … it has to be stoked'. Despite this, she praises *Gabriel's Gift* as an engaging novel by one of the most significant writers of our time.[7]

Few critics comment on how the creative imagination is explored through the father–son relationship, which is one of the striking aspects of the novel. Rex, left behind by Lester Young after falling from his platform shoes and breaking his leg, is still trying to be an artist. He is a talented musician, whose struggle to be creative and frustration at failing is movingly, if ironically described: his opera on rebirth is unlikely ever to be finished. As a father, he tries to foster his son's creativity by taking him to galleries ('The only canvas he saw was Tracey Emin's tent' (GG 26)), but is hampered by envy. Gabriel hopes that because he is a painter and his father a musician they can work 'in parallel, rather than in competition' (GG 28), but after the visit to Lester Jones (who shows no interest in Rex's music) the father is furious: ' "I wish I hadn't taken you, you little idiot! ... He hardly said two words to me" ' (GG 60). Like Karim and Haroon, the father–son relationship here is rivalrous and loving. It is only as the father achieves some measure of success that he can accept his son's talent without ambivalence.

David Jays, in the *Guardian*, also finds Kureishi has returned to his sunny side but is more convinced than Owen by the novella's treatment of talent and the artistic impulse. He notes the novel's eclectic range of artistic reference (Tarkovsky and Laurel and Hardy, *Così Fan Tutte* and Strawberry Fields) and sees the novel itself as a portrait in the style of Marc Chagall (whose paintings are mentioned in *Gabriel's Gift*). Jays describes *Gabriel's Gift* as sketch in pastels or a 'portrait in thin, bright colours', noting that the novel has only a few characters. He relishes the gentleness and humour with which the confused parents are represented and praises Kureishi's treatment of creativity and the muddle of ordinary life.[8]

In all three of these mainly appreciative reviews, there is also a sense that *Gabriel's Gift* does not mark a distinctively new phase in Kureishi's work and that it is slightly uneven or lacking in ambition. For Alex Clark the novel comes 'frustratingly close' to real seriousness but does not quite hit the mark; Katie Owen complains of a clichéd account of the creative process, and David Jays's references to light-textured sketches suggest that while *Gabriel's Gift* succeeds in charming and amusing the reader, it does not have the depth or the range of novels such as *The Buddha* and *The Black Album*.

THE BODY AND SEVEN STORIES

As suggested above, the title novella in *The Body and Seven Stories* represents something of a departure in Kureishi's *oeuvre*. Apart from occasional forays into the absurd, in stories such as 'The Tale of a Turd' (LBT) and 'The Penis' (MAD), or the Calvino-inspired fable of 'The Flies' (LBT), most of Kureishi's fiction uses the conventions of realism. But if the non-naturalistic form of this novella is different, the interest in the body itself is an enduring one. As a minor character in *The Buddha* discovers when she works in a massage parlour, ' "I soon realized that nothing human was alien to me" ' (BS 169), and the same could be said of Kureishi's treatment of physicality. As Elizabeth de Cacqueray notes, 'there is never repulsion for another's body' but rather 'physical acceptance of the other'. She gives examples from *My Beautiful Laundrette*, of

Omar expressing affection by helping his father to pee and cutting his toenails, and of the sensuality of Omar washing the blood from Johnny when he is beaten up.[9] Of his most recent film, *Intimacy*, Kureishi said: 'I was thinking about Bacon and Freud, about flesh – real flesh as opposed to advertising flesh – the idealisation and the use of sex in the media that seems to be corrupt, as opposed to what bodies and sexuality are really like in real people which I try to write about more seriously.'[10] Adam, the narrator of 'The Body', says he came to London 'because the bodies are closer; there is heat and magnetism' (B 33). Although reviewers have picked up on Adam's lusty enjoyment of his young body, he never stops loving his wrinkled and sagging wife. Even in his new incarnation, he desires her: 'I kissed her and felt her body against mine as we danced. I knew where to put my hands. In my mind, her shape fitted mine. I didn't want it to end. Her face was eternity enough for me. Her lips brushed mine and her breath went into my body' (B 118).

This preoccupation with desire, betrayal and intimacy connects 'The Body' with the stories in *Love in a Blue Time* and *Midnight All Day*, but it is written without bitterness. Indeed, while most critics see *Gabriel's Gift* revisiting *The Buddha*, *The Body* has been seen as an extension of Kureishi's middle-period preoccupations, although I would argue that it has far greater tenderness. Jessica Mann's review in the *Telegraph* finds Kureishi continuing to draw on his own experiences; 'the terror of decline' in 'The Body' and the struggle to fulfil male roles in the other stories: 'men trying and failing to be good fathers, husbands, lovers or sons'. Although she makes no specific criticisms of the collection, except to observe the prevalence of 'disappointment' as a theme, she seems less than wholly enthusiastic. Mann considers the plot of the title story derives from ancient myths and modern science fiction, but this attempt to pin down a source is too vague to be of any use: was she thinking of Adonis? Austin Powers? Her main focus is on the way Adam transforms from an intellectual to a hedonist, revelling in rough sex and ecstatic drugs, only to find that the thrill does not last. In this reading, although Mann does not mention it, Adam sounds like a descendant of Wilde's Dorian Gray. Indeed, Kureishi has long admired Wilde's writing and, after finishing *The Black Album*, he worked on an adaptation of *The Picture of Dorian Gray*. Like Wilde, he has always repudiated the worthy and the moralizing in favour of wit and style, and both writers are intensely engaged with morality beneath the mask of the dandy.[11] If, as I suggested in chapter four, Charlie is a latter-day Dorian, Adam is a Dorian in reverse. Even at his most Dionysian ('Narcissus singing into his own arse! Hello!' (B 59)), Adam learns (as Dorian does) that 'indulgence wasn't a full-time job and reality was a shore where dreams broke' (B 60). Mann concludes her review by conceding that Kureishi is 'an elegant writer with a unique vision of contemporary life' but asserts that the collection as a whole is 'dispiriting'.[12]

In contrast, Alexander Linklater, writing in the *Guardian*, is unequivocally appreciative. According to Linklater, Kureishi found his mature voice in *Intimacy*, with its 'continentally inspired, disciplined' prose, and he sees *The Body* as a continuation of Kureishi's sophisticated concern with private revelation. In the title novella, for example, Adam's question is a self-conscious move in an autobiographical game: 'What concealments and deceptions are there in the exhibition of self-pity? Isn't it tedious for you?' Adam is disturbed by the sense that his life had passed too quickly; he is a characteristic Kureishi persona, although older than the author himself. Like Jay in *Intimacy*, Adam is both Kureishi and not Kureishi. For Linklater, this 'confessional illusion' is given a further twist when Adam becomes younger. In the process of describing the loneliness of this 'phoney youth', the novella explores what Adam has lost: 'What I miss is giving people the pleasure of knowing about me.' Linklater notes the irony of this, given that Kureishi's trademark has become 'the feigning of personal revelation'.

Linklater sees the melancholy of 'The Body' spilling over into the other stories: a son struggling to forgive his dying mother, a father who cannot live with his son; but he notices too that love and redemption are allowed to creep in. The children do not have to repeat their parents' mistakes and the father understands his angry son. Above all, Adam comes to realize that his old body should have been a source of affection rather than the cause of his desperate attempt to avoid mortality. Linklater concludes that these compressed stories of family and the self may be less ambitious in scope that *My Beautiful Laundrette* and *The Buddha of Suburbia*, but that the writing in these 'blissfully readable cautionary tales' has become more concentrated and more durable.[13]

Jason Cowley is also enthusiastic about Kureishi's more compressed prose style ('his cool precision'), although he later considers that that his sentences are 'often very ordinary'. He begins with a discussion of 'the philosophically interesting' title story, which reminds him of the American poet Delmore Schwartz (1913–66), who wrote in his diary, on the eve of his thirtieth birthday: 'Too late, already too late.' Adam, the narrator of the title novella, is also burdened by an awareness of his own mortality; indeed, his memoir is entitled 'Too Late'. Cowley goes on to argue that although the Cartesian idea of the separation of mind and body is no longer credited, we remain aware of our duality. The soul may not, as Andrew Marvell (1621–78) wrote, be 'fettered in feet' and 'manacled in hands' (in the poem 'A Dialogue between the Soul and Body'), but Cowley sees Adam as exemplifying a common belief that identity is not corporeal; that the key to who we are lies in consciousness.

Elsewhere in this 'excellent' collection of stories, Cowley finds familiar Kureishi material: 'urban ennui', the complexities of love and sex, the confusion and pain of family life. In 'Straight' a man goes back to his old life of casual sex and drugs, after recovering from a near-fatal accident, but finds it empty. Like Adam, he tries to transform himself. Cowley considers that the best story is 'The Real Father' in which a film editor takes the young son he barely knows on holiday to the seaside. The father tries unsuccessfully to buy the son's affection and in the evening, he drifts down to a bar where he meets some youths and, after a few drinks, finds himself beginning to hop and then to pogo, 'alone of course, jumping up towards the sky'. As Cowley says, 'the next morning, he discovers that things are a little easier with his son, as if that moment of heightened self-abandon the previous night has awakened something in him, a subdued sense of fellow feeling and inchoate love for the boy'. Trying to define Kureishi's particular voice, Cowley argues: 'He can be very cold and cruel; but at the same time he understands essential truths about the drift and lassitude of modern life in cities. His is a fiction of wintry interiors, of emotional dislocation and of strangers seeking comfort with one another.'[14]

Although Julie Myerson confesses to an aversion to the short story form and her preference for something longer, she is won over by the work of the Japanese writer, Haruki Murakami (born 1949), and by Kureishi. She finds that they are both ruthlessly honest writers, who have a 'faintly feminine openness'; both see beauty in ordinary, urban lives. Myerson considers that the most surprising aspect of 'The Body' is that no one had thought of it before. The idea behind the story is a brilliant device for the exploration of philosophical, social and sexual questions and she believes that the tale suggests, not the joys of a recovered youth, but how much we might lose.

Myerson regards the shorter pieces in the collection as equally strong. There are struggling fathers and confused adults trying to make the most of their lives, described in unpretentious and convincing prose. She particularly admires Kureishi's ability to write about parental love, and she quotes a part-time father talking to his unhappy teenage son: ' "When we get to your house you won't want to say goodbye to me properly. But I want you to know that I will think of you when you're at school, or asleep, or with your friends." "I never miss you. I won't be thinking of you." "You don't have to. I'll do the thinking, okay?" '[15]

Interestingly, Ruvani Ranasinha connects 'The Body' with *The Buddha*, arguing that 'Kureishi has long been intensely interested in the extent to which our identity is ingrained in the physical, previously exploring the idea from a raced perspective.' She observes:

■ *The Buddha* turns on the ironies that arise from the gap between how Karim sees himself and how he is perceived. 'The Body' continues Kureishi's exploration of identity as performance in its delineation of Adam's false youth. Although the visible signifiers of youth and beauty, rather than racial difference, are the focus of this story, in an ironic aside, the surgeon pioneering this technique suggests to Adam: 'you could choose a black body. Think how much you'd learn about society'. Adam is instead preoccupied by his fascination with his flesh, vanity, ageing, deterioration and death. Kureishi approaches these fundamental questions of the human condition with intellectual curiosity, philosophical interest, as well as the clarity that informs his lively and trenchant essays. □   (Ruvani Ranasinha, review of *The Body*, 2003)[16]

Ranasinha also singles out the final story, 'Touched', as being the most reminiscent of Kureishi's early work:

■ It describes an adolescent half-Indian boy growing up in the 1950s. Kureishi retains his talent for precise evocation of era and locale. Ali is struck by the glamour, wealth and confidence of the visiting Bombay part of his family, who form a sharp contrast to his drab life in a council house. At first, the story seems to sketch the impact of the visit: the tensions created in Ali's parents' cross-cultural marriage, Ali's crush on his young cousin Zahida, and his response to taunts about the visiting 'darkies' from his 'friends'. Ali appears relieved to escape this derision during his visits to his blind neighbour Miss Beth, the only person who does not know he is half-Indian and so calls him Alan, another oblique insight into the absurdity of defining identity in a corporeal way. Gradually, another motive for the visits becomes clear, when Ali allows Miss Beth to molest him in exchange for pocket money. 'Touched' builds up to a climax that is not entirely unexpected, and perceptively evokes Ali's innocence and experience. Kureishi's mastery of the short story form is evident in his ability to suggest the complexity beneath the surface of the encounter, creating a story that is both complete and highly suggestive. □
(Ruvani Ranasinha, review of *The Body*, 2003)[17]

Although reviewers have responded positively to *Gabriel's Gift* and *The Body*, these books have not as yet received the same kind of academic attention as *The Buddha* and *The Black Album*. This may be in part because they cannot be viewed through the lens of postcolonial theory, which has formed so much of the critical debate over Kureishi's work. But in time the title novella of 'The Body' may well attract the kind of philosophical discussion about identity and authenticity that seems increasingly necessary in a postmodern culture of simulation where the fake is invariably indistinguishable from the natural. Adam imagines that when he is drunk, he understands the work of the intimidatingly obscure French philosopher and psychoanalyst, Jacques Lacan (1901–81) (B 4). Perhaps a sober critic, who understands Lacan's analysis of 'the Imaginary' (the phase prior to the acquisition of language and the sense of self), 'the mirror stage' (when the infant sees itself as an individual, separate from others), 'the Symbolic' (when the child enters into the language system and the social world of rules and restraints) and 'the Real' (which is unknowable), could usefully apply this to Kureishi's treatment of desire and identity. For Kureishi in these stories, desire is (as for Lacan) always about a lack of self; of how we want to live in the Imaginary but have to love in the lack that is the Symbolic. 'The Body' is full of dreams, mirrors, young children and the theorizing of narcissism:

> ■ A theory-loving friend of mine has an idea that the notion of the self, of the separate, self-conscious individual, and of any autobiography which that self might tell or write, developed around the same time as the invention of the mirror, first made en masse in Venice in the early six-teenth century. When people could consider their own faces, expressions of emotion and bodies for a sustained period, they could wonder who they were and how they were different from and similar to others.
>
> My children, around the age of two, became fascinated by their own images in the looking-glass. Later, I can remember my son, aged six, clambering onto a chair and then onto the dining table in order to see himself in the mirror over the fireplace, kissing his fingers and saying, as he adjusted his top hat, 'Masterpiece! What a lucky man you are, to have such a good-looking son!' Later, of course, they and their mirrors were inseparable. As I said to them: make the most of it, there'll be a time when you won't be able to look at yourself without flinching.
>
> According to my friend, if a creature can't see himself, he can't mature. He can't see where he ends and others begin. □ (B 28)

But it may also be that these stories owe more to self-help and therapy culture than they do to Lacanian theory. In 'Face to Face with You' (which recalls the short story, 'Neighbors', by Raymond Carver (1939–88)) a couple in their thirties, unsure if they really want to stay together, and working without passion in their careers, are thoroughly disconcerted when a couple exactly like themselves move into the flat above them. They are forced to look at themselves, as if in a mirror, but by facing the reality they discover not only that they are 'not so bad' but also that there is hope (B 155). In 'Goodbye, Mother' a middle-aged son finally manages to forgive his mother for her failure to express love or real interest in him, a lack which he feels has damaged his sense of self. He comes to terms with his past partly because his wife, who is engaged in hypnotherapy, encourages him to break out of the straitjacket of the so-called 'real' world and admit that the unconscious is what shapes lives. As she says of her clients: ' "After a bit, the self-knowledge will make them change" ' (B 198).

In an interview, Kureishi characterized his recent work as having 'greater interest in inner lives' and observed that 'in *The Buddha of Suburbia*, I was more interested in what people were wearing'.[18] But, paradoxically, the 'sartorial understanding' did give psychological depth to the characters in *The Buddha*. Since Adam changes bodies with almost the same ease as Karim changes his clothes, the transformation does not necessarily involve any deepening in the sense of an inner life. Moreover, there is very little sense of the inner lives of any characters other than the protagonist. In 'The Body', Adam feels that he has 'been failing as a writer. [He]'d become more skilful, but not better' (B 50). The same could possibly be said of Kureishi himself. Again, the tentatively experimental mode in *Gabriel's Gift* and 'The Body' suggests that he has been trying to find, as Adam says, 'interesting ways to make [the writing process] more difficult' (B 50). These books are, as many reviewers point out, more disciplined and compressed, but these qualities do not altogether compensate for the loss of ebullience and bravado. Craft cannot substitute for conviction, energy and creative engagement with others, even if the writing extols the virtues of uncertainty. Or again, as Adam puts it: 'Urgency and contemporaneity make up for any amount of clumsiness, in literature as in love' (B 50). But at the same time, it is characteristic of Kureishi's integrity as a writer that he should, as it were, give this ammunition to his critics. It could be said that Kureishi has gone from being an *enfant terrible* to something of an *éminence grise*, or that in his current writing these two roles are jostling for position. Possibly, like Adam, he does not feel the same urgency about contemporaneity as he once did and, for a writer whose reputation has always been bound up with pop culture, the expectation that his fiction will 'mainline the energies of metropolitan youth'[19] may be an inhibiting pressure. It is interesting to speculate on who Kureishi's readers are at this point in the early twenty-first century. At the time of *Sammy and Rosie*, in the late 1980s, Kureishi estimated that his audience was 'aged between 18 and 40, mostly middle class and well-educated, ... liberal progressive or leftish'.[20] Is he attracting the next generation of leftish liberals now, with these stories of middle age, or are his original readers growing older with him? Will he continue to be a distinctively contemporary writer or will he look back? Like Hanif Johnson in Salman Rushdie's *The Satanic Verses*, Kureishi's early work showed a control of 'the languages that mattered: sociological, socialistic, black-radical, anti-anti-anti-racist, demagogic, oratorical, sermonic: the vocabularies of power'.[21] Now his work has greater recourse to the languages of philosophy, aesthetics and the therapeutic (possibly another kind of contemporaneity), and with these vocabularies it is clear that he can tell different and equally powerful stories about the past and the future: 'The thing about being in the middle is you can see the end and the beginning and you think about what you'll leave behind.'[22]

Conclusion: Whatever Next?

It is impossible to 'conclude' about a writer who is still living, and writing at the height of his power, but it is possible to suggest what might be coming next. After *My Son the Fanatic*, it seemed that Kureishi had exhausted the fictional possibilities of the Asian side of his background. With *Love in a Blue Time* many reviewers considered that Kureishi had lurched from coming-of-age dramas to mid-life crises. In 'The Body' he makes both a leap forward and back to imagine an ageing, Kureishi-like protagonist whose brain is transplanted into a younger body. His most recent film, *The Mother* (2003), which was directed by Roger Michell and won joint first prize in the Director's Fortnight at Cannes in the same year, concerns the relationship between an older woman and a young man. This would seem to confirm Kureishi's abiding preoccupation with the 'odd couple', which has been such a fruitful focus since the transgressive relationship at the heart of *My Beautiful Laundrette*. But *The Mother* is also unusual for Kureishi, as the first work in which he has given centre stage to a female character and because it does not seem to have an autobiographical provenance. He has just finished writing his memoirs, *My Ear at His Heart*, which deals with his father's life through the latter's unpublished novels, and the connections between life and literature. Spanning three generations, it explores the contrast between his father's, Kureishi's, and his sons' lives in London. A remarkable text, which combines postcolonial and psychoanalytical perspectives with personal experience, it is moving and characteristically lucid. *My Ear at His Heart* (2004) involves a re-examination of British India and postwar immigration, and so might be considered a return to the preoccupations of the earlier work, but it is also, clearly, a continuation of Kureishi's autobiographical project.

Critics often distinguish between Kureishi's initial interest in 'cultural translation' and racial and sexual politics, and his later fictional explorations of relationships among (for the most part) middle-class white characters. But it is not the case that there was a sudden break from the social themes to the self: Kureishi has always experimented with autobiographical fiction; at different times the focus has been on ethnicity and racism, at other times less so. There is no reason why an Asian background will necessarily impinge on every aspect of life. Moreover, from the very beginning, Kureishi has highlighted the ways in which the personal is always political; an insight gleaned from the feminist movement. Although Kureishi seems more ambivalent about feminism now, the insight still informs his writing. Indeed, although his work clearly shows an interest in constructions of masculinity, his concentration on unhappy love, the frustrations of domesticity and the politics of personal relationships might be seen as traditionally female subjects.

The major difference between the early and middle period, I would argue, is not to do with 'race' but the greater breadth, humour and humanity of the earlier films and novels. The mid-life fictions seem not just darker but narrower in sympathies, lacking the interest in other people's stories which brims over in the early work and gives it vitality. *Love in a Blue Time, Intimacy* and *Midnight All Day* are compelling in their intensity, but many readers miss the brio and expansiveness with which Kureishi engaged with 'serious lying and betrayal' in *The Buddha*, and regret the more restricted canvas. Kureishi has always been willing to take risks as a writer, and with the renewal of optimism and energy manifest in his most recent fiction, it will be interesting to see where his restless attention will take him next: whether he looks back, within, or around him, maintains his austere style or allows a little comic exuberance, whether he deals with overtly political and racial questions or not, is anyone's guess. But judging by past form, it seems likely that Kureishi's work will continue to surprise.

Notes

INTRODUCTION

1 Hanif Kureishi, *The Late Show*, quoted in Susheila Nasta, *Home Truths: Fictions of the South Asian Diaspora in Britain* (Basingstoke: Palgrave Macmillan, 2002), p. 197.
2 Sukhdev Sandhu, *London Calling: How Black and Asian Writers Imagined a City* (London: Harper Collins, 2003), pp. 227 and 229.
3 Amitava Kumar, *Bombay London New York* (New York and London: Routledge, 2002), p. 151.
4 Sukhdev Sandhu, 'Paradise Syndrome', *London Review of Books* (18 May 2000).
5 Sandhu (2003), p. 230.
6 See Nasta (2002).
7 See Berthold Schoene, 'Herald of Hybridity: The Emancipation of Difference in Hanif Kureishi's *The Buddha of Suburbia*', *International Journal of Cultural Studies*, 1:1 (1998), p. 111.
8 For an account of Kureishi's influence on other writers and British culture generally see the 'Critical Overview and Conclusion', in Bart Moore-Gilbert, *Hanif Kureishi* (Manchester: Manchester University Press, 2001).
9 Hanif Kureishi, 'The Rainbow Sign', reprinted in *Dreaming and Scheming: Reflections on Writing and Politics* (London: Faber & Faber, 2002), pp. 25–6. Future page references are to this edition, hereafter cited as RS in brackets in the text.
10 See the discussion of 'The Rainbow Sign' in the context of diaspora identities in John McLeod, *Beginning Postcolonialism* (Manchester: Manchester University Press, 2000), pp. 205–38.
11 Kobena Mercer, *Welcome to the Jungle: New Positions in Black Cultural Studies* (London: Routledge, 1994), p. 214.
12 [*Editor's note*:] Yousaf refers the reader to Kobena Mercer (1994).
13 Nahem Yousaf, 'Hanif Kureishi and "the Brown Man's Burden" ', *Critical Survey*, 8:1 (1996), p. 20.
14 Hanif Kureishi, 'Dirty Washing', *Time Out* (14–20 November 1985), pp. 25–6.

CHAPTER ONE

1 This chapter focuses on the four plays currently in print in *Outskirts and Other Plays*. For reasons of space and availability of texts the following are not considered here: Kureishi's first play, *Soaking the Heat*, which was staged at the Royal Court Theatre Upstairs in 1976; *The Mother Country* (1980), about a Pakistani immigrant and his son, which was staged in the Riverside Studios' Plays Umbrella season (neither of these works has been published); a radio play, *You Can't Go Home*, which was broadcast on the BBC in 1980; the one-act play *Tomorrow-Today!* (1981), which was performed at the Soho Poly and was published in *Outskirts, The King and Me, Tomorrow-Today!* (London: John Calder and New York: Riverrun Press, 1983); Kureishi's co-adaptation of Janusz Glowacki's play, *Cinders*, which was put on at the Royal Court Theatre Upstairs in 1981; his translation and adaptation of a new version of Ostrovsky's *Artists and Admirers* with the director, David Leveaux, which was staged at the Riverside Studios in 1982; his adaptation for radio of Kafka's *The Trial*, which was broadcast in 1983 and his adaptation of Brecht's *Mother Courage*, which was staged at the Barbican

in 1984; his *Mother Courage*, which was produced as a mobile tour by the National's education department in 1993.

2 Kureishi was not alone. Simon Trussler observes that 'ethnic theatre was now able to draw upon a growing stable of writers of Afro-Caribbean or Asian roots – among them, Edgar White, Michael Abbensetts, Caryl Phillips, Tunde Ikoli, Mustapha Matura, Farrukh Dhondy, Barrie Reckord, Hanif Kureishi, and Jacqueline Rudet' (*The Cambridge Illustrated History of British Theatre* [Cambridge: Cambridge University Press, 1994], p. 371).

3 Moore-Gilbert (2001), p. 58.

4 Irving Wardle, '*The King and Me*', *The Times* (9 January 1980), p. 11.

5 Ruvani Ranasinha, *Hanif Kureishi* (Horndon: Northcote House, 2002), p. 22.

6 Ranasinha (2002), p. 24.

7 Ranasinha (2002), pp. 23–4.

8 Moore-Gilbert (2001), pp. 43–4.

9 [*Ranasinha's note*:] Irving Wardle, 'A Moral Tale that Carries Conviction', *The Times* (29 April 1981), p. 12.

10 Ranasinha (2002), p. 24.

11 Ranasinha (2002), p. 25.

12 Ranasinha (2002), pp. 25–6.

13 Moore-Gilbert (2001), p. 45.

14 Ranasinha (2002), pp. 26–7.

15 Moore-Gilbert (2001), pp. 51–2.

16 Ranasinha (2002), p. 28. [*Ranasinha's note*:] Avtar Brah, *Cartographies Of Diaspora: Contesting Identities* (London: Routledge, 1996), p. 43. For an account of the first-generation struggles, see A. Sivanandan, *From Resistance to Rebellion: Asian and Afro-Caribbean Struggles in Britain* (London: Institute of Race Relations), 1986.

17 Ranasinha (2002), p. 28.

18 Ranasinha (2002), pp. 29–30.

19 Moore-Gilbert (2001), p. 53.

20 Ranasinha (2002), pp. 30–1. [*Ranasinha's note*:] Kureishi observes: 'The real problem when I was growing up was that racism just wasn't a topic of understanding in England ... there was no wider understanding of racism. You felt it was your own personal and psychological problem.' Cited in Glenn Collins, 'Screen Writer Turns to the Novel to Tell of Race and Class in London', *New York Times* (24 May 1990), p. 17.

21 Moore-Gilbert (2001), p. 54.

22 Moore-Gilbert (2001), p. 28.

23 Moore-Gilbert (2001), p, 49.

24 Moore-Gilbert (2001), p. 50.

25 Kenneth Kaleta, *Hanif Kureishi: Postcolonial Storyteller* (Austin: University of Texas Press, 1998), pp. 24–5.

26 Kaleta (1998), p. 25.

27 Ranasinha (2002), p. 34.

28 See Ranasinha (2002), p. 127 n. 13.

29 Ranasinha (2002), p. 127 n. 13.

30 Moore-Gilbert (2001), p. 57.

31 Moore-Gilbert (2001), p. 227, n. 27.

32 See 'Can the Subaltern Speak?', in Patrick Williams and Laura Chrisman, eds., *Colonial Discourse and Post-Colonial Theory: A Reader* (Hemel Hempstead: Harvester Wheatsheaf, 1993), pp. 66–111.

33 [*Ranasinha's note*:] Gayatri Chakravorty Spivak, *Outside in the Teaching Machine* (London: Routledge, 1993), p. 250.

34 Ransinha (2002), pp. 35–6.

35 Ranasinha (2002), pp. 36–7.

36 [*Moore-Gilbert's note:*] This also has echoes of *The Caretaker* by Pinter (1960, revived at the Mermaid in 1972), a playwright whom Kureishi greatly admires. *Birds of Passage* has echoes of *The Homecoming* (1965, revived at The Garrick, 1978). Stella's homecoming is as ambivalently received as Teddy and Ruth's and Stella is further linked to Ruth through the theme of prostitution.

37 Moore-Gilbert (2001), pp. 59–61.

CHAPTER TWO

1 Interview with Jane Root, 'Scenes from a Marriage', *Monthly Film Bulletin*, 52 (November 1985), p. 333.

2 SS, p. 132.

3 Root (1985), p. 333.

4 See Kaleta (1998), pp. 40–1.

5 See Ria Julian, 'Brecht and Britain: Hanif Kureishi in Interview with Ria Julian', *Drama: Quarterly Theatre Review*, 155 (1987), pp. 5–7.

6 Introduction to *My Beautiful Laundrette* reprinted in *Dreaming and Scheming*, pp. 125–6.

7 David Robinson, 'Only sentiment', *Sight and Sound*, 55 (Winter 1985–6), p. 67.

8 Harlan Kennedy, *Film Comment*, 21 (November–December 1985), p. 76.

9 Leonard Quart, *Cinéaste*, 15:1 (1986), pp. 38–9.

10 Pam Cook, *Monthly Film Bulletin*, 52 (November 1985), p. 333.

11 Root (1985), p. 333.

12 Mahmood Jamal, 'Dirty Linen', *Artrage* (Autumn 1987). Reprinted in Kobena Mercer, ed., *Black Film, British Cinema* (London: Institute of Contemporary Arts, 1988), pp. 21–2.

13 *My Beautiful Laundrette* in *Collected Screenplays* 1, p. 67.

14 [*Dhillon-Kashyap's note:*] Interview in *Buzz*, 1986.

15 [*Dhillon-Kashyap's note:*] Rita Wolf, 'Beyond the Laundrette', *Guardian* (14 February 1987). For an alternative reading, see Pratibha Parmar's interview with Hanif Kureishi in *Marxism Today* (February 1988).

16 Perminder Dhillon-Kashyap, 'Locating the Asian Experience', *Screen*, 29 (1988), pp. 120–6.

17 Salman Rushdie, 'Minority Literatures in a Multi-Cultural Society' in Kirsten Holst Peterson and Anna Rutherford, eds., *Displaced Persons* (Sydney: Dangaroo Press, 1988), p. 37.

18 Rushdie (1987), p. 38

19 Rushdie (1987), pp. 40–1.

20 Norman Stone, 'Through a lens darkly', *Sunday Times* (10 January 1988), reprinted in Mercer (1988), pp. 22–3.

21 Sukhdev Sandhu, 'Pop Goes the Centre: Hanif Kureishi's London' in Laura Chrisman and Benita Parry, eds., *Postcolonial Theory and Criticism* (Cambridge: Brewer, 1999), p. 144.

22 For a full discussion of Raj Revival and Heritage cinema in relation to Kureishi's films, see Moore-Gilbert (2001), pp. 73–93.

23 Hanif Kureishi, 'England, bloody England', *Guardian* (22 January 1988), reprinted in Mercer (1988), pp. 24–5.

24 Kobena Mercer, 'Recoding the Narratives of Race and Nation', quoted in Anuradha Dingwaney Needham, *Using the Master's Tools: Resistance and the Literature of the African and Asian Diasporas* (Basingstoke: Palgrave Macmillan, 2000), p. 153.

25 George Mosse, *Nationalism and Sexuality: Middle Morality and Sexual Norms* (Madison: University of Wisconsin Press, 1985).

26 Radhika Mohanram, 'Postcolonial Spaces and Deterritorialized (Homo)Sexuality: The Films of Hanif Kureishi', in Gita Rajan and Radhika Mohanram, eds., *Postcolonial Discourse and Changing Cultural Contexts: Theory and Criticism* (Westport, CT and London: Greenwood Press, 1995), p. 120.

27 Mohanram (1995), p. 121.
28 Mohanram (1995), pp. 125–8.
29 Mohanram (1995), p. 132.
30 Stuart Hall, 'Old and New Identities, Old and New Ethnicities', in Anthony D. King, ed., *Culture, Globalization and the World System* (Basingstoke: Palgrave Macmillan, 1991), p. 44.
31 Hall (1991), p. 47.
32 Hall (1991), p. 49.
33 Hall (1991), pp. 52–3.
34 Hall (1991), pp. 55–6.
35 Hall (1991), p. 57.
36 Hall (1991), p. 60.
37 [*Ranasinha's note:*] Inderpal Grewal, 'Salman Rushdie: Marginality, Women and Shame', in M. D. Fletcher, ed., *Reading Rushdie: Perspectives on the Fiction of Salman Rushdie* (Amsterdam: Rodopi, 1994), p. 132 n. 12 (emphasis Ranasinha).
38 [*Ranasinha's note:*] Contrast Meera Syal's portrayals of British Asian women who attempt to redefine what being an Asian/woman means from within the community, 'always proud to be who they were, but not scared to push back the boundaries'. See Meera Syal, *Life Isn't All Ha Ha Hee Hee* (London: Doubleday, 1999), p. 84.
39 Ranasinha (2002), p. 48.
40 Ranasinha (2002), pp. 48–9.
41 Elizabeth de Cacqueray, 'Space for Dreams: the Use of Place and Space in Hanif Kureishi's Fictive Universes', in Francois Gallix, ed., *The Buddha of Suburbia* (Paris: Ellipses, 1997), pp. 196–7.
42 'The puritan and prurient theme of two outcast boys (outcast from society and having escaped the world of women) clinging together in passionate blood-brotherhood is a dream of American literature and film from *Huckleberry Finn* to the work of Walt Whitman and on to *Butch Cassidy and the Sundance Kid*', SS, p. 152.
43 *My Beautiful Laundrette* in *Collected Screenplays 1*, p. 58.
44 *My Beautiful Laundrette* in *Collected Screenplays 1*, p. 65.
45 Maria Pally, 'Kureishi Like a Fox', *Film Comment*, 22 (September–October 1986), p. 53.
46 See John Clement Ball, 'The Semi-Detached Metropolis: Hanif Kureishi's London', *Ariel*, 27:4 (1996), pp. 7–27.

CHAPTER THREE

1 Kureishi, 'Some time with Stephen: A Diary', reprinted in *Dreaming and Scheming*, p. 130. Hereafter cited as SS.
2 Gayatri C. Spivak, '*Sammy and Rosie Get Laid Get Laid*', in *Outside in the Teaching Machine* (London: Routledge, 1993), p. 244.
3 Colin MacCabe, 'Interview: Hanif Kureishi on London', *Critical Quarterly*, 41:3 (1999), p. 41.
4 See Colette Lindroth, '*The Waste Land* Revisited: *Sammy and Rosie Get Laid*', *Literature/Film Quarterly*, 17:2 (1989), pp. 95–8.
5 Ball (October 1996), p. 18.
6 Quoted by Kaleta (1998), p. 50.
7 [*Kaleta's note:*] Leonard Quart, 'The Politics of Irony', in Wheeler Winston Dixon, ed., *Reviewing British Cinema 1900–1992* (Albany: State University of New York Press, 1994), p. 242.
8 [*Kaleta's note:*] Vincent Canby, 'Chaotic London', *New York Times*, 30 (October 1987), C5:1.
9 [*Kaleta's note:*] Richard Corliss, 'The Empire Strikes Out', *Time*, 30 (9 November 1987), p. 91.
10 Kaleta (1998), pp. 53–4.
11 [*Kaleta's note:*] Leonard Quart [*Sammy and Rosie Get Laid* review], *Cinéaste*, 16:3 (1988), p. 40.
12 Sandeep Naidoo [*Sammy and Rosie Get Laid* review], *Bazaar*, 4:6 (Spring 1988), p. 16.

13 bell hooks, 'Stylish Nihilism: Race, Sex and Class at the Movies', in hooks, *Yearning: Race, Gender, and Cultural Politics* (Boston: South End Press, 1991), pp. 158–9.

14 hooks (1991), p. 160.

15 hooks (1991), pp. 160–1.

16 hooks (1991), pp. 162–3.

17 Spivak's 'In praise of *Sammy and Rosie Get Laid*', written after long discussions with Colin MacCabe, was first published in *Critical Quarterly*, 31:2 (1989), pp. 80–8. In a revised version of the essay, Spivak adds the reference to hooks's critique, but does not substantially change her reading. See '*Sammy and Rosie Get Laid*' in *Outside in the Teaching Machine* (London: Routledge, 1993), p. 245.

18 Spivak (1989), p. 80.

19 [*Spivak's note:*] Richard Miller, *Analyzing Marx* (Ithaca, NY: Cornell University Press, 1984), pp. 15–97.

20 Spivak (1993), pp. 245–7.

21 Spivak (1993), p. 248.

22 Spivak (1989), p. 83. I have used the first version of Spivak's essay here.

23 Mohanram (1995), p. 129.

24 Spivak (1993), pp. 251 and 252–3.

25 Spivak (1989), p. 85.

26 Spivak (1993), p. 253.

27 Spivak (1989), p. 86.

28 Spivak (1993), p. 253.

29 Spivak (1993), p. 253.

30 [*Spivak's note:*] Theodor Adorno, 'Commitment', in *The Essential Frankfurt School Reader*, pp. 300–18.

31 Spivak (1993), p. 254.

32 Spivak (1993), p. 253.

33 Spivak (1993), p. 243.

34 Susan Torrey Barber, 'Insurmountable Difficulties and Moments of Ecstasy: Crossing Class, Ethnic, and Sexual Barriers in the Films of Stephen Frears', in Lester Friedman, ed., *British Cinema and Thatcherism: Fires Were Started* (London: UCL Press, 1993), p. 221.

35 Barber (1993), pp. 228 and 229.

36 Barber (1993), p. 222.

37 Barber (1993), p. 231.

38 Barber (1993), p. 235.

39 Sandhu is contrasting Kureishi's London here with Sam Selvon, *The Lonely Londoners* (1956); George Lamming, *The Emigrants* (1954) and *The Pleasures of Exile* (1960); Linton Kwesi Johnson, *Dread Beat An' Blood* (1975) and *Inglan Is A Bitch* (1980).

40 [*Sandhu's note:*] Though it is rivalled by one of Sam Selvon's short stories. '[W]hen she asked me why I loved London I too shrugged … . The way St Paul's was, half-hidden in the rain, the motionless trees along the Embankment. But you say a thing like that and people don't understand at all. How sometimes a surge of greatness could sweep over you when you see something.' 'My Girl and the City', in *Ways of Sunlight* (London: MacGibbon & Kee, 1957).

41 Ignatius Sancho, *Letters of the Late Ignatius Sancho: an African, to which are Prefixed, Memoirs of his Life*, 2 vols. (London: J. Nichols, 1782). A modern edition, edited by Vincent Carretta, is available (New York: Penguin, 1998).

42 [*Sandhu's note:*] Paul Gilroy, *Small Acts: Thoughts on the Politics of Black Cultures* (London: Serpent's Tail, 1993), p. 120.

43 Sukhdev Sandhu, 'Pop Goes the Centre: Hanif Kureishi's London', in Laura Chrisman and Benita Parry, eds., *Postcolonial Theory and Criticism* (Cambridge: Brewer, 1999), pp. 141–3. A revised and expanded version of this essay appears in Sandhu's *London Calling: How Black and Asian Writers Imagined a City* (London: HarperCollins, 2003).

44 Sandhu (1999), p. 152.
45 Sandhu (1999), p. 153.
46 Sandhu (1999), p. 153.

CHAPTER FOUR

1 Robert Lee, 'Changing the Script: Sex, Lies and Videotapes in Hanif Kureishi, David Dabydeen and Mike Phillips', in A. Robert Lee, ed., *Other Britain, Other British: Contemporary Multicultural Fiction* (London and East Haven, CT: Pluto, 1995), p. 75.

2 Seminal work by Homi Bhabha includes: 'The Third Space', in Jonathan Rutherford, ed., *Identity, Community, Culture, Difference* (London: Lawrence & Wishart, 1990); 'DissemiNation: time, narrative, and the margins of the modern nation', in Homi K. Bhabha, ed., *Nation and Narration* (London: Routledge, 1990), pp. 291–322; and *The Location of Culture* (London: Routledge, 1994).

3 For a general discussion of hybridity in relation to Kureishi see Moore-Gilbert (2001), chapter six.

4 For a further discussion of 'hybridity' see Yu-Cheng Lee, 'Expropriating the Authentic: Cultural Politics in Hanif Kureishi's *Buddha of Suburbia'*, *EurAmerica: A Journal of European and American Studies*, 26:3 (1996), pp. 1–19.

5 Berthold Schoene, 'Herald of Hybridity': The Emancipation of Difference in Hanif Kureishi's *The Buddha of Suburbia'*, *International Journal of Cultural Studies*, 1:1 (1998), pp. 112–16.

6 Schoene (1998), p. 112.

7 Moore-Gilbert (2001), p. 206.

8 Paul Gilroy, *The Black Atlantic* (London: Verso, 1993), p. 3.

9 Ball (1996), p. 23.

10 Ranasinha (2002), p. 73.

11 Seema Jena, 'From Victims to Survivors: the Anti-Hero As a Narrative in Asian Immigrant Writing With Special Reference to *the Buddha of Suburbia'*, *Wasafiri*, 17 (Spring 1993), pp. 3–6.

12 Jena (1993), p. 6.

13 Michèle Hita makes the interesting point that by playing the son of an Indian shopkeeper in his mother's favourite genre of soap opera, Karim reconciles the two sides of his parentage. Moreover, Karim will 'transform the genre by placing an Indian at the heart of English popular culture' (editor's translation). Michèle Hita, 'Identité, vision et voyeurisme dans *The Buddha of Suburbia'*, in Gallix (1997), p. 44.

14 Sangeeta Ray, 'The Nation in Performance: Bhabha, Mukherjee and Kureishi', in Monika Fludernik, ed., *Hybridity and Postcolonialism: Twentieth Century Indian Literature* (Tübingen, Germany: Stauffenburg, 1998), p. 235.

15 Ray (1998), p. 235.

16 Ray (1998), p. 236.

17 Gayatri Spivak, 'The Burden of English Studies', in Rajeswari Sunder Rajan, ed., *The Lie of the Land: English Literary Studies in India* (Delhi: Oxford University Press, 1992), p. 293.

18 Ranasinha (2002), pp. 72–3.

19 Schoene (1998), p. 115.

20 See Waddick Doyle, 'The Space between Identity and Otherness in *The Buddha of Suburbia'*, and Jamel Oubechou, 'The Barbarians and Philistines in *The Buddha of Suburbia'*, both in *Commonwealth Essays and Studies*, 4 (1997), pp. 110–18 and 101–9.

21 Schoene (1998), pp. 121–2.

22 Moore-Gilbert (2001), p. 202.

23 Schoene (1998), p. 123.

24 Spivak (1992), p. 293, n. 26.

25 Schoene (1998), p. 123.

26 Schoene (1998), p. 117.

27 Elaine Dubourdieu, 'The Buddha, Britain and "Black" Immigration', in Gallix (1997), pp. 131–47. See also Moya Jones, 'The Immigrant is the Everyman of the 20th Century: Racial Tensions in *the Buddha of Suburbia*', in the same volume.

28 Cynthia Carey, '*The Buddha of Suburbia* as a Post-Colonial Novel', *Commonwealth Essays and Studies*, 4 (1997), pp. 122–3.

29 Nahem Yousaf, *Hanif Kureishi's The Buddha of Suburbia* (New York and London: Continuum, 2002), pp. 42–4.

30 Ranasinha (2002), p. 69.

31 [*Ranasinha's note:*] The racializing of gender becomes manifest in Helen's father's attempt to control her sexuality and protect her from the perceived threat posed to her by Karim. Similarly, Karim is 'ecstatic about [his] triumph in seducing' Helen who is now denied individuality and becomes simply 'the dog owner's daughter' (BS 82). The way women and their bodies function both biologically and symbolically as the boundaries of the ethnic groups and/or the nation is further underlined in Karim's attempts to defy exclusion by 'possessing' white women (BS 227). See Nira Yuval-Davis and Floya Anthias, eds., *Women-Nation-State* (London: Macmillan, 1998).

32 [*Ranasinha's note:*] Paul Gilroy, *The Black Atlantic* (London: Verso, 1993), p. 32.

33 Ranasinha (2002), p. 73–4.

34 Schoene (1998), p. 114.

35 Rita Felski, 'Nothing to Declare: Identity, Shame, and the Lower Middle Class', *PMLA*, 115 (January 2000), p. 34.

36 Felski (2000), p. 42.

37 Felski (2000), p. 34.

38 Felski (2000), pp. 37–8.

39 Felski (2000). p. 42.

40 Quoted by David Nicholson, 'My Beautiful Britain', *Films and Filming* (January 1988), pp. 9–10.

41 The full text of this article is available in French in Gallix (1997), pp. 26–36.

42 Terry L. Allison and Renée R. Curry, ' "All Anger and Understanding": Kureishi, Culture, and Contemporary Constructions of Rage', in Allison and Curry, eds., *States of Rage: Emotional Eruption, Violence and Social Change* (New York: New York University Press, 1996), p. 162. For a further discussion of humour in *The Buddha* see Marc Porée, *Hanif Kureishi: The Buddha of Suburbia* (Paris: CNED-Didier Concours, 1997).

43 Sandhu (2003), p. xxiii.

44 See Jack P. Rawlins, 'Great Expiations: Dickens and the Betrayal of the Child', in Michael Cotsell, ed., *Critical Essays on Charles Dickens's Great Expectations* (Boston: G. K. Hall, 1990), pp. 170–1.

45 See Seema Jena (1993). For more on the picaresque see Matthew Graves, 'Subverting Suburbia: the Trickster Figure in Hanif Kureishi's *The Buddha of Suburbia*' and Jan Borm, ' "Thank God I Have an Interesting Life": Le Picaresque Dans *The Buddha of Suburbia*', both in Gallix (1997), pp. 70–8 and 79–87.

46 Moore-Gilbert (2001), p. 113.

47 [*Moore-Gilbert's note:*] However Karim, 17 when *The Buddha* opens, is roughly Kim's age at the end of his adventures.

48 Moore-Gilbert (2001), pp. 126–7.

49 Moore-Gilbert (2001), p. 127. Moore-Gilbert sees the enabling precedent of Kipling in Rushdie's work: 'a further area in which Rushdie's influence on Kureishi can be detected', p. 127.

50 Moore-Gilbert (2001), p. 127.

51 Nasta (2002), p. 195.

52 Nasta (2002), p. 203.

53 Steven Connor, *The English Novel in History: 1950–1995* (London: Routledge, 1996), p. 94.
54 Connor (1996), p. 95.
55 Connor (1996), p. 96.
56 Kaleta (1998), p. 63.
57 Connor (1996), p. 98.
58 Alamgir Hashmi, 'Hanif Kureishi and the Tradition of the Novel', *The International Fiction Review*, 19:2 (1992), p. 91.
59 Nasta (2002), p. 197.
60 Dominique Vinet discusses *The Buddha* in relation to Voltaire and Molière in 'Le Candide des faubourgs: anatomie d'un humoriste', *Gallix* (1997), pp. 103–17.
61 Kaleta (1998), pp. 34–5 and 77–80.
62 Donald Weber, ' "No Secrets Were Safe From Me": Situating Hanif Kureishi', *Massachusetts Review*, 38:1 (1997), p. 130.
63 Jörg Helbig, ' "Get back to where you once belonged": Hanif Kureishi's Use of the Beatles-myth in *The Buddha of Suburbia*', in Wolfgang Kloos, ed., *Across the Lines: Intertextuality and Transcultural Communication in the New Literatures in English* (Amsterdam: Rodopi, 1998), pp. 77 and 80.
64 Moore-Gilbert (2001), p. 8.
65 Quoted in MacCabe (1999), p. 43.
66 For a full account of the adaptation see Kaleta (1998), chapter five.
67 Kaleta (1998), p. 85.

CHAPTER FIVE

 1 Kaleta (1998), p. 214.
 2 Quoted in Philip Dodd, 'Requiem for a rave', *Sight and Sound*, 1 (September 1991), p. 12.
 3 Quoted in Dodd (1991), p. 12.
 4 Dodd (1991), pp. 9–13.
 5 Dodd (1991), p. 13.
 6 [*Kaleta's note:*] J. D. Considine [*London Kills Me* review] *Rolling Stone*, 6 August 1992), p. 66.
 7 [*Kaleta's note:*] Jonathan Romney, 'The Sound of Silence', *New Statesman and Society*, 4 (13 December 1991), p. 30.
 8 [*Kaleta's note:*] William Parante [*London Kills Me* review] *Scotsman* (28 December 1991).
 9 [*Kaleta's note:*] 'United Kingdom 1991/Director: Hanif Kureishi', *The Times* (12 December 1991).
10 Kaleta (1998), pp. 89–90. [*Kaleta's Note:*] Tom Dewe Mathews [*London Kills Me* review] *Sight and Sound*, 1:5 (December 1991), p. 13.
11 [*Kaleta's note:*] Derek Malcolm, 'Capital Punishment', *Guardian* (12 December 1991), p. 29. Quoted by Kaleta (1998), p. 91.
12 Kaleta (1998), p. 213.
13 Kaleta (1998), pp. 92–5.
14 Kaleta (1998), p. 88.
15 Kaleta (1998), p. 103.
16 Ranasinha (2002), p. 77.
17 Ranasinha (2002), p. 80.
18 Sandhu (1999), pp. 151–2.
19 MacCabe (1999), p. 42.

CHAPTER SIX

 1 Schoene (1998), pp. 124, 125 and 126.
 2 Maya Jaggi, 'A buddy from suburbia', *Guardian* (1 March 1995).

3 [*Ranasinha's note:*] Tariq Modood, ' "Difference", Cultural Racism and Anti-Racism', in Pnina Werbner and Tariq Modood, eds., *Debating Cultural Hybridity: Multi-Cultural Identities and the Politics of Anti-Racism* (London: Zed Books, 1997), p. 164.

4 [*Ranasinha's note:*] Tariq Modood, 'British Muslims and the Rushdie Affair', in James Donald and Ali Rattansi, eds., *Race, Culture and Difference* (London: Sage Publications in association with the Open University, 1992), p. 261. The Labour Force Survey (1992–99) reports that Pakistani and Bangladeshi communities have the highest unemployment rate and lowest economic activity and employment rate of all Britain's ethnic minorities (Office for National Statistics).

5 [*Ranasinha's note:*] Modood, 'British Muslims', in Donald and Rattansi (1992), p. 268.

6 [*Ranasinha's note:*] Modood, ' "Difference" ', in Werbner and Modood (1997), pp. 164–5.

7 [*Ranasinha's note:*] Commission for Racial Equality, 'Stereotyping and Racism in Britain – an Attitude Survey', *Impact* (October/November 1999), p. 41. The Runnymede report observes that aggressive hostility to Islam is expressed in ways unthinkable in relation to other beliefs; see 'The Runnymede Report', *Guardian* (11 October 2000), p. 6.

8 [*Ranasinha's note:*] Tariq Modood, 'Introduction', in Tariq Modood and Pnina Werbner, eds., *The Politics of Multiculturalism in the New Europe: Racism, Identity and Community* (London: Zed Books, 1997), p. 3. Ranasinha (2002), pp. 81–2.

9 MacCabe (1999), p. 50.

10 MacCabe (1999), p. 51.

11 Ranasinha (2002), p. 82.

12 Ranasinha (2002), pp. 84–5.

13 Ranasinha (2002), p. 84

14 Kaleta (1998), p. 144.

15 Ranasinha (2002), p. 85.

16 Ranasinha (2002), p. 88.

17 Ranasinha (2002), p. 90.

18 [*Ranasinha's note:*] Robert Stam and Ella Shohat, *Unthinking Eurocentrism* (London: Routledge, 1994), p. 215.

19 Ranasinha (2002), pp. 90–1.

20 [*Ransinha's note:*] Cited in Harvey Porlock, 'Critical List', *Sunday Times* (19 March 1995), Books Section, p. 7.

21 [*Ranasinha's note:*] Karen Robinson, 'Talking Books', *Sunday Times* (4 August 1996), Books Section, p. 10.

22 [*Ranasinha's note:*] Donald Weber, ' "No Secrets Were Safe from Me": Situating Hanif Kureishi', *Massachusetts Review*, 38:1 (1997), pp. 119, 129, 125, 127 and 125.

23 Ranasinha (2002), pp. 91–2.

24 [*Holmes's note:*] Quoted in Kaleta (1998), p. 124.

25 Frederick M. Holmes, 'The Postcolonial Subject Divided between East and West: Kureishi's *The Black Album* as an Intertext of Rushdie's *The Black Album*', *Papers on Language and Literature*, 37:3 (Summer 2001), p. 308.

26 Adnan Ashraf, ' "Into the Unknown": A Conversation with Hanif Kureishi' (October 1995), http://www.walrus.com/~adnan/kureishi.html, p. 3.

27 Moore-Gilbert (2001), pp. 135–6.

28 Moore-Gilbert (2001), p. 136.

29 Moore-Gilbert (2001), p. 148.

30 See Moore-Gilbert (2001), p. 238 n. 56.

31 Moore Gilbert (2001), p. 122.

32 [*Moore-Gilbert's note:*] Kureishi's text corroborates the anxieties expressed by Gayatri Spivak about the 'benevolence' of western feminists towards the 'subaltern'. See 'Can the Subaltern Speak?' [reference in note 34 below] and 'French Feminism in an International Frame' (1981), in Spivak, *In Other Worlds: Essays in Cultural Politics*

(London: Routledge, 1997), pp. 134–53. Compare Chandra Talpade Mohanty, 'Under Western Eyes: Feminist Scholarship and Colonial Discourse', *Boundary*, 2 (Spring/Autumn, 1984), pp. 71–92; and Avtar Brah, *Cartographies of Diaspora: Contesting Identities* (London: Routledge, 1996), pp. 84–127.

33 [*Moore-Gilbert's note:*] On the tropes associated with the colonial gaze, see Mary Louise Pratt, *Imperial Eyes: Travel Writing and Transculturation* (London: Routledge, 1992).

34 [*Moore-Gilbert's note:*] Spivak, 'Can the Subaltern Speak?', in Patrick Williams and L. Chrisman, eds., *Colonial Discourse and Post-Colonial Theory: A Reader* (Hemel Hempstead: Harvester Wheatsheaf, 1993), p. 93.

35 Moore-Gilbert (2001), pp. 140–3.

36 Bronwyn T. Williams, ' "A State of Perpetual Wandering": Diaspora and Black British Writers', *Jouvert*, 3 (1999). Page references are to the online publication http://152.1.96.5/jouvert/v3i3/willia.htm, p. 8.

37 Williams is referring here to Dipesh Chakrabarty's essay, 'Postcoloniality and the Artifice of History: Who Speaks for "Indian" Pasts?', *Representations*, 37 (1992), pp. 1–25.

38 Williams (1999), pp. 10–11.

39 Williams (1999), p. 2.

40 Maria Degabriele, 'Prince of Darkness Meets Priestess of Porn: Sexual and Political Identities in Hanif Kureishi's *The Black Album*', *Intersections*, 2 (May 1999). Page references are to the online publication http://wwwsshe.murdoch.edu.au/intersections/issue2/Kureishi.html, p. 2.

41 [*Degabriele's note:*] Madonna, *Vogue*, US: WEA/Warner Brothers, 1990.

42 [*Degabriele's note:*] Akbar S. Ahmed, *Postmodernism and Islam* (London: Routledge, 1992), p. 178.

43 [*Degabriele's note:*] Iain Chambers, *The Metropolitan Experience* (London: Methuen, 1986), p. 177.

44 Degabriele (1999), pp. 3–6.

45 Kureishi quoted in Kaleta (1998), p. 140.

46 Holmes (2001), p. 297.

47 Holmes (2001), pp. 301–2.

48 [*Holmes's note:*] Quoted in Kaleta (1998), p. 139.

49 [*Holmes's note:*] Fredric Jameson, *Postmodernism, or, the Cultural Logic of Late Capitalism* (Durham: Duke University Press, 1991), p. x.

50 [*Holmes's note:*] 'Some time with Stephen: A Diary', in *London Kills Me: Three Screenplays and Four Essays* (Harmondsworth: Penguin, 1992), p. 163.

51 [*Holmes's note:*] James Saynor, 'Mirror Shades' [Review of *The Black Album*], *New Statesman & Society* (3 March 1995), p. 40.

52 [*Holmes's note:*] Marlena G. Corcoran, 'Salman Rushdie's Satanic Narration', *Iowa Review*, 20:1 (1990), pp. 157–8.

53 Holmes (2001), pp. 309–10.

54 Holmes (2001), p. 311.

CHAPTER SEVEN

1 See Kaleta (1998), p. 161.

2 Kureishi, 'Introduction: Sex and Secularity', *Collected Screenplays 1*, p. vii.

3 'Bradford', reprinted in *Dreaming and Scheming*, pp. 57–80.

4 Ranasinha (2002), p. 93.

5 *Collected Screenplays 1*, pp. viii–x.

6 'The Road Exactly: Introduction to *My Son the Fanatic*', reprinted in *Dreaming and Scheming*, pp. 219–20.

7 Moore-Gilbert (2001), p. 164.

8 Moore-Gilbert (2001), pp. 164–9.

9 See Amy Gutmann, ed., *Multiculturalism: Examining the Politics of Recognition* (Princeton, NJ: Princeton University Press, 1992).

10 Ranasinha (2002), pp. 94–6.

11 Ranasinha (2002), p. 93.

12 [*Ranasinha's note:*] Nigel Andrews, 'Cinema's Cinderella No More', *Financial Times* (12 May 1997), p. 15.

13 Ranasinha (2002), pp. 96–8.

14 For a detailed discussion of subaltern secularism see Ranasinha (2002), pp. 98–100. [*Ranasinha's note:*] Homi Bhabha, 'Unpacking my library ... again', in Iain Chambers and Lidia Curti, eds., *The Post-Colonial Question: Common Skies, Divided Horizons* (London: Routledge, 1996), p. 209.

15 Ranasinha (2002), p. 89.

16 Maya Jaggi, 'A buddy from suburbia', *Guardian* (1 March 1995).

17 [*Ranasinha's note:*] To date Professor Akbar Ahmed is alone in his comments on the 'tired stereotypes' of the Muslim community in *My Son the Fanatic*, in 'Public purse funds distorted drama about Muslim condition', http//www.q-news

18 Harvey Thompson [review of *My Son the Fanatic*], wsws.org (29 May 1998).

19 Sukhdev Sandhu, http://www.23–59.co.uk/script/hanif-art.htm (1999).

20 Udayan Prasad speaks of the scene's importance in showing how immigrants rarely see the countryside because they are always working. See Michael Sragow [review of *My Son the Fanatic*], *Salon Review* (8 July 1999), available online at salon.com

21 *Collected Screenplays 1*, p. 381

22 Moore-Gilbert (2001), pp. 169–71.

23 Kureishi, 'Sex and Secularity', in *Collected Screenplays 1*, p. xi.

24 *Collected Screenplays 1*, p. 382.

25 Kaleta (1998), p. 194.

CHAPTER EIGHT

1 Bruce Dessau, 'The Buddha of Bromley', *Time Out* (19 April 1999), p. 11. Quoted in Ranasinha (2002), p. 111.

2 'Filming *Intimacy*', in *Dreaming and Scheming*, p. 228.

3 Interview with Kureishi in Nahem Yousaf, *The Buddha of Suburbia: A Reader's Guide* (New York, London: Continuum, 2002), p. 22.

4 Sukhdev Sandhu, [Untitled Document] published online (1999) at http://www.23–59. co.uk/script/hanif-art.htm

5 Moore-Gilbert (2001), p. 153.

6 Kureishi email to Guide author.

7 Jenny Turner, *Independent* (13 April 1999).

8 Robbie Clipper Sethi, [Untitled review] *IndiaStar: A Literary-Art Magazine* (1999) available online at http://www.indiastar.com/

9 Andrew Gallix, 'Et in Suburbia Ego: Hanif Kureishi's Semi-Detached Storeys', in Gallix (1997), p. 161.

10 Charles Taylor, *Salon* (19 November 1997).

11 See Kureishi's 'Filming *Intimacy*', in *Dreaming and Scheming*, pp. 223–33.

12 Yousaf (2002), p. 25.

13 David Sexton, *Evening Standard* (14 May 1998).

14 Suzanne Moore, 'Why I Applaud the Books of Men Who Tell It Like It Is', *Independent* (15 May 1998), p. 21.

15 Sylvia Brownrigg, 'High Infidelity: An Interview with Hanif Kureishi', *The Village Voice Literary Supplement* (April–May 1999).

16 Polly Rance, *The Richmond Review* (1999), available online at www.richmondreview.com/

17 Laura Cumming, 'Charity begins at Home', *Guardian* (9 May 1998).
18 Moore-Gilbert (2001), p. 173.
19 Kureishi email to Guide author.
20 Moore-Gilbert (2001), p. 175.
21 Moore-Gilbert (2001), p. 179.
22 Ranasinha (2002), p. 109.
23 Ranasinha (2002), pp. 110, 111.
24 Ranasinha (2002), pp. 111–12.
25 Ranasinha (2002), pp. 112, 113.
26 Ranasinha (2002), p. 114.
27 Amitava Kumar, *Bombay London New York* (New York, London: Routledge, 2002), p. 159.
28 Kumar (2002), pp. 160 and 163.
29 Michael Billington, 'Glittering Ponces', *Guardian* (23 April 1999), p. 18.
30 Paul Taylor, 'Nod off and Die', *Independent* (24 April 1999).
31 Moore-Gilbert (2001), p. 184. Moore-Gilbert provides a detailed comparison of *Sleep with Me* and specific works of Orton and Chekhov.
32 Moore-Gilbert (2001), p. 185.
33 Paul Binding, 'Masks and Rituals', *Independent* (31 October 1999), p. 10.
34 James Hopkin, 'The Horror of being Hanif', *Guardian* (30 October 1999).
35 Sandhu (2000), pp. 33–5.

CHAPTER NINE

1 Kureishi, Interview with Robert McCrum, 'I got out of the suburbs, but did they get out of me?', *Observer* (25 February 2001).
2 McCrum (2001).
3 Ball (1996), p. 15.
4 Kureishi, 'Music was our common culture in the 60s and 70s', *Guardian* (16 March 2001).
5 McCrum (2001).
6 Alex Clark, 'Mood Swings', *Guardian* (3 March 2001).
7 Katie Owen, 'They muck you up', *Daily Telegraph* (3 March 2001).
8 David Jays, 'Never trust a man in platform heels', *Guardian* (25 February 2001).
9 Elizabeth de Cacqueray, 'Space for Dreams: the Use of Place and Space in Hanif Kureishi's Fictive Universes', in Gallix (1997), p. 195.
10 Yousaf (2002), pp. 19–20.
11 For the reference to Kureishi's adaptation of *Dorian Gray*, see Kaleta (1998), p. 148. The continued influence of Wilde, 'that exemplary dissident', is evident in Kureishi's speech 'Loose Tongues and Liberty' given at the Hay Festival and published in the *Guardian* (7 June 2003).
12 Jessica Mann, 'Peter Pan's Midlife Crisis', *Daily Telegraph* (20 October 2002).
13 Alexander Linklater, 'Death of the ego', *Guardian* (16 November 2002).
14 Jason Cowley, 'You're as young as you feel', *Guardian* (3 November 2002).
15 Julie Myerson, 'Nobody reads 'em', *Daily Telegraph* (16 November 2002).
16 Ruvani Ranasinha, [review of *The Body and Seven Stories*] *Wasafiri* 39 (Summer 2003), p. 69.
17 Ranasinha (2003), pp. 69–70.
18 Kureishi, Cheltenham Literary Festival (17 October 1997). Quoted by Ranasinha (2002), p. 106.
19 Sandhu (1999).
20 'Some time with Stephen', *Dreaming and Scheming*, p. 138.
21 Salman Rushdie, *The Satanic Verses* (London: Viking, 1988), p. 281.
22 Kureishi, 'Interview with Robert McCrum', *Observer* (25 February 2001). Quoted by Ranasinha (2003), p. 68.

Select Bibliography

www.hanifkureishi.com (the official website)

SELECTED TEXTS BY HANIF KUREISHI
FICTION
The Black Album (London: Faber & Faber, 1995).
The Body and Seven Stories (London: Faber & Faber, 2002).
The Buddha of Suburbia (London: Faber & Faber, 1990).
Gabriel's Gift (London: Faber & Faber, 2001).
Intimacy (London: Faber & Faber, 1998).
Love in a Blue Time (London: Faber & Faber, 1997).
Midnight All Day (London: Faber & Faber, 1999).

SCREENPLAYS
Collected Screenplays 1 (London: Faber & Faber, 2002).
London Kills Me (London: Faber & Faber, 1991).
The Mother (London: Faber & Faber, 2003).
My Beautiful Laundrette and Other Writings (London: Faber & Faber, 1996).
My Son the Fanatic (London: Faber & Faber, 1997).
Sammy and Rosie Get Laid: The Script and the Diary (London: Faber & Faber, 1988).

STAGE PLAYS
Outskirts and Other Plays (London: Faber & Faber, 1992).
Sleep with Me (London: Faber & Faber, 1999).
Tomorrow-Today! (1981) in *Outskirts, The King and Me, Tomorrow-Today!* (London: John Calder and New York: Riverrun Press, 1983).

ESSAYS (for ease of consultation, individual essays referred to in the text are cited separately)
'Bradford' (1986), reprinted in *Dreaming and Scheming*, pp. 57–79.
'Dirty Washing', *Time Out*, 795 (14–20 November 1985), pp. 25–6.
Dreaming and Scheming: Reflections on Writing and Politics (London: Faber & Faber, 2002).
'England, Bloody England', *Guardian* (22 January 1988), reprinted in Mercer (1988), pp. 24–5.
'Filming *Intimacy*', in *Dreaming and Scheming*, pp. 223–33.
'Introduction to *My Beautiful Laundrette*' (1986), reprinted in *Dreaming and Scheming*, pp. 123–6.
'Introduction: Sex and Secularity', *Collected Screenplays 1*, pp. vii–xi.
'Loose Tongues and Liberty', speech given at the Hay Festival (2003), edited version in the *Guardian* (7 June 2003).
'The Rainbow Sign' (1986), reprinted in *Dreaming and Scheming*, pp. 25–56.
'The Road Exactly: Introduction to *My Son the Fanatic*', in *Dreaming and Scheming*, pp. 215–21.
'Some time with Stephen: A Diary' (1988), reprinted in *Dreaming and Scheming*, pp. 127–99.

INTERVIEWS

Ashraf, Adnan, ' "Into the Unknown": A Conversation with Hanif Kureishi' (October 1995), http://www.walrus.com/-adnan/kureishi.html

Brownrigg, Sylvia, 'High Infidelity: An Interview with Hanif Kureishi' [about *Intimacy*], *The Village Voice Literary Supplement* (April–May 1999).

Dessau, Bruce, 'The Buddha of Bromley', *Time Out* (19 April 1999), p. 11.

Dodd, Philip, 'Requiem for a rave' [about *London Kills Me*], *Sight and Sound*, 5:1 (September 1991), pp. 9–11.

Jaggi, Maya, 'A buddy from suburbia' [about *The Black Album*], *Guardian* (1 March 1995), pp. 6–7.

MacCabe, Colin, 'Interview: Hanif Kureishi on London', *Critical Quarterly*, 41:3 (1999), pp. 37–56.

McCrum, Robert, 'I got out of the suburbs, but did they get out of me?', *Observer* (25 February 2001).

'Music was our common culture in the 60s and 70s', *Guardian* (16 March 2001).

Pally, Marcia, 'Kureishi Like a Fox', *Film Comment*, 22:5 (September–October 1986), pp. 50–5.

Root, Jane, 'Scenes from a Marriage: Hanif Kureishi in Interview with Jane Root', *Monthly Film Bulletin*, 52 (November 1985), p. 333.

Treneman, Ann, 'I thought, I'll be a writer', *The Independent* (15 April 1997), p. 10.

EDITED WORKS

The Faber Book of Pop, ed. with Jon Savage (London: Faber & Faber, 1995).

VHS/DVD

Buddha of Suburbia, two tapes (1998)
London Kills Me (1993)
My Beautiful Laundrette (2001)
My Son the Fanatic (2002)
Sammy and Rosie Get Laid (1994)

SELECTED CRITICISM AND REVIEWS
BOOKS ON KUREISHI THAT OFFER AN OVERVIEW

Kaleta, Kenneth C., *Hanif Kureishi: Postcolonial Storyteller* (Austin: University of Texas Press, 1998).

Moore-Gilbert, Bart, *Hanif Kureishi* (Manchester: Manchester University Press, 2001).

Ranasinha, Ruvani, *Writers and Their Work: Hanif Kureishi* (Plymouth: Northcote House, 2002).

ESSAYS ON KUREISHI THAT DISCUSS MORE THAN ONE WORK

Allison, Terry L. and Curry, Renée R., ' "All Anger and Understanding": Kureishi, Culture, and Contemporary Constructions of Rage', in Allison and Curry, eds., *States of Rage: Emotional Eruption, Violence and Social Change* (New York: New York University Press, 1996), pp. 146–66.

Ball, John Clement, 'The Semi-Detached Metropolis: Hanif Kureishi's London', *Ariel*, 27:4 (October 1996), pp. 7–27.

De Cacqueray, Elizabeth, 'Space for Dreams: the Use of Place and Space in Hanif Kureishi's Fictive Universes', in Gallix (1997), pp. 186–99.

Moore-Gilbert, Bart, 'London in Hanif Kureishi's Films', *Kunapipi*, XXI.2 (1999), pp. 5–14.

Sandhu, Sukhdev, 'Pop Goes The Centre: Hanif Kureishi's London', in Laura Chrisman and Benita Parry, eds., *Postcolonial Theory and Criticism* (Cambridge: Brewer, 1999), pp. 133–54.

Weber, Donald, ' "No Secrets Were Safe from Me": Situating Hanif Kureishi', *Massachusetts Review*, 38:1 (1997), pp. 119–35.

Yousaf, Nahem, 'Hanif Kureishi and "the Brown Man's Burden" ', *Critical Survey*, 8:1 (1996), pp. 14–25.

REVIEWS OF *THE KING AND ME, OUTSKIRTS, BORDERLINE* AND *BIRDS OF PASSAGE*

Billington, Michael [review of *Outskirts*], *Guardian* (29 April 1981), p. 10.

Fenton, James, 'Okay, as a Favour, Tell You What I'll Do' [review of *Birds of Passage*], *Sunday Times* (25 September 1983), p. 39.

Wardle, Irving [review of *The King and Me*], *The Times* (9 January 1980), p. 11.

Wardle, Irving 'A Moral Tale that Carries Conviction' [review of *Outskirts*], *The Times* (29 April 1981), p. 12.

Wardle, Irving [review of *Borderline*], *The Times* (6 November 1981), p. 18.

Wardle, Irving [review of *Birds of Passage*], *The Times* (17 September 1983), p. 9.

REVIEWS AND ESSAYS ON *MY BEAUTIFUL LAUNDRETTE*

Canby, Vincent, 'Chaotic London', *New York Times*, 30 (October 1987), C5:1.

Cook, Pam, untitled review, *Monthly Film Bulletin*, 52 (November 1985), p. 333.

Dhillon-Kashyap, Perminder, 'Locating the Asian Experience', *Screen*, 29:4 (1988), pp. 120–6.

Hall, Stuart, 'Old and New Identities, Old and New Ethnicities', in Anthony D. King, ed., *Culture, Globalization and the World System* (Basingstoke: Macmillan, 1991), pp. 41–68.

Jamal, Mahmood, 'Dirty Linen', *Artrage*, in Mercer (1988), pp. 21–2.

Kennedy, Harlan, *Film Comment*, 21 (November–December 1985), p. 76.

Kennedy, Harlan, 'Gritty Brit' [interview with Stephen Frears], *Film Comment*, 23 (March–April), pp. 15–17.

Mercer, Kobena, ed., *Black Film, British Cinema* (London: Institute of Contemporary Arts, 1988).

Quart, Leonard, *Cinéaste*, 15:1 (1986), pp. 38–9.

Rushdie, Salman, 'Minority Literatures in a Multi-Cultural Society', in Kirsten Holst Peterson and Anna Rutherford, eds., *Displaced Persons* (Sydney: Dangaroo Press, 1988), pp. 33–42.

Wolf, Rita, 'Beyond the Laundrette', *Guardian* (14 February 1987).

REVIEWS AND ESSAYS ON *SAMMY AND ROSIE*

Aldama, Frederick Luis Aldama, *Postethnic Narrative Criticism: Magicorealism in Oscar 'Zeta' Acosta, Anna Castillo, Julie Dash, Hanif Kureishi, and Salman Rushdie* (Austin: Texas University Press, 2003).

Corliss, Richard, 'The Empire Strikes Out', *Time*, 30 (9 November 1987), p. 91.

hooks, bell, 'Stylish Nihilism: Race, Sex and Class at the Movies', in hooks, *Yearning: Race, Gender, and Cultural Politics* (Boston: South End Press, 1991), pp. 155–63.

Lindroth, Colette, '*The Waste Land* Revisited: *Sammy and Rosie Get Laid*', *Literature/Film Quarterly*, 17:2 (1989), pp. 95–8.

Naidoo, Sandeep, *Bazaar*, 4:6 (Spring 1988), p. 16.

Parma, Pratibha, '*Sammy and Rosie Get Laid*', *Marxism Today*, 32 (February 1988).

Quart, Leonard, *Cinéaste*, 16:3 (1988), p. 40.

Spivak, Gayatri Chakravorty, 'In Praise of *Sammy and Rosie Get Laid*', *Critical Quarterly*, 31:2 (1989), pp. 80–8.

Spivak, Gayatri Chakravorty, '*Sammy and Rosie Get Laid*', in *Outside in the Teaching Machine* (London: Routledge, 1993), pp. 243–54.

REVIEWS AND ESSAYS ON BOTH *MY BEAUTIFUL LAUNDRETTE* AND *SAMMY AND ROSIE*

Barber, Susan Torrey, 'Insurmountable Difficulties and Moments of Ecstasy: Crossing Class, Ethnic, and Sexual Barriers in the Films of Stephen Frears', in Lester Friedman, ed., *British Cinema and Thatcherism: Fires Were Started* (London: UCL Press, 1993), pp. 221–36.

Mohanram, Radhika, 'Postcolonial Spaces and Deterritorialized (Homo)Sexuality: The Films of Hanif Kureishi', in Gita Rajan and Radhika Mohanram, eds., *Postcolonial Discourse and Changing Cultural Contexts: Theory and Criticism* (Westport, CT and London: Greenwood Press, 1995), pp. 117–34.

Quart, Leonard, 'The Politics of Irony: The Frears-Kureishi Films', in Wheeler Winston Dixon, ed., *Re-viewing British Cinema 1900–1992* (Albany: State University of New York Press, 1994), pp. 241–8.

Sampat-Patel, Niti, 'Unmasking Masquerade: Home and Exile in the Films of Hanif Kureishi', in Sampat-Patel, *Postcolonial Masquerades: Culture and Politics in Literature, Film, Video, and Photography* (New York: Garland, 2001), pp. 3–46.

Stone, Norman, 'Through a lens darkly', *Sunday Times* (10 January 1988), reprinted in Mercer (1988), pp. 22–3.

REVIEWS, BOOKS AND ESSAYS ON *THE BUDDHA OF SUBURBIA*

Borm, Jan, ' "Thank God I have an Interesting Life": Le picaresque dans *The Buddha of Suburbia*', in Gallix (1997), pp. 79–87.

Carey, Cynthia, '*The Buddha of Suburbia* as a Post-Colonial Novel', *Commonwealth Essays and Studies*, 4 (1997), pp. 119–25.

Collins, Glenn, 'Screen Writer Turns to the Novel to Tell of Race and Class in London', *New York Times* (24 May 1990), p. 17.

Connor, Steven, *The English Novel in History: 1950–1995* (London: Routledge, 1996).

Doyle, Waddick, 'The Space between Identity and Otherness in Hanif Kureishi's *The Buddha of Suburbia*', *Commonwealth Essays and Studies*, 4 (1997), pp. 110–18.

Dubourdieu, Elaine, 'The Buddha, Britain and "Black" Immigration', in Gallix (1997), pp. 131–47.

Felski, Rita, 'Nothing to Declare: Identity, Shame, and the Lower Middle Class', *Proceedings of the Modern Language Association*, 115 (January 2000), pp. 33–45.

Gallix, Andrew, 'Et in Suburbia Ego: Hanif Kureishi's Semi-Detached Storeys', in Gallix (1997), pp. 148–64.

Gallix, François, ed., *The Buddha of Suburbia* (Paris: Ellipses, 1997).

Graves, Matthew, 'Subverting Suburbia: the Trickster Figure in Hanif Kureishi's *The Buddha of Suburbia*', in Gallix (1997), pp. 70–8.

Hashmi, Alamgir, 'Hanif Kureishi and the Tradition of the Novel', *International Fiction Review*, 19:2 (1992), pp. 88–96.

Helbig, Jörg, ' "Get Back to Where You Once Belonged": Hanif Kureishi's Use of the Beatles-myth in *The Buddha of Suburbia*', in Wolfgang Kloos, ed., *Across the Lines: Intertextuality and Transcultural Communication in the New Literatures in English* (Amsterdam: Rodopi, 1998), pp. 77–82.

Hita, Michele, 'Identité, vision et voyeurisme dans *The Buddha of Suburbia*', in Gallix (1997), pp. 37–44.

Jena, Seema, 'From Victims to Survivors: the Anti-Hero As a Narrative Strategy in Asian Immigrant Writing With Special Reference to *The Buddha of Suburbia*', *Wasafiri*, 17 (Spring 1993), pp. 3–6.

Jones, Moya 'The Immigrant is the Everyman of the 20th Century: Racial tensions in *The Buddha of Suburbia*', in Gallix (1997), pp. 131–47.

Langford, Barry, 'Margins of the city: towards a dialectic of suburban desire', in Richard Phillips, ed., *De-Centring Sexualities: Politics and Representations Beyond the Metropolis* (London and New York: Routledge, 2000), pp. 64–80.

Lee, Yu-Cheng, 'Expropriating the Authentic: Cultural Politics in Hanif Kureishi's *Buddha of Suburbia'*, *EurAmerica: A Journal of European and American Studies*, 26:3 (1996), pp. 1–19.

Moore-Gilbert, Bart, 'Hanif Kureishi's *The Buddha of Suburbia*: Hybridity in Contemporary Cultural Theory and Artistic Practice', *Q/W/E/R/T/Y: Arts, Littératures & Civilisations du Monde Anglophone*, 7 (Octobre 1997), pp. 191–208.

Oubechou, Jamel, 'The Barbarians and Philistines in *The Buddha of Suburbia'*, *Commonwealth Essays and Studies*, 4 (1997), pp. 101–9.

Porée, Marc, *Hanif Kureishi: The Buddha of Suburbia* (Paris: CNED-Didier Concours, 1997).

Ray, Sangeeta, 'The Nation in Performance: Bhabha, Mukherjee and Kureishi', in Monika Fludernik, ed., *Hybridity and Postcolonialism: Twentieth Century Indian Literature* (Tübingen, Germany: Stauffenburg, 1998), pp. 219–38.

Schoene, Berthold, 'Herald of Hybridity: The Emancipation of Difference in Hanif Kureishi's *The Buddha of Suburbia'*, *International Journal of Cultural Studies*, 1:1 (1998), pp. 109–27.

Spivak, Gayatri Chakravorty, 'The Burden of English', in Rajeswari Sunder Rajan, ed., *The Lie of the Land: English Literary Studies in India* (Delhi: Oxford University Press, 1992).

Vinet, Dominique, 'Le Candide des faubourgs: anatomie d'un humoriste', in Gallix (1997), pp. 103–17.

Yousaf, Nahem, *Hanif Kureishi's The Buddha of Suburbia* (New York and London: Continuum, 2002).

REVIEWS OF *LONDON KILLS ME*

Considine, J. D., *Rolling Stone* (6 August 1992), p. 66.

Malcolm, Derek, 'Capital Punishment', *Guardian* (12 December 1991), p. 29.

Mathews, Tom Dewe, *Sight and Sound*, 1:5 (December 1991), p. 13.

Parante, William, *Scotsman* (28 December 1991).

Romney, Jonathan, 'The Sound of Silence', *New Statesman and Society*, 4 (13 December 1991), p. 30.

REVIEWS AND ESSAYS ON *THE BLACK ALBUM*

Appiah, Anthony K., 'Identity Crisis', *New York Times*, Section 8 (17 September 1995), p. 42.

Degabriele, Maria, 'Prince of Darkness Meets Priestess of Porn: Sexual and Political Identities in Hanif Kureishi's *The Black Album'*, *Intersections*, 2 (May 1999), online at http://wwwsshe.murdoch.edu.au/intersections/issue2/Kureishi.html

Holmes, Frederick M., 'The Postcolonial Subject Divided between East and West: Kureishi's *The Black Album* as an Intertext of Rushdie's *The Black Album'*, *Papers on Language and Literature*, 37:3 (Summer 2001), pp. 296–313.

Porlock, Harvey, 'Critical List', *Sunday Times* (19 March 1995) Books Section, p. 7.

Robinson, Karen, 'Talking Books', *Sunday Times* (4 August 1996), Books Section, p. 10.

Saynor, James, 'Mirror Shades', *New Statesman & Society* (3 March 1995), pp. 40–1.

Williams, Bronwyn T., ' "A State of Perpetual Wandering": Diaspora and Black British Writers', *Jouvert*, 3 (1999). Page references are to the online publication http://152.1.96.5/jouvert/v3i3/willia.htm

REVIEWS OF *MY SON THE FANATIC*

Ahmed, Professor Akbar, 'Public purse funds distorted drama about Muslim condition', http//www.q-news

Andrews, Nigel, 'Cinema's Cinderella No More', *Financial Times* (12 May 1997), p. 15.

Thompson, Harvey, 'A moving and unconventional love story' (29 May 1998), available online at http://www.wsws.org

Sragow, Michael [interview with Udayan Prasad], *Salon* (8 July 1998) available online at http://www.salon.com

REVIEWS OF *LOVE IN A BLUE TIME, MIDNIGHT ALL DAY* AND *INTIMACY*

Binding, Paul, 'Masks and Rituals' [review of *Midnight All Day*], *The Independent* (31 October 1999), p. 10.

Cumming, Laura, 'Charity Ends at Home' [review of *Intimacy*], *Guardian* (9 May 1998).

Hopkin, James, 'The Horror of Being Hanif' [review of *Midnight All Day*], *Guardian* (30 October 1999), p. 10.

Moore, Suzanne, 'Why I applaud the Books of Men who Tell it like it is' [review of *Intimacy*], *Independent* (15 May 1998), p. 21.

Rance, Polly [review of *Intimacy*], *Richmond Review* (1999) available online at http://www.richmondreview.com/

Sandhu, Sukhdev [Untitled Document], available online (1999) at http://www.23-59.co.uk/script/hanif-art.htm

Sandhu, Sukhdev, 'Paradise Syndrome' [review of *Midnight All Day*], *London Review of Books* (18 May 2000), pp. 32-5.

Sethi, Robbie Clipper [review of *Love in a Blue Time*], *IndiaStar: A Literary-Art Magazine* (1999), available online at http://www.indiastar.com/

Sexton, David, 'What do these authors have in common? They all hate women' [review of *Intimacy*], *Evening Standard* (14 May 1998).

Taylor, Charles [Review of *Love in a Blue Time*], *Salon* (19 November 1997), available online at http://www.salon.com

Turner, Jenny, 'All about the babe they lack' [review of *Love in a Blue Time*], *The Independent* (13 April 1999).

REVIEWS OF *SLEEP WITH ME*

Billington, Michael, 'Glittering Ponces', *Guardian* (23 April 1999), p. 18.

Taylor, Paul, 'Nod off and die', *The Independent* (24 April 1999).

REVIEWS OF *GABRIEL'S GIFT AND THE BODY*

Clark, Alex, 'Mood Swings' [review of *Gabriel's Gift*], *Guardian* (3 March 2001).

Cowley, Jason, 'You're as young as you feel' [review of *The Body*], *Observer* (3 November 2002).

Jays, David, 'Never trust a man in platform heels' [review of *Gabriel's Gift*], *Guardian* (25 February 2001).

Linklater, Alexander, 'Death of the ego' [review of *The Body*], *Guardian* (16 November 2002).

Mann, Jessica, 'Peter Pan's Midlife Crisis' [review of *The Body*], *Daily Telegraph* (20 October 2002).

Myerson, Julie, 'Nobody reads 'em' [review of *The Body*], *Daily Telegraph* (16 November 2002).

Owen, Katie, 'They muck you up'[review of *Gabriel's Gift*] *Daily Telegraph* (3 March 2001).

Ranasinha, Ruvani (review of *The Body*), *Wasafiri*, 39:1 (Summer 2003), pp. 68-70.

BOOKS AND ESSAYS WITH WORTHWHILE DISCUSSIONS OF KUREISHI

Bald, Suresht Renjen, 'Negotiating Identity in the Metropolis: Generational Differences in South Asian British Fiction', in Russell King *et al.*, eds., *Writing Across Worlds: Literature and Migration* (London: Routledge, 1995), pp. 70-88.

Chaudhuri, Una, 'The Poetics of Exile and the Politics of Home', in Patrick Hogan and Lalita Pandit, eds., *Literary India: Comparative Studies in Aesthetics, Colonialism and Culture* (Albany: State University of New York Press, 1995), pp. 141–9.

Gikandi, Simon, *Maps of Englishness* (New York: Columbia University Press, 1996).

Julian, Ria, 'Brecht and Britain: Hanif Kureishi in Interview with Ria Julian', *Drama: Quarterly Theatre Review*, 155 (1987), pp. 5–7.

Kumar, Amitava, *Bombay London New York* (New York and London: Routledge, 2002).

Lee, A. Robert, 'Changing the Script: Sex, Lies and Videotapes in Hanif Kureishi, David Dabydeen and Mike Phillips', in A. Robert Lee, ed., *Other Britain, Other British: Contemporary Multicultural Fiction* (London and East Haven, CT: Pluto Press, 1995), pp. 69–89.

McLeod, John, *Beginning Postcolonialism* (Manchester: Manchester University Press, 2000).

Nasta, Susheila, *Home Truths: Fictions of the South Asian Diaspora in Britain* (Basingstoke: Palgrave Macmillan, 2002).

Needham, Anuradha Dingwaney, *Using the Master's Tools: Resistance and the Literature of the African and South Asian Diasporas* (Basingstoke: Palgrave Macmillan, 2000).

Punter, David, *Postcolonial Imaginings: Fictions of a New World Order* (Edinburgh: Edinburgh University Press, 2000).

Sandhu, Sukhdev, *London Calling: How Black and Asian Writers Imagined a City* (London: HarperCollins, 2003).

OTHER WORKS CITED

Ahmed, Akbar S., *Postmodernism and Islam* (London: Routledge, 1992).

Bhabha, Homi 'Unpacking my library ... again', in Iain Chambers and Lidia Curti, eds., *The Post-Colonial Question: Common Skies, Divided Horizons* (London: Routledge, 1996).

Bhabha, Homi, ed., *Nation and Narration* (London: Routledge, 1990).

Bhabha, Homi, *The Location of Culture* (London: Routledge, 1994).

Anthias, Floya and Yuval-Davis, Nira, eds., *Women–Nation–State* (London: Macmillan, 1998).

Blake, William, 'There Is No Natural Religion [Second Series]', in Geoffrey Keynes, ed., *Blake: Complete Writings with Variant Readings* (Oxford: Oxford University Press, 1969), p. 97.

Brah, Avtar, *Cartographies Of Diaspora: Contesting Identities* (London: Routledge, 1996).

Chakrabarty, Dipesh, 'Postcoloniality and the Artifice of History: Who Speaks for "Indian" Pasts?', *Representations*, 37 (1992), pp. 1–25.

Chambers, Iain, *The Metropolitan Experience* (London: Methuen, 1986).

Chrisman, Laura and Williams, Patrick, eds., *Colonial Discourse and Post-Colonial Theory: A Reader* (Hemel Hempstead: Harvester Wheatsheaf, 1993).

Commission for Racial Equality, 'Stereotyping and Racism in Britain – an Attitude Survey', *Impact* (October/November 1999).

Corcoran, Marlena G., 'Salman Rushdie's Satanic Narration', *Iowa Review*, 20:1 (1990), pp. 157–8.

Gilroy, Paul, *Small Acts: Thoughts on the Politics of Black Cultures* (London: Serpent's Tail, 1993).

Gilroy, Paul, *The Black Atlantic* (London: Verso, 1993).

Grewal, Inderpal, 'Salman Rushdie: Marginality, Women and *Shame*', in M. D. Fletcher, ed., *Reading Rushdie: Perspectives on the Fiction of Salman Rushdie* (Amsterdam: Rodopi, 1994).

Gutmann, Amy, ed., *Multiculturalism: Examining the Politics of Recognition* (Princeton, NJ: Princeton University Press, 1992).

Jameson, Fredric, *Postmodernism, or, the Cultural Logic of Late Capitalism* (Durham, NC: Duke University Press, 1991).

Koestler, Arthur, 'Humour et esprit', *Janus: A Summing Up* (Paris: Calmann-Levy, 1979), chapter VI.

Mercer, Kobena, *Welcome to the Jungle: New Positions in Black Cultural Studies* (London: Routledge, 1994).

Miller, Richard, *Analyzing Marx* (Ithaca, NY: Cornell University Press, 1984), pp. 15–97.

Modood, Tariq, 'British Muslims and the Rushdie Affair', in James Donald and Ali Rattansi, eds., *Race, Culture and Difference* (London: Sage Publications in association with the Open University, 1992).

Modood, Tariq, ' "Difference", Cultural Racism and Anti-Racism', in Pnina Werbner and Tariq Modood, eds., *Debating Cultural Hybridity: Multi-Cultural Identities and the Politics of Anti-Racism* (London: Zed Books, 1997).

Modood, Tariq, 'Introduction', in Tariq Modood and Pnina Werbner, eds., *The Politics of Multiculturalism in the New Europe: Racism, Identity and Community* (London: Zed Books, 1997).

Mohanty, Chandra Talpade, 'Under Western Eyes: Feminist Scholarship and Colonial Discourse', *Boundary*, 2 (Spring/Autumn, 1984), pp. 71–92.

Mosse, George, *Nationalism and Sexuality: Middle Morality and Sexual Norms* (Madison: University of Wisconsin Press, 1985).

Pratt, Mary Louise, *Imperial Eyes: Travel Writing and Transculturation* (London: Routledge, 1992).

Rawlins, Jack P., 'Great Expiations: Dickens and the Betrayal of the Child', in Michael Cotsell, ed., *Critical Essays on Charles Dickens's Great Expectations* (Boston: G. K. Hall, 1990).

Rushdie, Salman, *The Satanic Verses* (London: Viking, 1988).

Said, Edward, *Orientalism* (1978; Harmondworth: Penguin, 1991).

Sancho, Ignatius, *Letters of the Late Ignatius Sancho: an African, to which are Prefixed, Memoirs of his Life*, 2 vols. (London: J. Nichols, 1782). A modern edition, edited by Vincent Carretta, is available (New York: Penguin, 1998).

Sayyid, Bobby, *A Fundamentalist Fear: Eurocentrism and the Emergence of Islamism* (London: Zed Books, 1997).

Sivanandan, A, *From Resistance to Rebellion: Asian and Afro-Caribbean Struggles in Britain* (London: Institute of Race Relations, 1986).

Spivak, Gayatri Chakravorty, 'Can the Subaltern Speak?', in Patrick Williams and L. Chrisman, eds., *Colonial Discourse and Post-Colonial Theory: A Reader* (Hemel Hempstead: Harvester Wheatsheaf, 1993), pp. 66–111.

Spivak, Gayatri Chakravorty, *In Other Worlds: Essays in Cultural Politics* (London: Routledge, 1997).

Stam, Robert, and Shohat, Ella, *Unthinking Eurocentrism* (London: Routledge, 1994).

Syal, Meera, *Life Isn't All Ha Ha Hee Hee* (London: Doubleday, 1999).

Trussler, Simon, ed., *The Cambridge Illustrated History of British Theatre* (Cambridge: Cambridge University Press, 1994).